THE TRUE NORTH STRONG & FREE?

THE TRUE NORTH STRONG & FREE?

*Proceedings of a Public Inquiry into
Canadian Defence Policy and Nuclear Arms*

Sponsored by The True North
Strong and Free Inquiry Society

Introduction by Mel Hurtig

Gordon Soules Book Publishers Ltd., West Vancouver, Canada

Canadian Cataloguing in Publication Data

Main entry under title:

The True north strong & free?

Conference held Nov.8–9, 1986 in Edmonton.
ISBN 0-919574-83-1

1. Canada - Defenses - Congresses. 2.
Canada - Military policy - Congresses. 3.
Nuclear weapons - Canada - Congresses. I.
True North Strong and Free Inquiry Society.
UA600.T78 1987   355'.033071   C88-091039-9

Published by:
Gordon Soules Book Publishers Ltd.
1352-B Marine Drive,
West Vancouver, B.C., Canada
V7T 1B5

Information regarding programs and activities of The True North Strong and Free Inquiry Society should be addressed to:
The True North Strong and Free Inquiry Society
#203, 10006 - 149th Street
Edmonton, Alberta, Canada
T5P 1K8

Designed by Chris Bergthorson
Typesetting by Joy Woodsworth and The Typeworks
Printed and bound in Canada by Hignell Printing Limited

Table of Contents

Panelists Cynthia Cannizzo, Major-General (Ret.) Leonard Johnson, and Lois Wilson participated in question sessions in the following chapters: 6, 7, 8, 9, 12, 13, 15, 16, 17, 18, 19 and 22.

Acknowledgments

The True North Strong and Free? comprises the speeches given at the True North Strong and Free?—A Public Inquiry into Canadian Defence Policy and Nuclear Arms, held November 8 and 9, 1986, in Edmonton, Alberta.

The inquiry was successful because many individuals and organizations contributed time, energy and funds.

The event was sponsored by the Northern Alberta Chapter of the Council of Canadians and the Edmonton Chapter of the Canadian Physicians for the Prevention of Nuclear War (then known as the Physicians for Social Responsibility). Special credit goes to Mel Hurtig for initiating the idea and recruiting speakers, and to the coordinators of the inquiry, Lois Hammond and Irene Clay, who, with incomparable patience and matchless organizational skills, saw a good idea become a grand event. Other members of the tireless Steering Committee were Roberta Carey, Karen Farkas, Clyde Hurtig, Evelyn Levine, Brock Macdonald, Elizabeth McBride, Ian McBride, Elizabeth Munroe, Joyce Sorochan, Brian Sproule and Bill Stollery.

Thanks also to office assistants Susan Schutta and Lorna Dawson, registrar Don Horne, production manager John Sproule, display manager Kathy Radchuck, evaluation manager Karel Bennett and volunteer Bill Berezowski. Special thanks go to the art class students at St. Joseph's High School, Edmonton, who, under the direction of teacher Hank Zyp, produced all the colourful banners and signs for the event.

The inquiry was made possible by the financial support of the following organizations: Canadian Institute for International Peace and Security; Department of External Affairs, Government of Canada; Wild Rose Foundation, an Alberta Government Foundation; Government of the Northwest Territories; Students' Union, University of Alberta (sponsoring "The Three-Party Debate: Can Canada Really Be an Effective Peacekeeping Middle Power?); Clifford E. Lee Foundation; and the University of Alberta.

The following community groups also contributed generously through fund-raising efforts: Alberta Nurses for Nuclear Disarmament; Edmonton Peace Council; Franciscans of Western Canada; Gabriola Island Peace Association; Students' Union, Holy Trinity Catholic Community High School; Nanoose Conversion Campaign; Ponoka Peace CAPP Gang; Psychologists for Peace; Rio Terrace Moravian Church, Peace Ministry; Southminster United Church; Temple Beth Ora; and the United Church of Canada, Peace and Disarmament Task Force.

Support from ACCESS Alberta enabled the inquiry to be videotaped and broadcast repeatedly. The highlights of each speech are given in a one-hour videotape, available for purchase from Filmwest Associates Ltd., P.O. Box 11028, Edmonton, Alberta T5J 3K3.

Grant MacEwan Community College generously shared the Universiade Pavilion. Studio Graphics contributed the logo and artwork, and Resistance Graphics, the typesetting.

Thank you also to the 180 individuals who contributed financially, to the 165 hard-working volunteers, and to the 60 community groups that endorsed the inquiry.

Many students became involved in the inquiry. We congratulate Natasha Affolder of Sedgewick Central High School, the winner of The True North Strong and Free? School Essay Contest.

We thank the many people who helped to make the proceedings of the inquiry available in book form, particularly Roberta Carey, whose editing of the original transcripts and constant attention to detail contributed enormously to the quality of the book. We are also indebted to Colin Park for his contributions to the footnotes; to Elizabeth Munroe, Maureen Colclough and Anne Norman for editorial assistance; and to Lois Hammond for special assistance. Dr. James Foulks gave of his time to read and comment on the manuscript.

The Steering Committee is especially grateful to the speakers, who waived their customary fees and took time out of their busy schedules to join in the event. The inquiry was fortunate to have as moderators Bishop Remi De Roo and Jean Forest, who handled their difficult task with intelligence, humour and grace. Their presence was very important in maintaining the inquiry as an informed dialogue among people of differing views.

Lastly, a special thanks to the more than five thousand people who attended the inquiry, listened attentively for two days and responded so enthusiastically during the discussions and in their letters following the inquiry.

The True North Strong and Free Inquiry Society

Mel Hurtig

Introduction

MEL HURTIG

On Saturday, November 8, 1986, at 8:30 in the morning, over five thousand people gathered in Edmonton at the University of Alberta's huge athletic auditorium. Hazarding the minus 26° chilling cold and wind of the winter's worst snowstorm, they came to hear David Suzuki, Brigadier-General Don Macnamara, George Ignatieff, Bishop Remi J. De Roo, Gwynne Dyer and many others debate Canada's foreign and defence policy at a public inquiry, The True North Strong and Free?

They came from Halifax in the east and Yellowknife in the north and Victoria in the west to listen and to talk, mostly about Canada's defence policy and nuclear arms. Men and women from all walks of life gathered

Mel Hurtig is a leading Canadian publisher, and founder and honorary chairman of the Council of Canadians, a national organization dedicated to preserving Canadian economic, political, cultural and social sovereignty. He is also one of the founding members and a past national chairman of the Committee for an Independent Canada. In 1985, Mel Hurtig published the Canadian Encyclopedia, *the largest publishing project in the history of Canada. Over the past fifteen years, he has frequently spoken in all ten provinces on economic, social and political issues, on the future of Canada, on the dangers of excessive foreign ownership and on the development of Canadian natural resources. He has received much recognition for his work, including four honorary degrees, an appointment as an officer in the Order of Canada, the Association for Canadian Studies Award of Merit, the Royal Society of Canada's Centennial Medal, and the Canadian Booksellers Association President's Award.*

to learn about Canada's policies and possible alternatives to these policies, as well as about new ways individuals might participate in the decision-making process.

Sponsored by the Northern Alberta Chapter of the Council of Canadians and the Edmonton Chapter of the Canadian Physicians for the Prevention of Nuclear War, the two-day event was primarily concerned with two fundamentals — the risk of nuclear war and the possibilities for peace. The world has been caught in a protracted, dangerous and costly arms race that threatens its survival. Because Canada is geographically located between the superpowers, Canadians are in particular danger. In any serious military confrontation between the Soviet Union and the United States, Canada would become the "incinerated meat in the nuclear sandwich." But while our location makes us particularly vulnerable, it also presents an opportunity for us to play an important role in the search for international peace.

The inquiry was developed and presented with the firm belief that issues of Canadian security and world peace are everyone's business. Defence and foreign policy decisions are too important to leave to only the generals and politicians. As George Ignatieff told the audience, to thunderous applause, "There can be no incineration without representation."

Balanced dialogue was the essence of the inquiry. As well as being chosen for their expertise, speakers were carefully selected so that varied and often conflicting points of view were presented. Government, labour, all three major federal political parties, the military, research organizations and community peace groups were all represented.

To begin the inquiry, Bishop Remi De Roo set forth the requirements for meaningful dialogue:

> I invite you then to pursue an open dialogue, the condition for
> which is primarily the respect of persons. That means willingness
> on the part of each one of us to listen to the full range of opinions
> that will be expressed. I invite you to listen, not simply with your
> ears, but with your heart, and thus to be receptive to the fullness
> of truth.

This book is a record of the proceedings. Rather than being a series of technical or scientific research papers, it is a collection of impassioned speeches and the transcripts of a very lively debate. These are presented with minimal changes made by the editors for clarity and stylistic uniformity.

The many important questions that were discussed remain as critical and unsettled today as they were in November of 1986. Does Canada have the right kind of defence resources? Do we or should we have defence policies independent of our superpower neighbour to the south, and, if so, what should they be? Are NATO and NORAD fulfilling their stated purposes? Is Canada involved in nuclear proliferation through industrial and military cooperation with nuclear powers?

Those who approach this book with firmly preconceived ideas about the presentations made at the inquiry will likely be surprised. The inquiry audience listened carefully to the military voices—on the one hand, the articulate remarks of the officers presently in command, represented by General Don Macnamara, and, in contrast, the voice of those who have fought for Canada in past wars, represented by Major-General (Ret.) Leonard Johnson, C. G. Gifford, plus several former armed forces members who spoke from the floor. William Arkin from the Institute for Policy studies in Washington, D.C., reviewed Canadian government defence agreements with the United States, agreements that are not widely known, if at all. Ernie Regehr from Project Ploughshares revealed little-known facts about Canadian arms production.

Accustomed as we are to hearing only about the terrible dangers of nuclear war and the complicated problems in foreign policy that prevent us from changing defence policy, perhaps the most important surprise was the wealth of concrete alternatives the speakers offered. Gwynne Dyer's eloquent proposal for Canadian neutrality is thought-provoking. George Ignatieff called on a lifetime of experience in international relations to propose other specific alternate policies. Laurie MacBride outlined economic alternatives to arms production. The three-party panel of MPs engaged in a very lively, focused debate about alternatives.

Following their presentations, speakers were questioned first by the panelists—Dr. Cynthia Cannizzo, Major-General (Ret.) Leonard Johnson and the Very Reverend Lois Wilson—and then by the audience. The dialogue resulting from the questions was particularly informative. In this book, when the speaker was questioned right after the speech, the question-and-answer dialogue is at the end of the speaker's chapter. When two or three speeches were followed by a joint question period, then the question session forms a separate chapter.

The text alone, however, cannot convey the intense atmosphere of the active audience participation, which was one of the most important aspects of the inquiry. A white-haired veteran would speak, then a middle-aged woman from a small town, then a concerned high school student. All spoke with passion and a remarkable depth of knowledge and feeling that dramatically underlines the broad Canadian concern for world peace.

After two intense days, by late Sunday afternoon, the thousands of participants still listened attentively. They had worked hard through a most demanding program that was tightly scheduled to a fault, with hardly a break. They stayed to vote on the final resolutions, presented by moderator Jean Forest, which would make their opinions known to the Canadian government, the media and the public.

There are many reasons why The True North Strong and Free? inquiry was so successful. The inquiry was planned and organized by a truly grass-roots community. Inspired by the People's Enquiry into a Canadian Forces facility at Nanoose Bay, held in Nanaimo, British Columbia, in January 1986 (which dealt with nuclear submarine activities in the inland waters of the Pacific Coast), I suggested that a broader defence inquiry be held in Edmonton. A group of enthusiastic, talented and diverse people formed a large steering committee, and the Edmonton Chapter of the Canadian Physicians for the Prevention of Nuclear War offered financial support and office facilities.

The next few months saw hundreds of volunteers join in organizing the event. Many had never been involved with peace groups or political activities. They all came forward for the same reason—they care about our country and our world.

Early funding came from the Canadian Institute for International Peace and Security, the Bureau of International Security and Arms Control of the Department of External Affairs, the Students' Union at the University of Alberta, and the Government of the Northwest Territories.

The questions raised in Edmonton remain open today, and the inquiry continues with each person who reads this book. But one point is clear. An elderly man in the audience asked General Macnamara, "Would you please identify for us Canada's enemy?" The general replied, "Canada's enemy today is the potential for a nuclear war."

I sincerely hope that you will agree that the pages following are a valuable contribution to the vital debate about our country, our future and the search for world peace.

Resolutions

Panel members drafted resolutions based on submissions from the audience. In addition, each panel member submitted a resolution. Resolutions were voted upon by the audience at the end of the two-day public inquiry.

1. *Resolved,* that Canada seek an arms control agreement regulating all categories of cruise missiles.
   Carried

2. *Resolved,* that Canada rescind the cruise missile test agreement immediately.
   Carried

3. *Resolved,* that Canada endorse the Soviet nuclear test moratorium and urge the United States to respond in kind.
   Carried

4. *Resolved,* that Canada establish an international crisis management centre to reduce the risk of accidental nuclear war.
   Carried

5. *Resolved,* that the Canadian government establish an independent commission to examine alternative security policies for Canada, including the possibilities of non-alignment and neutrality. The commission would hold public hearings and make the study available through Parliament to the people.
   Carried

6. *Resolved,* that Canada acquire ice-capable submarines and other forms of underwater surveillance for the Arctic.
Defeated

7. *Resolved,* that annually the Department of External Affairs report to Parliament on what military commodities have been exported and to what destinations.
Carried

8. *Resolved,* that Canada withhold all financial, political and moral support for SDI.
Carried

Resolution presented by the Very Reverend Lois Wilson:

9. *Resolved,* that this conference request and encourage full, frank and informed participation of more government personnel in future consultations on peace and security, and that this be communicated to the Government of Canada.
Carried

Resolution presented by Major-General (Ret.) Leonard Johnson:

10. *Resolved,* that the government restore funding to the CBC in order to enhance international coverage and thus its ability to give Canadians clear windows on the world.
Carried

Resolution presented by Dr. Cynthia Cannizzo:*

11. *Resolved,* that in order to protect its sovereignty and serve its interests at home and abroad, Canada should (a) maintain an adequate defence capability, and (b) continue to work within its alliances and elsewhere to promote both nuclear and conventional arms control.
Defeated

---

* It was pointed out that the audience might wish to vote differently on the two parts of Dr. Cannizzo's resolution. The inquiry asked her if she wished to put forward two separate resolutions. Dr. Cannizzo declined.

A copy of the resolutions passed by the conference was sent to Prime Minister Brian Mulroney. Here is his reply:

February 20, 1987

Dear Mses Clay and Hammond,

I would like to thank you for your recent letter. There have been many dramatic changes which have shaped our world in recent years and our Government has recently concluded a formal study of our nation's foreign policy.

Submissions by Canadians to the Special Parliamentary Committee on Canada's International Relations covered a wide range of topics including such areas as security and arms control, trade, development assistance, relations with the U.S.A., human rights and the Northern dimension of Canada's foreign policy. Your writing to me is another indication that Canadians want their country to follow an independent, active and internationalist approach to our foreign policy.

I appreciate your taking the time to bring your particular concerns to my attention and have forwarded a copy of your correspondence to my colleague, The Right Honourable Joe Clark, Secretary of State for External Affairs, so that he too may have the benefit of your comments.

With every good wish,

Yours sincerely,

Brian Mulroney

PART I

The Issues

Panelists Cynthia Cannizzo, Major-General (Ret.)
Leonard Johnson, and Lois Wilson participated
in question sessions in the following chapters:
6, 7, 8, 9, 12 and 13.

Ambassador Douglas Roche

CHAPTER 1
Opening Remarks

AMBASSADOR DOUGLAS ROCHE

I have come to this platform first as an Albertan to welcome this great assembly to my home city of Edmonton and to congratulate the Council of Canadians and the Canadian Physicians for the Prevention of Nuclear War. I am here also as Canada's ambassador for disarmament to tell you how proud I am of the peace movement in Canada, to thank you for this tremendous expression of public concern about the most important issue of our time and to ask you for your continued help. I am here finally as a citizen of the world, as a member of the global human community, as a father, and as one person who is conscious of the beauty of God's planet

Douglas Roche was appointed Canada's ambassador for disarmament in 1984. In that capacity, he represents Canada at international meetings on disarmament, is a special advisor to the government and is the chief liaison between the government and non-governmental organizations. He heads the Canadian delegation to the Disarmament Committee at the United Nations. From 1972 until 1984, Douglas Roche was a Conservative member of Parliament for Edmonton South; while an MP, he joined Parliamentarians for World Order and was elected its international chairman in 1980. Douglas Roche is the author of eight books, including Justice Not Charity: A New Global Ethic for Canada *(Toronto: McClelland & Stewart, 1976). He gives a contemporary examination of the United Nations amidst the global crises of the nuclear arms race and economic development in* United Nations: Divided World *(Toronto: NC Press, 1984). He has received various honours, including the World Federalists Peace Award (1983).*

and our responsibility to protect it, yet who is determined to develop it and hand it on intact to the generations yet unborn.

This meeting shows that I am not alone in this hope and that no single member of this audience is alone. This outstanding gathering is not an isolated event, for across our great country, from the Atlantic to the Pacific, there is a rising concern about ending the nuclear arms race and there is more public involvement in these issues than ever before. I have seen this upsurge while touring Canada during this International Year of Peace. Together, we are helping to develop a stronger public opinion, to support policies and to build a world where national security is brought about by fewer arms, not more, and where personal security for the disadvantaged people of the world is obtained by spending more on development and less on arms.

Increasingly, people across our land and across our world understand that a radical reduction in the nuclear weapons held by the superpowers is an essential priority today. This reduction must come about by sincere negotiations in the continuing summit process that produced such a dramatic moment in Iceland. The summit in Iceland made the abolition of nuclear weapons a respectable subject.[1] That is a big step forward, and it is now unacceptable for the superpowers to fall back into rigid positions. Canada wants the productive summit process to continue, for there is now an extraordinary opportunity to achieve what only recently seemed to be a dream—concrete accomplishments in disarmament, stability and peace, paralleled by radical reductions in nuclear arms.

Canada wants a negotiated, verifiable, comprehensive test-ban treaty, one that will end all nuclear testing by all countries in all environments for all time. At the United Nations, Canada supports concrete, realistic steps towards such a treaty. Canada's agenda for arms control and disarmament includes support of the Treaty on the Non-Proliferation of Nuclear Weapons,[2] a chemical weapons treaty, the protection of outer space from weapons, and measures to build confidence and trust between nations. What is needed now is our unflagging determination as a people, as a government, and as a free society to make progress on the long journey to peace with security, freedom and social justice. All my experience in travelling throughout the world for three decades as a journalist, parliamentarian and diplomat tells me that there is scarcely any other country with Canada's strength, reputation and potential to give leadership to the world. This world—*our* world—is clearly at a turning point. Never before have we possessed the power to annihilate a nation or the power for such sweeping creativity. We live in an age of disruption, trying to find the ways not only to survive but also to bring the global society to a new and higher level of civilization. It is a political, economic and social struggle of massive proportions, and it is, at its core, an ethical problem that all of us face.

We must stimulate a new ethic based on global cooperation and the reconciliation of people. Such an ethic is not some vague concept, but it is very precise. Through global cooperation, countries in every region could implement those strategies for collective security and international economic development that have been so painstakingly laid out by the United Nations. Through reconciliation fostered by more international exchanges, we could widen the understanding that the planet is common ground that must be protected. Our concern with the number and type of nuclear weapons held by each side must not be allowed to stand in the way of deepening our understanding of the needs of the human family in a technological era. People everywhere have the same joys and sorrows, the same griefs and hopes. Our common purpose is to live in peace so that our common home, the planet, can continue to glisten with the glories of nature and resound with the vibrancy of its inhabitants.

Let our message from this weekend go out across the land to inspire even more Canadians. We will never lose hope, and our work will build the conditions for peace and development. Do not leave this meeting without renewing your own sense of hope. Determine to be part of the process for peace. Find new ways to inspire young people. Finally, whatever your background, whatever your role in life, never lose courage in creating the world of our dreams.

Notes

1. In October 1986, President Reagan and General Secretary Gorbachev met in Reykjavik, Iceland. There was no formal agreement, but the two reached broad agreement on a wide range of weapons reductions and testing matters—until the Strategic Defense Initiative was discussed. Gorbachev saw elements of SDI as threatening—it is widely agreed that the entire "protective shield" cannot work—while Reagan remained firmly committed to continued SDI research and possible development. The talks broke down.

2. This 1968 treaty is intended to limit the spread of nuclear weapons to non-nuclear countries. Under its provisions, the process of disarmament in nuclear countries must show progress or non-nuclear countries will cease to be bound by the treaty. It also guarantees non-nuclear countries access to nuclear technology for peaceful purposes.

Bishop Remi J. De Roo

CHAPTER 2
Moderator's Welcome

BISHOP REMI J. DE ROO

Our purpose today is to seek together the truth that will guide us all towards peace, the truth that will be the foundation for a lasting peace. So we are invited first to listen to each other as we inquire into Canadian defence policy and the issues surrounding nuclear arms, and second to combine our continued efforts to keep Canada our "True North, Strong and Free."

My role is to serve as your moderator, that is, as a facilitator and enabler. My contribution will be in the service of good order and punctuality so that all may be heard to the best of our abilities. I invite you then to pursue an open dialogue, the condition for which is primarily the respect of persons. That means willingness on the part of each one of us to listen to the full range of opinions that will be expressed. I invite you to

The Most Reverend Remi De Roo is Bishop of Victoria and the president of the Western Conference of Catholic Bishops. Growing up on a prairie farm in the 1930s, he witnessed the poverty of the Depression. As a result, he has been a passionate champion of poor and underprivileged people in Canada and other parts of the world. Bishop De Roo holds a doctorate in theology from the Angelicum University in Rome and has been Bishop of Victoria since 1962. In 1983, the Social Affairs Commission of Canada's Catholic Bishops, chaired by Bishop De Roo, issued a New Year's statement calling for a new and ethical approach to economic planning in Canada. Bishop De Roo has followed up this approach in Cries of Victims—Voice of God *(Ottawa/Toronto: Novalis/Lorimer, 1986).*

23

listen, not simply with your ears, but with your heart, and thus to be receptive to the fullness of truth.

True peace is a condition of harmony whereby all people are treated as responsible agents, as subjects of their own destiny, sharing common goals and promoting values recognized as meaningful by the majority. Peace, then, is both a project to be achieved and a gift to be received. So I invite you now, as we begin this momentous event, to pause for a moment to create an atmosphere of openness, of joy and, as Ambassador Roche said, of hope; to pause for a moment of quiet, a moment of prayer, a moment of listening in the silence of your heart. I invite you to raise your thoughts and aspirations to the Divine Giver of the gift of peace. I invite you to pause also to remember all those throughout the world who gave their talents and their lives so that you and I might enjoy the peace and freedom we experience today and so that you and I might be inspired to continue building peace in each generation.

CHAPTER 3
Facing the Possibility of Nuclear War

DOROTHY GORESKY, M.D.

Part of my responsibility this morning is to inform you about the possibility of laying waste our planet by destructive nuclear energy. But we must also become aware of the potential we humans have for an overwhelming constructive power to heal our planet.

I wish I could show you a poster called "Ultimate Beauty, Ultimate Disaster," by Kamekura, a Japanese graphic artist.[1] Your eyes would be drawn to many beautiful butterflies, only then to be repelled. The butterflies are all falling—because their wings are on fire. Kamekura experienced the bombing of Hiroshima. But how, without actually being victims, do *we* attempt to comprehend the devastating potential of nuclear weapons? For comprehend them we must, if we and our planet are to survive.

Imagine a planetary giant who has within his being all the potential for such destructiveness. His hair glows yellow like the sun because his surface temperature is 5500°C; his internal temperature is ten to thirty million degrees. That is the range of temperatures produced by the detonation of a nuclear bomb. Half of the energy released is a blast composed of two parts: static overpressure and dynamic overpressure. Static overpressure is like a great wall pressing on objects from all sides. The arms of our giant possess a crushing strength of up to twenty pounds per square inch of pressure beyond the fifteen pounds normally exerted on us by the earth's atmosphere. As little as one pound per square inch over normal pressure will shatter glass into millions of pieces. Dynamic overpressure means the super, hurricane-force winds that can be created by the giant's breath. Real hurricane winds may reach velocities of 160 miles per hour. Our giant can create winds from 500 to 600 miles per hour.

Dorothy Goresky, M.D.

The surface of our giant can give off radioactive elements. These we can neither see, nor smell, nor hear, nor touch, nor taste, but they affect our bodies in mysterious and frightening ways. These elements spontaneously emit particles which persist in our environment, some for only a few hours, some for thousands of years. Radioactivity affects the body by destroying cells or by damaging the way they function.

If we could be onlookers to a nuclear explosion, what would we see? Within two seconds, the heat from the giant's head would vaporize everything at the centre of a nuclear explosion. Everything would simply disappear. Radioactive material would immediately start spreading into the atmosphere. Beyond the central area of destruction there would be a zone in which our giant's arms, like a colossal nutcracker, would squeeze and crush everything within their embrace. The slightly lesser heat there would convert animals and humans into charcoal masses. All inflammable material would burst into flame. And now our giant's breath would hurl this part of the shattered, burning city and all its occupants into the air.

If a bomb were to drop on downtown Edmonton now, how long would it take for the destruction I have just described to happen? Ten seconds. This building would not likely be in the area of total obliteration, but in our area, and in an area of fifty or sixty square miles, fifty per cent of the people would be killed immediately. Four out of five of the remaining victims would receive unimaginable injuries—crushed chests and limbs, skull fractures, penetrating wounds, ruptured lungs and internal organs, crushed vertebrae, severed spinal cords, and profound hemorrhages. Up to two thousand of those injuries would be third-degree burns, one of the most painful conditions to endure and one requiring treatment at hospitals

Dr. Dorothy Goresky was born in Battleford, Saskatchewan, and received her medical training at the University of Alberta. After spending three and a half years as a rural medical practitioner in Saskatchewan, she worked in public health for eight years. In 1965 she was the first woman physician to join the staff of the Student Health Service at the University of British Columbia, where she continues to practise. Dr. Goresky was founding president of the B.C. Chapter of Physicians for Social Responsibility (now called Canadian Physicians for the Prevention of Nuclear War) and was the third president of the National Executive; she continues to serve on the national Board of Directors. In 1983, she was one of five Canadian delegates to the Third Congress of the International Physicians for the Prevention of Nuclear War in Holland. In 1985, she joined seven other Canadian PSR members attending the ceremonies in Oslo at which the International Physicians for the Prevention of Nuclear War were awarded the Nobel Peace Prize.

with special burn beds. Even if all the hospitals in Edmonton remained intact, there would be only about twelve special burn beds available. In all of North America there are only two thousand.

Over the next days and weeks, thousands of survivors would die of their injuries and acute radiation sickness. Because of their greater resistance to radiation, the insects and rodents would flourish, spreading the more resistant bacteria and viruses. Infections would then rapidly decimate the remaining survivors, whose immune systems would have been damaged, not only by radiation, but by malnutrition and by the physical and psychological trauma.

These are stories from the survivors of Hiroshima.

Here is an account from a schoolteacher on the outskirts of the city: "I climbed Hijiyama Mountain and looked down. I saw a few buildings standing, but Hiroshima didn't exist. That was mainly what I saw. Hiroshima didn't exist." And as she went to look for her family, she remembers: "The most impressive thing was the expression in people's eyes—in bodies badly injured which had turned black—their eyes looking for someone to come and help them—the emptiness—the helpless expression, was something I will never forget."[2]

Another survivor said: "I came upon, I don't know how many, soldiers burned from the hips up, and where the skin had peeled, their flesh was wet and mushy. They must have been wearing their military caps because the black hair on the top of their head was not burned. And they had no faces. Their eyes, noses and mouths had been burned away and it looked like their ears had melted off. It was hard to tell front from back."

What are the possibilities of providing medical help to survivors? Unlike 1945, there may well be no outside world to respond, for we are told that the possibility of a "limited nuclear war" is unlikely. Canadian Physicians for the Prevention of Nuclear War makes one clear statement, "There is no possible medical response to a nuclear war." This conclusion is based on a diversity of facts, but the one incontrovertible fact is that the most sophisticated hospitals, medical supplies and equipment, and the most skilled physicians and nursing teams, would be required to treat such injuries. Many of these personnel would be among the victims. The complete disruption of all civic systems—electricity, water, sewage, transportation, police—would preclude all hope of help. There would be none.

The number of nuclear weapons that can perpetrate such devastation has grown to many thousands. If the weapons from only one Trident submarine were released, they could wreak such destruction on *all* the major cities in the United States. We seek security from these very things that will destroy us. Do you know of any bird crazy enough to take the eggs of a deadly reptile into its nest and incubate them? Yet we humans nurture the seeds of our own destruction.

Never before has a threat existed that removed the certainty with which humans have always lived—the certainty that no matter what else happened in our lives, there would always be other generations to follow us and a life-sustaining planet to nourish them. That certainty has been removed from us forever, no matter whether we are advocates for nuclear arms buildup or for dismantling nuclear weapons. To be aware of this, at any level, is to feel pain for our world and for our collective future.

This experience of pain for the world is something new and strange for most of us. But I believe the survival of our earth depends on our experiencing such pain. My experience happened about six years ago, when a group of physicians returned from a conference in San Francisco and showed a film on Hiroshima. It was like a physical blow to realize that all there was left of that city was its burned-out, rubble-strewn streets and the only indication that humans had ever walked those streets was their shadows on the walls. The strange thing was that, even as I was experiencing the pain, I was aware that the overwhelming sadness engulfing me was not for possessions or people, not for my children or myself. It was for the earth. At that moment, no matter how impossible it seemed, I knew I had to do whatever little I could to prevent such destruction of our earth.

How do we evaluate that phenomenon? I can only guess that our innermost being recognizes the true relationship between ourselves and the universe.

Joanna Rogers Macy, in her book *Despair and Personal Power in the Nuclear Age* (Philadelphia: New Society, 1983) states: "No one is exempt from that pain, any more than one could exist alone in empty space. We are not closed off from the world but integral components of it, like cells in a larger body." Macy reports a brainstorming session on the question of why we avoid expressing in our daily lives our deep concern about the threat of nuclear war. Some ten categories of fear were elicited. It is valuable to go to Macy's book to help discover the degree to which each one of us holds those fears. It is essential that we acknowledge these feelings, for if we are cut off from our feelings, we are fragmented. We are less than whole. Being less than whole prevents the possibility of acquiring emotional maturity.

Therein lies the problem. Our sense of security is an emotional perception and has little to do with our reasoning mind. Our sense of vulnerability is also determined less by fact than by feelings. If this were not true, surely those who promote nuclear weapons as our security would, themselves, have felt secure long ago with their thousands of nuclear weapons.

One model for bringing about change suggests that there are three steps: awareness, acceptance and responsible action. We are unlikely to change our lifestyle if we are not aware, for instance, that we have high blood pressure and that our lifestyle is probably contributing to it. One might say that at this public inquiry we will be examining our country's blood pressure and how our lifestyle is making it what it is. That will be the awareness step. The acceptance step is being able to say, "Like it or not, that's the way it is." If we find ourselves in agreement with what we hear and learn about our country's blood pressure, there will be little need for action on our part.

But what if we don't like the level of our country's blood pressure? Can we leave the responsible action to others? The answer to that, of course, is no. As the medical model shows, only when you and I, in cooperation with our doctor and family and friends, decide to take charge is there any possibility of altering our blood pressure. How fortunate that in this country, too, we have the power to influence Canada's blood pressure. We can choose leaders who will effect the changes we believe necessary.

But perhaps you believe there is nothing that you can do. Take a moment to use your imagination. See yourself walking in the woods on a beautiful winter's day with a gentle snow falling all around you. You are caught by the beauty of each snowflake as it lingers for a moment in its crystal clarity on your outstretched hand before melting into nothingness. Suddenly you are startled by a loud crash and you look around to discover that the weight of the snow has torn a branch from the largest tree in the forest. *Which* snowflake did it? Each one of us is as unique, as insignificant *and* as powerful as a snowflake.

Another Japanese graphic artist, Shimooka, eloquently portrays the hope and faith he places in each individual. In his poster there are many snow-white doves fluttering above a pair of hands; the caption reads, "You are a remarkable magician because peace is concealed in your hand."

Let us learn to walk more softly on this earth. Let us learn to deal more gently with ourselves and with one another. Let us learn to release the magic in our hands.

Notes

1. Yusaka Kamekura, "Hiroshima Appeals 1983," in *Peace—Images for Survival* by Japan Graphic Designers Association (Washington, D.C.: Shoshin Society).
2. Eric Chivian et al., eds. *Last Aid: The Medical Dimensions of Nuclear War* (San Francisco: W. H. Freeman, 1982).

CHAPTER 4
The Debate in Canada on Issues of Peace and Security

GEOFFREY PEARSON

The role of the Canadian Institute for International Peace and Security is to increase knowledge and understanding of issues of peace and security from a Canadian perspective. We are not an advocacy organization; we do not advocate one particular policy or another. We do our best to help the debate on peace and security through information and activities such as this conference.

My task this morning is to set the stage for what is to follow. I first want to say a few things about the issues before us in Canada. The speakers at the conference fall into two categories. There are people here who are officials, who work for the federal government, and there are people outside the government. I was an official for thirty years and I'm very sensitive to the distinction between those outside the government who can speak freely and openly about what they want to do and those who represent government and are, in effect, speaking for others.

Let me tell you what is, in my view, a major question: What are the chances of a nuclear war and what can we do to prevent it? Dr. Goresky has told you something about what a nuclear war might be like. Let's assume that her scenario is correct. A nuclear war would probably be the end of civilization as we know it. What is the likelihood of it happening? I can't give you an answer to that question. I don't think anybody would dare to give you an answer to that question in any precise way, but the most important fact is that western governments, including the Canadian government, do not think that the chances of a nuclear war happening are very high. But many people think that the chances of a nuclear war happening are quite high. This gap between what governments think and what a lot of people think is a major reason for holding this kind of in-

Geoffrey Pearson

quiry. It's the responsibility of governments to do their best to answer this question. It is also the responsibility of every national government to defend the sovereignty and independence of its people. If nuclear war is a real possibility, then it is the supreme responsibility of governments to explain to their people what nuclear war is and what can be done about it.

What can Canada do? What should we as individuals do? Suppose that the best way of preventing a nuclear war was for Canada to cooperate as closely as possible with the United States. If the greatest priority is to prevent nuclear war and if the best way to do that is to cooperate as closely as possible with our ally and neighbour, then clearly that is the best thing to do. This illustrates the problem that results when you mix up the notion of independence with the notion of security.

If I've got the priorities right, then nuclear war is the supreme issue before us and everything else takes second place. That was the reason that our politicians in the 1940s and 1950s thought that the North Atlantic Treaty Organization was such a good thing. They thought that close cooperation with our NATO allies would prevent war. That is still the view of most people in our government. If that is the case, how can Canada be both strong and free?

Douglas Roche referred to the Iceland summit. What are the issues that we as Canadians might want to consider from that summit?

I'll mention two issues: one is the Strategic Defense Initiative (SDI), which appears to have been the obstacle to agreement in Reykjavik; and the other is the air-launched cruise missile. As Canadians we must make up our minds about these two issues. If it is true that the Strategic Defense Initiative is blocking progress on disarmament (and it may not be true), then we as Canadians have to decide where we stand on that issue. The testing of the air-launched cruise missile is an issue that goes to the heart of what I might call Canada's nuclear allergy. We do not have any nuclear weapons ourselves. Should we be helping others to test weapons

Geoffrey Pearson is executive director of the Canadian Institute for International Peace and Security. He was born in Toronto and educated at the University of Toronto and at Oxford University. He joined the Department of External Affairs of Canada in 1952. In Ottawa, Geoffrey Pearson served in a range of senior assignments in the Department of External Affairs, including chairman of the Policy Analysis Group, director-general of the Bureau of United Nations Affairs, and advisor on Disarmament and Arms Control Affairs. He held diplomatic appointments at Canadian embassies in Paris and Mexico City and at the High Commission in New Delhi. From 1980 to 1983 he served as Canada's ambassador to the Soviet Union.

that are capable of carrying nuclear weapons? If what governments believe is correct—that deterrence of the so-called enemy, the balance of power, and the alliance system are the right ways to prevent war—then we should agree to test that weapon. But if this belief is incorrect—if these policies will only lead to further conflict and competition—then we would be wrong to test those weapons.

I lived for three years in the Soviet Union as Canada's ambassador. I had not given much thought to what the Soviet people think about these issues. I came back convinced that their basic perceptions—of war, peace and nuclear war—are very much the same as those of Canadians. I'm talking here about the Soviet *people*. I'm not talking necessarily about their government, although I think their government also reflects this. In any event, the Soviet people have much more reason for not wanting war than we have. When Soviet leader Gorbachev was fourteen, his father was killed in the war; every Soviet family has a similar story to tell. Nevertheless, the Soviet Union has five million people in the armed forces. It has almost as many nuclear weapons as the United States does. It looks very threatening to its neighbours. The problem is that, although both sides desire peace, the situation remains tense, difficult and potentially disastrous.

In Canada's case, I hope we will consider how we can best use our influence, both in defending North America with our allies in NATO and in exerting as much influence as we can on some of the questions Doug Roche talked about: speaking out where we think it is right to speak out; not linking these issues to other short-term issues; remembering that the prevention of war is the supreme public good.

Finally, let us not be hypnotized only by the threat to Canada. I have also lived in India. In India the problem is not nuclear war. The problem is getting through the day and having enough energy and enough food. Wars are not caused only by rivalries between great powers. They are caused by injustice, poverty and unfairness. Most people in the world are poor. For longer than our lifetimes, we will have a world where most people are going to be poor. So when we think about what Canada can and should do, think about sharing the wealth. Think about the future in terms of a more just international order in the world and what we, as citizens of a rich and lucky country, can do to bring that about.

CHAPTER 5
Canada's Defence Policy

BRIGADIER-GENERAL DON MACNAMARA

My military colleagues and I feel privileged to have the opportunity to attend this large gathering of Canadians interested in discussing matters that are so near and dear to the hearts of our profession. I say that because we are wearing the uniforms of Canada's oldest and largest peace movement—the Canadian Armed Forces. We are here because we share the same goals as the sponsoring organizations of this conference [Our goal is the prevention of war, particularly a superpower nuclear war that could destroy our country. Our job is the protection of Canada's interests and the prevention of war.]

It is appropriate that we are holding this conference on the weekend preceding Remembrance Day, when we remember the 115,000 Canadians who were killed in or died as a result of the wars of this century. That was indeed a heavy price for a small and growing nation. But we are fortunate that war has not touched our shores for 170 years. Canada's losses in the three wars of this century pale in comparison with those sustained in the bombings of London, Coventry, Dresden, Hamburg, Tokyo, Hiroshima or Nagasaki. Nor must we forget that there are forty-three wars being waged today, although we are not directly involved. War and violence, in the eyes of many, continue to be useful means to achieve political objectives. The prevention of war, therefore, must remain at the top of our agenda.

I will touch on several elements involved in discussing defence policy in both theoretical and practical terms and will set the foundation for subsequent discussion.

As Geoffrey Pearson has said, a national security policy, of which a defence policy is an integral part, must be seen as the most important ele-

Brigadier-General Don Macnamara

ment of a country's business. The first and fundamental responsibility of a sovereign government is to ensure the survival and security of the nation—its people, their values, their institutions and their assets. These values and the institutions that they have spawned, although espoused by many if not most nations in the world, are in fact practised in only about twenty per cent of the world's countries.

I would like to remind you what those fundamental values are, because we as Canadians often forget them. First, we accept that we live in a country with a freely elected representative and responsible government—a democratic government. Second, we have the individual and personal freedom to pursue our own interests as long as they don't interfere with the rights of others, and that includes the freedom of choice and the freedom to protest. Third—something that is very Canadian—we recognize the ultimate value of human life, which we express in our sense of social justice, both domestically and internationally. These are the values that we seek to protect. These are what are at stake.

Defence policy is an integral part of our Canadian security policy, which, through a succession of governments, has been a three-pronged effort. First of all, it has involved the deterrence of war through collective defence arrangements such as the North Atlantic Treaty Organization (NATO) and the North American Aerospace Defence Command (NORAD). Second, the government has sought the peaceful settlement of disputes through mechanisms such as diplomacy, world courts, the United Nations and even military intervention in the form of peacekeeping forces. And the third prong is the quest for verifiable arms control and disarmament agreements, the aims of which are to achieve enhanced, or at least undiminished, security at a lower level of armaments and expenditure.

The matter of arms control will be addressed in detail by my colleague, Ralph Lysyshyn, from the Department of External Affairs, but remember that defence and arms control policies cannot be separated. Prime Minister Brian Mulroney reinforced this in a speech in 1985 to the Consultative Group on Disarmament and Arms Control Affairs. He said, "The

Don Macnamara is currently director of curriculum at the National Defence College in Kingston, Ontario. His thirty-five years of service in the RCAF and Canadian Forces have included eighteen years as a scientist in military research and development, positions on the directing staff of both the Canadian Forces Command and Staff College and the National Defence College, and several appointments in National Defence Headquarters, including director of strategic policy planning and director of arms control policy.

world at large should recognize that arms control is a component of, and not a substitute for, a healthy national security policy."

To explain our defence policy, I will list the stated roles of the Canadian Forces since the early 1950s. First, protecting Canadian sovereignty, that is national self-defence, or, as some political scientists call it, unilateral defence. Second, defending North America in conjunction with the United States through NORAD and other agreements, which could be called bilateral defence arrangements. Third, contributing to collective defence through NATO, a multilateral effort. And finally, contributing to the United Nations' work of collective security through peacekeeping forces, which political scientists might call an omnilateral approach.

This hierarchy of roles is not uniquely Canadian, because political scientists would also point out that the unilateral-bilateral-multilateral-omnilateral approach is an option open to any nation. Nor is the order necessarily a priority for the assignment of resources. The threats to the nation's security set the priorities, or at least they should. Thus Canadian defence policy should be considered as the sum of our national self-defence, collective defence and international security initiatives.

Statements regarding the security policy and the roles of the Canadian Forces are most often the beginning and the end of discussions of defence policy. Recently, however, a number of editors and letter-writers have indicated a need to assess defence commitments from the point of view of the threats to Canadian security. What are these threats to Canadian security, and where might they arise?

I believe that this level of analysis merits much more discussion than time permits, and to do a complete analysis we would have to discuss in detail the essential strategic factors as we see them today. Canadians are and should be concerned because of our location between the nuclear-armed superpowers. As Walter Gordon said, Canada is "the meat in the sandwich." Nuclear weapons are real—they are here and they cannot be "disinvented"—and in order to prevent, limit or control the use of nuclear weapons, we must concern ourselves primarily with the potential causes of a superpower nuclear war.

In our strategic analyses, the potential causes of a superpower nuclear war are seen to be, first of all, the possibility of a NATO—Warsaw Pact war in Europe; secondly, the escalation of other regional conflicts in which the superpowers' interests may become engaged; third, destabilization of the deterrent forces, that is, if either side perceived imbalances or opportunities; and finally, miscalculation, the misinterpretation of each other's intentions.

NATO's political and military strategy is based on the twin concepts of collective defence and deterrence. Canadian membership in NATO and our commitment of forces to the defence of Europe are aimed at the prevention of a NATO–Warsaw Pact war threat by contributing to the maintenance of the balance of forces that will deter aggression by the Warsaw Pact. Through this membership and this commitment of forces to Europe, Canada also has a voice at major arms control events—for example, at the Mutual Balanced Force Reduction talks in Vienna,[1] at the successful Stockholm Conference on Confidence- and Security-Building Measures and Disarmament in Europe[2] and at the Review Conference of the Helsinki Accord in Vienna.[3] Canada is present at these talks because we are a member of NATO and have troops in Europe. We also have access to the many and various councils and committees in NATO.

The second potential cause of a superpower nuclear war, the escalation of regional conflicts, is really one of the foundations of Canada's involvement in peacekeeping activities. Putting the cap on potentially dangerous regional conflicts can be in Canada's direct national security interest. Our involvement in every UN peacekeeping force, including Korea, should speak for itself. Our particular concern for major flashpoints, especially the Middle East, is reflected in our long-term and multifaceted commitment there.

The third potential cause, the destabilization of the deterrent forces or creation of perceived imbalances, is a component of our rationale for the European force commitments, not only in terms of absolute numbers but also as an expression of our will, a contribution to the very important psychological dimension of the alliance strategy. In addition, our participation in NORAD is very much aimed at the protection of the United States' deterrent forces and at providing these forces with early warning of attack through radar surveillance of the approaches to North America. A similar rationale has supported our involvement in the testing of the cruise missile.

The fourth potential cause, miscalculation or misinterpretation by the superpowers or alliances of each other's intentions, can also be reduced through our collective defence efforts in NATO and through our military and diplomatic voice at consultations with the United States and other NATO allies. We have a voice at the table, and this is especially important when instability may cause a potential conflict, such as we have seen in Poland, Czechoslovakia and Hungary. Also important are the confidence-building measures reached in Stockholm in 1986.

While Canada's primary defence concern, therefore, is the prevention of superpower nuclear war, we must also look at some other potential risks to Canadian security.

The first of these may be stated under an umbrella heading of challenges to Canada and Canadians, which includes the full range of concerns for protecting our sovereignty, such as safeguarding our fisheries and other offshore resources, maintaining surveillance of our aerospace, dealing with direct threats to Canadian residents abroad and ensuring our ability to evacuate them in times of danger. The last heading is, for lack of a better title, domestic turmoil. Realistically, we must take into account the effect of major natural disasters that require giving military aid to civil authorities.

I hope that this rather quick analysis provides some rationale for the choice of roles and the deployment of the Canadian Forces; however, the challenges of a complex, interdependent, international security situation and the very high costs of modern military equipment place real strains on our strategic analyses and defence budgets.

The Honourable Perrin Beatty, the Minister of National Defence, has stated:

> Our capacity as a country, and as an alliance, to conduct effective arms control negotiations with the Soviet Union and its allies rests on a confidence in our own strength and security, which is in turn based on shared values and true partnership. It is in these terms that Canada approaches national defence and arms control: not as two solitudes, but as priorities which share a common logic and a similar purpose.

We in the Canadian Forces take this responsibility seriously.

Finally, I observe with some pride that the Canadian Armed Forces is the largest organization in this country in which Canadians of both language groups, both sexes, all ethnic and educational backgrounds, are working together towards a common and honourable aim—the defence of our country, Canada.

Notes

1. In 1973, negotiations between the Warsaw Pact and NATO began in Vienna with the objective of mutual reductions of forces and armaments and associated measures in Central Europe. There is no treaty as yet.

2. The Stockholm conference successfully concluded with a treaty, signed by all Warsaw Pact and NATO countries and by every other European country except Albania, in September 1986. It contains agreements regarding the use and movement of ground forces and supporting forces and requires forewarning and certain kinds of observation by adversary staff.

3. The third review of the signatories' adherence to the terms of the first Accord of 1975 was held in Vienna in November 1986.

CHAPTER 6
Question Session

DOROTHY GORESKY, M.D.,
GEOFFREY PEARSON AND
BRIGADIER-GENERAL DON MACNAMARA

Members of the panel and the audience had an opportunity to question the three speakers. The panel consisted of Cynthia Cannizzo, The Very Reverend Lois M. Wilson and Major-General (Ret.) Leonard Johnson. Bishop De Roo was the moderator.

Cynthia Cannizzo

Dr. Goresky, fear is not one of your three steps of awareness, acceptance and action (nor is it the best way to promote awareness), yet you admitted that the disarmament movement itself promotes fear and then uses that fear of nuclear war as a tool to pressure the government. However, as a stress-management expert, you must know that fear can be a very dangerous emotion. It can cause the wrong action. It can cause panic or paralysis, can distort our perceptions and can decrease our ability to make decisions. Is it not, therefore, somewhat irresponsible to promote fear as a political tool?

Dorothy Goresky

Fear has not been the motivation behind exposing the dire consequences of nuclear war. Until we are aware of such things, there is no potential motivation for us to act. So fear is not the motivation. We realize very strongly, however, that by presenting these types of things to people we may, indeed, be paralysing them with fear. There has been no kind of motivation to use that fear as a political weapon in any way. Physicians —and I'm sure many, many other groups—recognize that there is a great need to help people get beyond the question of fear, but I emphasized that the need to experience the anguish of what could happen to our planet is

Cynthia Cannizzo

absolutely vital if we are to become involved in any way in trying to prevent this kind of event from happening.

Lois Wilson
Geoffrey Pearson mentioned the critical imbalance between the rich and the poor in the world, and since the majority of people in the world are poor, this imbalance is one of the causes of tension and wars. Last week I attended the first National Conference on Hunger in Canada, which revealed some horrifying facts about the disparities in our own country. So my question to General Macnamara concerns the nature of security. When you mentioned security, you said that we recognize the value of human life in the sense of social justice, both domestically and internationally. What kind of consensus about social issues do you think exists? Is social justice linked to Canada's defence policy, or is it ever even talked about?

Don Macnamara
About social issues and defence policy discussions—I assure you that the social dimensions of defence strategy are actively discussed. If one is going to do an adequate strategic analysis of the sources of conflict in the world, one does not simply look at the military causes. As Geoffrey Pearson has mentioned, the underlying causes are many. In our own analyses we look at political, economic, military, social and cultural underpinnings of the sources of conflict within and between nations. These are essential components of our analyses. What we are doing is identifying the sources and causes of conflicts and whether or not military intervention should be necessary, either in terms of collective security or in our own national defence interests. After that, we are the instrument of military power and we have neither the authority nor the resources to take action

Cynthia Cannizzo is assistant director of the strategic studies program at the University of Calgary. She has a Ph.D. from the University of Michigan and completed post-doctoral fellowships at the University of Lancaster, England, and the University of Calgary. Publications include a number of articles and The Gun Merchants *(New York: Pergamon, 1980). She is currently finishing a book on NATO. She is a member of the Consultative Group on Arms Control and Disarmament for External Affairs Office, Canadian Branch of the Inter-University Seminar on Armed Forces and Society (chairperson), International Institute for Strategic Studies, and other professional strategic and arms control organizations. She testified to the Standing Committee on External Affairs and National Defence on NORAD and to the joint parliamentary committee on Canadian defence.*

The Very Reverend Lois M. Wilson

in those other dimensions. That is the responsibility of other departments of government, but all of these factors are indeed taken into account in the analyses.

Leonard Johnson
General Macnamara, in your description of the strategic analysis and potential causes of a superpower nuclear war you gave us four potential causes. I suggest that there's a fifth: the danger of accidental war. This has been brought out in the last couple of years in the writings of people such as Paul Bracken and Daniel Ford. In addition, in May 1986, a conference at the University of British Columbia on accidental nuclear war brought together political scientists who had been working with quantitative data to try to come to grips with the probability of a nuclear war, and some of them have concluded that the risk is very much greater than we thought. If we continue as we are—and there's the qualifier in it—what they described as a nuclear time bomb may go off within about twenty-five years. I would like to know what the Department of National Defence's assessment is of that factor.

Macnamara
When one talks about accidental nuclear war, two dimensions are normally addressed. One is accidental nuclear war in terms of the technical aspects, that is, whether a weapon can go off or be set off inadvertently; the second is accidental nuclear war by miscalculation, which is one of the causes I mentioned. Within the Defence Department, and to the degree that we are privy to the control mechanisms of nuclear weapons on

The Very Reverend Lois M. Wilson is president of the World Council of Churches and co-director of the Ecumenical Forum of Canada. She is also a national board member of Amnesty International, the Canadian Institute for International Peace and Security, and the Refugee Status Advisory Board in Canada. Since she was ordained a minister of the United Church of Canada in 1965, Lois Wilson has worked on many issues within the United Church, the World Council of Churches and the United Nations. These issues have included world peace initiatives, the North-South dialogue, human rights, the changing role of women, and ecumenical and inter-religious dialogue. Since her election in 1983 as president of the World Council of Churches, she has travelled extensively in many developing countries. She is an expert on social and economic conditions in the Third World. She has received many honours, including ten honorary degrees, the Order of Canada, the World Federalists Peace Award (1985) and the Pearson Peace Medal (1985).

Major-General (Ret.) Leonard Johnson

either side, we are satisfied, as far as I am aware, that all feasible, technical means are in place—the use of redundant systems—to ensure that there is virtually no risk of such a technical accident occurring. And as to a risk of war between the superpowers, even should such a technical accident occur, there is the Accidental Nuclear Weapons Agreement between the Soviet Union and the United States, which was signed in 1971. It was aimed at the prevention of general nuclear war should a single nuclear event occur. This treaty was also aimed at neither side reacting reflexively should a third party launch a nuclear weapon at either the United States or the Soviet Union, thus leading one to think that the other superpower had initiated war.

As to the other form of accidental war, through miscalculation, it is very much in our interest, and very much our concern, to be able to participate in the various venues for discussion of the prevention of accidental war. The Stockholm Conference on Confidence- and Security-Building Measures, for example, was wholly aimed at the prevention of surprise attack at the conventional level—the creation of conditions that would increase trust. So both of these dimensions are indeed addressed.

Cannizzo

Geoffrey Pearson, if, as you have argued, the root causes of warfare and conflict are a very complex set of factors, such as great powers, human nature and the structure of the international system, how do we get people to move away from advocating simple, one-track solutions that would only address part of the problem, and get them to move towards the construction of politically viable and strategically sound solutions that address most, if not all, of the causes of warfare and conflict?

Leonard Johnson grew up in northern Saskatchewan, joined the Royal Canadian Air Force in 1950, and served in flying, staff and command appointments until his retirement in 1984. Promoted to brigadier-general while commanding Canadian Forces Base Edmonton in 1974, he commanded the Canadian Forces Training System, served as associate assistant deputy minister for policy at National Defence Headquarters, and commanded the National Defence College at Kingston from 1980 to 1984. Now living in retirement near Westport, Ontario, Major-General Johnson is a member of Generals for Peace and Disarmament, the Group of 78, the Pugwash Movement, Veterans Against Nuclear Arms, and other public interest groups. He is a member of the Royal Canadian Legion and a lay reader in the Anglican parish of Nowboro-Westport.

Geoffrey Pearson

I don't know. One of the problems in disarmament negotiations is that we tend either to say that *everything* must be settled at once or to say that we'll go step by step and one piece at a time. The danger of the latter approach is that people forget what the goal is and think that one step at a time is okay. The partial test-ban treaty in 1963 was predicated on the assumption that there would be a comprehensive test-ban treaty soon afterwards.[1] That was twenty-three years ago. People tend to forget, if you do it one piece at a time, what it is that the whole is all about.

On the other hand, you can try to settle everything at once. Soviet leader Gorbachev tried that at the Iceland summit at Reykjavik. He put proposals on the table that would, in effect, lead to the abolition of strategic nuclear weapons in ten years. That was a revolutionary proposal. President Reagan apparently said, "Okay, I agree to that," but at the last moment said, "But wait, there's one other factor I forgot and that is, I won't give up the Strategic Defense Initiative." So the whole thing fell apart, and the Soviet Union has gone back to saying: "Okay, we won't settle these issues one by one. We're only going to settle them on the basis of a package of the kind we put forward in Iceland." So in a sense we're not as far ahead now as we were before Reykjavik. There's no clear answer to your question. What it comes down to is a matter of gradually building up a sense of confidence and trust so that these issues become less difficult.

Husbands and wives don't bargain with each other each morning about whether they're going to settle all problems today or just one or two problems. We have recently reached an agreement in Stockholm that is leading to greater confidence there. Without that sense of greater confidence, it's going to be difficult to agree on even small things. So this is where people come in, I think. People can lead and help governments to take some risks.

Cheryl McKercher (Edmonton, Alberta)

Geoffrey Pearson, how much effect can Russian peace movements have on changing Russian foreign policies compared to the effects of western peace movements?

Pearson

They couldn't hold this meeting in Moscow, that's for sure. It's not easy for people there who oppose the policies of their government to make their opposition clear in any public way. If they hang a banner outside their apartment window, they are liable to be arrested for subversion. On the other hand, there is discussion and debate underneath the surface. It goes on outside the public view, and as I said in my talk, I think the Soviet people are just as interested as you are in these questions, if not more so, but their opinions are expressed in different ways than they are in the West. There is now evidence of somewhat more public debate. The newspapers are publishing letters that do challenge official views. This is a new development. Although we may see a gradual change in the way the Soviets conduct public discussion, at the moment the Soviet peace movement is really not able to influence the discussion. In addition, the Soviets say everybody in their country is for peace, so why should we have a separate peace movement.

Ron Aspinall (Green Party and Canadian Physicians for the Prevention of Nuclear War, Tofino, British Columbia)
Geoffrey Pearson alluded to this topic. Is it not hypocritical for Canadians to boast of themselves as emissaries of peace when it was Canadian uranium that was in the Hiroshima and Nagasaki bombs? Our government allows testing of submarine and air delivery systems for nuclear weapons, and our industries work and derive profit from these immoral weapons of megadeath.

Pearson
I can't speak for the government. If you want to address the question to the government, then you'll have to find somebody to speak for the government. And I can't really comment in any detail on the subject that you raised, because I don't feel that I know enough about these matters. But I think that behind your question is the assumption that anything Canada has to do with nuclear weapons—I'm not sure whether you're including peaceful nuclear energy—is bad and we should get out of it. That assumption really leads to the conclusion that we should probably be a neutral country without any cooperation on defence matters with the United States. You saw what happened in the case of New Zealand, which banned vessels carrying nuclear weapons from its ports. This led to a virtual breakdown in their defence cooperation with the United States. Now whether that solution is acceptable to the Canadian people is something that has to be decided in elections, but so far there's no evidence that that the majority of Canadians are willing to do that.

Tim Nixon (Project Ploughshares, Edmonton, Alberta)
General Macnamara, you've stated that your mandate is to protect our freedom and sovereignty. How may we ensure that our free country, our sovereign country, might make an independent contribution to world peace when our own democratically elected representatives are not al-

lowed access to documents such as the renewal of the NORAD agreement, which our generals in the Defence Department officially have made with the United States Defense Department?

Macnamara

I think that the essence of the question is whether or not there should be public disclosure of all defence agreements between Canada and its allies. It is very difficult to effect a strategy, a defence policy, against a perceived threat from an adversary if you are going to tell your adversary in public exactly how it is you intend to prevent him from reaching his objectives. So there has to be, at some stage of the game, for better or for worse, secrecy and confidentiality in terms of government policy and agreements on national security affairs.

Kevin O'Reilly (Nuclear Free North, Yellowknife, Northwest Territories)

I would like to know why the Department of National Defence is not giving northerners any detailed information on recent and proposed military initiatives such as cruise missile testing, low-level flights and the North Warning System. Not only are we not given adequate information, but we are not even consulted about these initiatives, although we will bear the brunt of them if they are used. Why?

Macnamara

Discussions can arise from your requests to have such a consultation. One of the great gifts of democracy is that we can participate in this way. If you feel that the government has not consulted with you, then you are quite at liberty to write to your member of Parliament and ask for consultation; and indeed the Defence Department takes its direction from our elected representatives.

Emlen Littell (Vancouver Island Veterans Against Nuclear Arms)

How can Canadian sovereignty and defence be controlled by Canadians if we are linked to NORAD, SDI, and Strategic Defense Architecture 2000 Plan,[2] which can lead to first-strike capabilities for the United States without Canadian participation?

Macnamara

We are in NORAD, and the responsibility and contribution that we make to that command is to provide strategic warning—that is, to identify whether an attack is taking place against North America across our territory, to characterize the nature of that attack, and to give advance warning to strategic forces in the United States. That is our contribution to deterrence in North America.

The Canadian government's policy is that there is not a government-to-government relationship concerning the Strategic Defense Initiative. I do not know of any Canadian company that has received an SDI contract. There has been no official participation in SDI. The Strategic Defense Initiative is a research program, and its future is still up in the air. There is a whole host of technologies, many of which have to work together to make SDI succeed. Some of these, incidentally, can be in Canada's best interests, such as the capability to maintain surveillance of our own territory from space-based radar satellites. We do not have any involvement in SDI. Also SDA 2000 was prepared by the United States virtually without consultation with Canada. The fact is that we are not implicated in the way in which you implied.

Jim Baldwin (Greenpeace, Vancouver, British Columbia)
General Macnamara, you suggested that Canada would be destroyed in the event of a nuclear war between the superpowers. If this is so, it would appear that Canada's defence policy, based as it is on weaponry, is functionally irrelevant. Wouldn't it be appropriate to phase out our armed forces and instead spend our defence budget of approximately ten billion dollars a year to create alternatives for building world peace?

Macnamara
I know of no country in the world that is without armed forces, with the exception of Costa Rica, which has phased out its armed forces but has a fairly large police force. So I do not see any possibility that Canada's armed forces will cease to exist, whatever reallocation of resources you might have in mind. Second, with regard to whether or not the current posture contributes to the defence of Canada, it's important to recognize that the posture is aimed at doing what we can to defend ourselves. Now if you look at the size of the forces, the size of our population and the size of our country, our independent defence of ourselves is virtually impossible. What is really in our best interest is being able to contribute where we can to international security and international stability, and that is indeed what we do through peacekeeping operations. It is also what we do as part of the consultations that take place within the alliance structures, and for us to abrogate those opportunites—for us to back away—would not, I believe, increase our security one whit. We would still be exposed to exactly the same risk, and the difference would be that we wouldn't have a voice in controlling that risk. So I cannot see any sense in going in the direction you suggest.

John Guy (Project Ploughshares, Calgary, Alberta)
Mr. Pearson, you said that if drawing closer to the United States would help to prevent nuclear war, then Canada should do it. If drawing closer to the Soviet Union would help to prevent nuclear war, should we consider doing that? You didn't pose that question in your speech. Why not? And would you now care to comment on it?

Pearson
I didn't leave it out deliberately. I just didn't think about it. I was trying to think out loud, which is always a dangerous thing to do. Logically, you're absolutely correct. I put the question in terms of what is the supreme issue, and the issue I said was how to prevent nuclear war. If you agree that that is the issue, then what is the best way of going about it? And I said that if it meant a "free defence policy" with the United States (somewhat like free trade), then that would be the right thing to do. If it also meant drawing closer to the Soviet Union, I agree that that would also be the right thing to do. I'm only asking us all to think anew about this question, get the question right, and then think about the answers. And I'm not saying that governments don't do that. They do. After all, governments are just as concerned as citizens; governments are made up of citizens who have the responsibility to prevent nuclear war. Maybe we're reaching a stage where we should have a better dialogue between governments and citizens on this issue, and the presence of General Macnamara and his colleagues here is a step in the right direction.

Lawrence Dombro (Edmonton, Alberta)
Dr. Goresky, if Star Wars were operating at its full capacity, with its primary, secondary and tertiary shields in place, would it be a shield against all nuclear weapons, or is there a certain percentage of warheads that would still get through, thus causing the cold death of the planet? If this is the case, then shouldn't it be stressed that Star Wars is not only a complete waste of technology, money and human effort, but also that it should not be used as a hindrance to arms reductions the way it was used at the Reykjavik summit by President Reagan?

Goresky
My detailed knowledge of SDI is very limited, but I gather that there is absolutely no potential for SDI being totally effective at present, in the near future, or even in the far-distant future. Eugene Carroll[3] addressed this question when he spoke at the 1986 Vancouver Centennial Peace and Disarmament Symposium,[4] and I believe that he said that several former U.S. secretaries of defence had stated that if Star Wars ever went past its present stages, then all hopes of negotiations for nuclear disarmament

would vanish. Therefore, as far as I can make out, the chief danger of the SDI program is the jeopardy in which it places nuclear disarmament.

Lieutenant-Colonel (Ret.) Woodrow Coward (Veterans Against Nuclear Arms, Galiano Island, British Columbia)
General Macnamara, this meeting has to do with Canadian sovereignty. Would you please identify for us Canada's enemy? Canada's enemy—not the enemy of our allies, but *Canada's* enemy. Would you identify the specific hostile acts against Canada that form the basis of that identification?

Macnamara
In a technical context you have an enemy when you are at war. Until you are at war, you don't really have an enemy as such. Perhaps you have an adversary. Perhaps you have someone with whom you have a confrontation, but you do not necessarily have an enemy. Canada's enemy today is the potential for a nuclear war. There is no one country that stands to be an enemy to Canada. An enemy of Canada at the present time is a conceptual threat. Within that, there are a number of other enemies: the causes of unrest, the causes of conflict, the causes of instability and the causes of poor international relations, which can bring country against country. Dr. Wilson made reference to this earlier. We do, indeed, have to take account of the whole spectrum of military, political, social, economic and cultural enemies. In the whole range of policies of the Canadian government—defence and otherwise—we attempt to address all of these enemies in Canada's interests.

George Dajenais (Edmonton, Alberta)
General Macnamara, in view of the stated goal of the armed forces to preserve Canadian security, can you explain the deletion of a clause banning NORAD involvement in anti-ballistic missile systems in a recently signed NORAD agreement between Canada and the United States.[5] Can you explain how this helps or enhances this goal, and are the armed forces in full agreement with this deletion, which seems to set the stage for Canadian involvement in this SDI morass?

Macnamara
I can't comment on why this clause was deleted or on whether it is something that the Canadian Forces agrees with or disagrees with. The NORAD treaty is a government-to-government agreement. With regard to whether or not Canada should be interested in anti-ballistic systems—within the Anti-Ballistic Missile Treaty there is provision for both sides to undertake certain research, and both the Soviet Union and the United

States are undertaking such research.[6] The Soviet Union has deployed an anti-ballistic missile defence around Moscow. The United States had a system in place at a missile silo base in North Dakota, which it dismantled in the early 1970s. If we are to be participants in the protection of our sovereignty and if the defence of North America at some stage or another involves the discussion between the two superpowers of anti-ballistic missile systems (within or outside the treaty), it is in our strong interest to be able to participate in those discussions and not be left outside the door.

Notes

1. This treaty betwen the United States and the Soviet Union banned tests in the atmosphere, underwater and outer space. Additionally, the Outer Space Treaty of 1967 more explicitly banned *orbiting* weapons of mass destruction, and the Seabed Treaty of 1971 banned the placement of nuclear weapons on the seabed.

2. Strategic Defense Architecture 2000 (SDA 2000) is the command and technical system to coordinate defence against ballistic missiles, cruise missiles, bombers and sea-launched missiles.

3. Rear-Admiral (Ret.) Eugene P. Carroll of the U.S. Navy, with experience as commander of a nuclear-armed fleet and strategic nuclear war planning for the Pentagon, is now the deputy-director of the Center for Defense Information in Washington, D.C. This independent centre for military analyses and lobbying is used even by members of the U.S. Congress to balance the views of the National Security Council and the Pentagon.

4. See *End the Arms Race: Fund Human Needs* (West Vancouver: Gordon Soules, 1986), pp. 29–36.

5. The NORAD agreement was redefined by a simple "exchange of notes," in force from March 11, 1981. Parliament was not consulted and few Cabinet ministers knew what the changes meant. NORAD was officially renamed North American Aerospace Defence Command (formerly North American Air Defence Command). The previous agreement had been a detailed, point-by-point document. Its replacement was very general and brief, and in particular *omitted* a 1968 clause that prohibited any involvement with anti-ballistic missile systems. This omission was widely viewed as a possible precursor to bringing SDI technology into Canada.

6. The recognition of ABM defences as destabilizing led to the ABM Treaty. Both superpowers were permitted to retain one specified installation, and the Soviet Union retained a dense protective system around Moscow. The United States allowed its protection of a North Dakota missile site to go into disuse.

CHAPTER 7
Is Canada a Silent Nuclear Power?

ROBERT PENNER

Is Canada a silent nuclear power? Does Canada participate actively in the nuclear arms race? Is this country silent about that participation? Are we silent about international matters that should concern us? In my opinion, the answer to all these questions is yes.

Are we, as a nation, rising to the huge challenge of the arms race? Are we adequately evaluating what our role in it could or should be? Is this country doing all it should to prevent nuclear war? Unfortunately the answer here is a rather sad and disappointing no.

Canada is heavily involved in the arms race in three main ways. First, we're involved in the production, testing and development of nuclear weapons, and their related systems and other technical and material support. Second, Canadian military systems are integrated into the United States' nuclear war-fighting plans. Third, we provide political support for the nuclear arms race.

We all know that Canada doesn't possess its own nuclear weapons, but most of us also know that Canada indirectly fuels the arms race through its own involvement in the nuclear weapons and war-fighting infrastructure of NATO and the United States. For example —

• We allow the United States to test the cruise missile and other weapons systems under the umbrella weapons-testing agreement of 1983.[1]

• We accept U.S. plans to disperse nuclear-armed bombers to airfields on Canadian soil in times of crisis.

• We routinely allow the United States to put nuclear-armed vessels in Canadian ports.

• We allow Canadian waters to be used for deep-water testing of torpedoes for nuclear-attack submarines. Virtually the entire Canadian fleet

55

Robert Penner

and a substantial part of our air force are geared to anti-submarine warfare.
• The United States has been allowed to fire mock neutron bomb artillery shells in Canada.
• The United States has regularly used Canadian territory to communicate with its nuclear bomber force.
• The United States is allowed to use Ellesmere Island for high-frequency testing so that it can create a satellite system to control weapons delivery during a protracted nuclear war.
• The United States plans to expand its air-survival communication network to include Canada so that when the world is destroyed, members of the military can still communicate with each other.
• Although refusing to give direct support to Star Wars, the Canadian government has described Star Wars research, the key stumbling block to arms control today, as "prudent."
• With virtually no public debate, Canada agreed to participate in the North Warning System, an integral part of the nuclear war–fighting plans of the U.S. military.
• We allow an extremely high percentage of Canadian uranium and uranium by-products to find their way into nuclear bombs.

Other than that, there's hardly any involvement at all!

In fact, this list is just the beginning of our involvement. A colleague of mine, Steve Shallhorn, has just produced a map which shows more than 140 locations in Canada where nuclear war is the business of Canada, and that's just the tip of the iceberg.

Obviously the answer to the question, Is Canada a silent nuclear power? must be yes, but the real question is, Where does that silence come from? It's the silence that's the problem.

The points I've listed are mainly technical matters; these are symptoms of the disease. The disease can be more clearly identified in the word *silent*. With only rare exceptions, Canada is silent to the buildup of the arms race, silent to the wrong-headed actions of our neighbour to the south, silent to the wishes of the vast majority of people of this country,

Robert Penner is the coordinator of the Canadian Peace Alliance, an association of four hundred peace-related groups from across Canada. He was a national spokesperson for the Peace Petition Caravan Campaign in 1984 and the coordinator of the Toronto Disarmament Network from 1983 to 1986. He has been an organizer of several national and local anti-cruise protests. Bob Penner was formerly a student of classical guitar at the Royal Conservatory of Music.

and silent at a time when the world cannot afford to be silent. Because we won't take a strong political stand against the arms race, we end up with these nuclear war–fighting support systems in our country.

This country and our leaders are keeping quiet at the very moment they should be shouting. They're dabbling when they should be leading. They're studying when they should be acting, and they're acquiescing when they should be rebelling. It seems to me that Canadian disarmament policy can be summed up in three words: lack of courage.

I believe that nuclear war is likely. I believe that the world could be destroyed quite easily. It's frightening to imagine the time when it's too late to do anything more. Thinking of a time when there is nothing more we can do should compel us to action now. But we musn't do just anything; we must do everything possible. We must act before it's too late.

Here is a quote from Martin Luther King, Jr.:

> We are faced with the fact that tomorrow is today. There is such a thing as being too late. Over the bleached bones of numerous civilizations are written the pathetic words, "Too Late". If we do not act, we shall surely be dragged down the dark corridor of time reserved for those who possess power without compassion, might without morality, and strength without sight.

The human race does not have the luxury of small steps when the world is in crisis. It's *our* bleached bones King is referring to. Faced with the risk of the end of the human race, we must take risks ourselves and stand up and be counted. Refusing to test the cruise missile would have been a risk for the Canadian government, and it would have been difficult, but that's precisely why it would have been so meaningful.

The Canadian government could take a risk today and support the Soviet proposals made at the summit in Reykjavik. They're good proposals. We should support them. I'm taking a small risk even saying that. The first rule of being in the peace movement is that you can never say anything positive about the Soviet Union, so I've violated that rule already. The second rule of being in the peace movement is that if you do say anything positive about the Soviet Union, you immediately have to qualify it by saying three bad things about human rights or other things the Soviets do wrong, but I'll take a further risk and avoid that for now.

I think the Canadian government should take a small risk and support the Soviet Union's unilateral moratorium on the testing of nuclear weapons, which is one of the most important arms control initiatives in recent years. Can you imagine a country that purports to have a comprehensive test-ban treaty at the top of its agenda saying nothing positive about such a large concession by the Soviets? I'd like a Canadian government representative to explain how a unilateral cessation of nuclear testing by the

Soviet Union is not a good thing. Do we think that the moratorium is not a good thing only because the Soviet Union has done it? What a shame if such a significant opportunity is missed.

Even if the United States doesn't agree with us, why does Canada not stand up and be counted? Why not stand up like New Zealand and say: "We don't care if you threaten us. We don't care if you retaliate. We don't even care if you aren't nice to us anymore. We are going to end our support for the nuclear arms race because we believe it's the right thing to do."

With all due respect to some previous speakers, it's not just a question of wanting peace—we all want peace—but we're talking about what specific policies Canada needs to put forward to help us achieve peace. It's just not good enough to say that all the speakers at this public inquiry are on the same side. There are very serious differences of opinion. The Canadian government has a list of disarmament policies that it supposedly supports, but its actual policy contradicts almost all of these points. Point four is that Canada supports a comprehensive test ban, but when the Soviet Union moves on this question, the Canadian government says nothing. Point five is that Canada is against an arms race in outer space, but the government says Star Wars research is prudent. Point three is that Canada supports a ban on chemical weapons, but when the United States asks Canada to lead the charge within NATO for support of a new chemical weapons production plan, Canada does so. Former Defence Minister Erik Nielsen urged his NATO colleagues to "share in the moral burden" of this decision to proceed with chemical weapons. To their credit, six of the fifteen NATO allies had their own morality to worry about and opposed this decision. But the problem goes beyond Canada's lack of response to each particular issue. Canadian complicity in the arms race goes to the heart of the policy we support and defend through NATO and other international military agreements.

Our country supports nuclear war not just indirectly but directly. Our government, our External Affairs Minister [Joe Clark], our Prime Minister [Brian Mulroney], and their representatives at this inquiry support the initiation of nuclear war.

The policy of NATO is to reserve the right to use nuclear weapons not just to deter a nuclear attack but to respond to a conventional attack in Europe or elsewhere. Our government, through NATO, subscribes to the policy that states that the West could be the first to use nuclear weapons. In other words, if the Soviet Union invades Europe, NATO will destroy the world—because once nuclear weapons begin to be used, there's no stopping them. There will very quickly be global thermo-nuclear death. I hope the Soviet Union doesn't invade Western Europe, but somehow I don't think the destruction of the planet is an adequate response.

I submit that all who do not oppose a policy that allows nuclear war to be initiated are committing a criminal act. Our government does not oppose that policy.

Here's a good statement from a prominent Canadian leader on precisely this issue.

> Canada had no defence policy, so to speak, except that of NATO, and our defence policy had determined all our foreign policy. We had no foreign policy of any importance except that which flowed from NATO, and this is a false perspective for any country. It is a false perspective to have a military alliance determine your foreign policy. It should be your foreign policy which determines your military policy.

Pierre Elliott Trudeau said that shortly after being elected prime minister. Later he also said we had to test the cruise missile because the NATO allies wanted us to. Canadian policy is a timid policy, and our allies know that.

Canada is a member of NATO and NORAD, is on the Joint Board of Defence, and has made more than three hundred secret bilateral defence arrangements with the United States, and a special provision for the cooperation and sharing of military intelligence. Our role seems to be that of a follower, rather than a former, of policy of these bodies.

For example, Star Wars cannot be implemented without the use of Canadian territory. Clearly the U.S. military expects little trouble in using our territory. In fact, many of the agreements that will tie us to Star Wars are already in place, for example NORAD and the North Warning System.

In fact, the U.S. military needn't ask Canada's approval for very much. The more we become integrated with the U.S. military, the more we lose control of our defence policy. The United States has plans to disperse nuclear bombers in Canada in times of crisis. These plans call for no prior consultation until the crisis, at which time the Canadian government could supposedly say no.

It sounds good in theory. Let's look at the practice. During the Cuban missile crisis in 1962,[2] the United States asked Canada to put its forces on full alert. Prime Minister John Diefenbaker said no. Defence Minister Douglas Harkness disagreed and, in defiance of the Prime Minister, ordered the alert himself. However, the armed forces had already decided to put themselves on alert without the knowledge or approval of the Prime Minister or the Minister of Defence. One would assume that this instruction came directly from the U.S. military. So much for our right to say no.

If the problem is a lack of courage, what's the solution? How do we get our political leaders to act more courageously? This is a problem we won't solve easily. By definition, politicians are followers rather than leaders of the will of a society, but it's amazing how much courage develops in a situation when two options are equally unpleasant. Jumping out of a window of a four-storey building is suddenly a lot easier when the house is burning. And that's the role of the peace movement and public opinion in Canada—to make it more difficult to say yes than to say no to the nuclear arms race. We have to make it clear that politicians who do not respond to the public's concern about the arms race face political consequences.

If you want to bring about change by being nice to people and hoping they'll listen to you, then the strategy of the Canadian government is right on course, although it doesn't seem to be bringing many results. If you want to bring about change by doing what's right, refusing to participate in criminal plans, speaking out when you disagree and building public opposition to policies you oppose, then this government has a long way to go.

Being a nation means more when you stand for something. This country should stand for an end to the arms race, not just in words but in actions. As a sovereign country, we should not be afraid to act on such crucial questions.

One thing that's certain is that if each person at this inquiry did something about it, this country wouldn't be silent any longer. If all the people who oppose the arms race acted together, Canada's involvement would end tomorrow. No government could withstand that challenge. The house would be on fire, and the politicians would jump out of the window; they would begin to take a few risks in bringing Canada out of the arms race and bringing the world closer to real peace and nuclear disarmament.

We must remember what Martin Luther King said, and we must demand that our elected leaders remember it as well. King had the privilege of judging from the future the mistakes of the past. No human being will ever have that luxury should we fail to prevent nuclear war. We must make the necessary judgements today. Such judgements can only lead to one conclusion: we aren't doing enough. Canada can be silent no longer. We must act more decisively, more courageously and more honestly. We must support any action that slows the arms race and must oppose any action that does not. We must get nuclear weapons and all the assorted paraphernalia out of this country and do everything possible to ensure that our influence is effective now.

"Tomorrow is today." Martin Luther King knew the only road to civil rights. He also knew that destruction could come before change. He knew he could not be tentative. Millions in Canada and around the world know that we cannot afford to be tentative either, nor should our government.

We must act together, consistently and courageously. We are compelled as citizens of this country and of this planet to use whatever means are available to us to stop the madness before we share the pathetic epitaph, "Too Late."

QUESTIONS

Lois Wilson

I'd like you to comment on the confidence you have in the political processes in this country. I sense a deep cynicism about political processes and the record of the present and future governments on the issues we are discussing. Is it worth restoring credibility to the political process, and if so, how? In the previous question period, Kevin O'Reilly asked about getting information from the government, and he was told to go to his member of Parliament. We all know that if you write a letter to your MP, you get a form letter saying: "We will take it under advisement." So how do you break through the logjam of what we perceive to be democracy? Are there alternatives? You said we should use whatever means are available. What are those means?

Robert Penner

Democracy in this country is imperfect. I think we all recognize that. But we have to use the options that are available. We have the electoral process as one avenue. We also have the process of this type of meeting, of public information, of mobilizing a large number of people. Although I think we all share a healthy cynicism about this political process, we can see in a very big way that the work of those who are concerned about the issue of nuclear disarmament is having its effect. If we had called a meeting such as this four or five years ago, we certainly wouldn't have the turnout that we have today. I think that's a sign of the growing public awareness. We wouldn't have five high-ranking officials from the Department of National Defence participating in such a meeting. That's a sign of the government responding to public pressure—maybe the government is not moving enough, but this response is a sign. Progress is slow, but if we look around we certainly can see that progress is being made.

Members of the peace movement in Canada and all those who are concerned about the issue have a tremendous opportunity in the next federal election, which will be held in a couple of years. All the political parties are looking for new avenues of support, and they're looking to the disarmament issue. They're reading the polls. The latest one I saw said that almost one in ten Canadians thinks nuclear disarmament is the top issue in this country. One in ten as the *top* issue. That's more than any other single issue. Those of us concerned about peace have a real opportunity to focus on political issues at the time when the rest of the country is also focused on political issues. That's an important avenue for us to follow.

Cynthia Cannizzo

Recent organizational changes in the United States Space Command have further institutionalized the separation of NORAD from Space Command in order to retain NORAD's independent role for strategic warning and air defence of the North. No Canadian company has an SDI contract. Canada did not participate in Strategic Defense Architecture 2000. How then can you argue that Canada is heavily involved in SDI?

Penner

You said that the Canadian government had no involvement in SDA 2000. General Macnamara said earlier that the Canadian government had "virtually" no involvement. Maybe we could find out what the difference is between "no involvement" and "virtually no involvement." I think that was a carefully chosen word. I'd be surprised if we weren't involved. If NORAD has no relation to Star Wars, then why was the clause that specifically would have made sure that NORAD couldn't be used for Star Wars secretly removed several years ago and not replaced? It does make me suspicious. If NORAD were to have absolutely no involvement with Star Wars, the clause that would have prevented that possibility from occurring should have been reinserted.

I'm skeptical of the statement that there's no Canadian involvement in Star Wars. Thanks to the pressure of a large number of Canadians, that involvement is less than it might have been. I'm very glad that there is no Canadian company that has yet received a Star Wars contract, and I hope that continues. The fact is that Star Wars is dependent on the territory between the superpowers, and Canada has a huge amount of that territory. There's very little doubt that the U.S. military wants to use that territory, needs that territory and is going to put a lot of pressure on this country to get what it wants. It's our role to make sure it doesn't.

Gerri Lynne Benoit (Calgary, Alberta)

As you've clearly pointed out, the Soviet peace movement can only be in a positive position since their government is putting forth the very position and campaigns that the Canadian peace movement is striving for. What can Canadian peace organizations do to help alleviate the paranoia from anti-communist propaganda and to persuade our government to align itself with peace interests rather than U.S. interests?

Penner

That's a difficult question. I don't think there's any doubt that the parameters of the peace work in this country and of the peace movement throughout the world are in some way defined by the Cold War. We're certainly limited in what we can or can't do by people's perceptions of the peace movement. It's not the role of the peace movement to take one side or the other. The role of the peace movement is to put forward the positions that we subscribe to, regardless of who else subscribes to them, and if that means favouring a Soviet policy, then so be it. It's a challenge we all have to face. We have to remember that we are all products of a Cold War environment; we all carry that baggage with us. We all have our misconceptions, and I think that the peace movement and the rest of the interested public and the government have to be more forthright on this. It's a risk, but it's an important risk to take. That certainly doesn't mean being uncritical, but it means responding to the situation as it is.

We talk about the Soviet peace movement and pressure on the Soviet government. I don't know why it isn't very obvious that the Soviet government directly feels the pressure from the West. Isn't it obvious that the Soviet government is always playing to western public opinion and responding to the demands of the western peace movement? We have a lot of influence on the Soviet government. It was western peace groups, not the Soviet government, that first proposed a moratorium on nuclear testing, and the Soviet government felt that pressure from the West as much as a western government would. So I don't think we can underestimate the role of the western peace movement; the test-ban moratorium is one example of its effect on other countries.

Nina Boychuk (Thorhild, Alberta)

You talked about all the nuclear technology that Canada has and how it's involved in the nuclear arms race. How can we reconcile the conflict between the use of nuclear energy for good purposes and the risks of its misuse because of nuclear proliferation?

Penner

My interest is in the question of nuclear weapons, not particularly in the question of nuclear power, but there has been effective documentation to show that the by-product of our nuclear power program, weapons-grade uranium, is finding its way into nuclear bombs. Later today we'll hear from Bill Arkin. He has shown very clearly that the Canadian government is not ensuring that this uranium finds its way into peaceful purposes when it's exported to the United States. It is undeniable that Canadian uranium that's supposed to go into nuclear reactors finds its way into nuclear bombs. Although I am not here to address the nuclear power question, the Canadian government should absolutely insist that no Canadian uranium or nuclear technology has the remotest possibility of finding its way into nuclear weapons. Unfortunately that's just not the case right now.

Gina Shimizu (Youth Parliament of Alberta, Edmonton, Alberta)
Although being nuclear-arms-free seems to be the goal of most of Canada, can you justify this goal in light of the possible effects on trade and on our economy that could result from refusing the United States the cooperation that it has been getting?

Penner
I can justify it because I don't think it matters how good the Canadian economy is if the world is destroyed in a nuclear exchange. We've often heard the argument that producing more weapons is good for the economy, but I like the quotation from a business executive in the United States: "Being dead is bad for business."

There are risks. Canada would suffer economically if we decided to get out of the arms race. It would be only a short-term risk, because many studies have shown that the development of alternatives to military production is a more effective use of our resources, in the long term producing more jobs and more goods that improve the quality of life. In the short term we might suffer some consequences if Canada pulled out of the arms race, but in the long term it would be better for our economic interests and it would certainly be better for our security interests.

Richard Dougherty (Citizens for Constitutional Reform, Spruce Grove, Alberta)
The overwhelming majority of scientists in the United States, with full access to classified information, say that an effective defence against Soviet missiles is possible; the Soviets already have a major investment in research, development and eventual deployment of strategic defence systems of their own; and the record of Soviet violation of disarmament treaties is very clear — in view of all these facts, why doesn't the Canadian peace movement strongly recommend to the Canadian government that it officially participate in the research and deployment of the Strategic Defense Initiative?

Penner
I'm not here to speak for the entire Canadian peace movement. I'll speak for myself. First of all, I reject all three of your premises. There is a huge body of overwhelming scientific opinion that says Star Wars can't work. Your claim that the Soviet Union has an advanced Star Wars program is

unsubstantiated and untrue. I don't think there's evidence of that. There's evidence of some research on a limited level. Most technical experts would say that the Soviet Union doesn't have the technological capability of the West and couldn't possibly be ahead in the Star Wars race.

The Soviet Union's record on arms control treaties, by and large, is pretty good. It's not perfect, but it's pretty good. I don't think that any of us are basing our policies on the idea that the Soviet Union should be blindly trusted. We're saying that arms control treaties are in the interest of all countries. They'll support them because it's in their security interests in the long run. We have to develop means to make sure that all countries are supporting the treaties, and the Soviet Union has made a very major concession, agreeing to all sorts of verification in the last year or two, in response, I think, to western public opinion. That is an important step. It's not enough in itself—it has to be followed up—but it's an important step.

Salvatore Corea (Archbishop O'Leary High School, Edmonton, Alberta)
By allowing U.S. nuclear weapons testing in Alberta, is Canada not endangering Canadians' peace because of the risk of nuclear war and endangering our relations with other nations, such as the Soviet Union, for the mere purpose of helping out the United States and the Reagan administration? If a problem arises, such as the Soviet Union asking permission to be allowed to test nuclear arms, what do you think Canada's response should or would be? Finally, who would take responsibility if nuclear weapons testing backfires, thus endangering Canadians' lives and health—like the Chernobyl nuclear power plant explosion?

Penner
If the Soviet Union asks Canada for permission to test nuclear weapons in Canada, I think Canada should say no. Canada should have said no to the United States and should say no to the United States now. The issue of the cruise missile is again in the forefront. Since there is unilateral cessation of testing on the side of one superpower, it would be an important contribution for the Canadian government to say, "We'll take a modest step in support of your cessation of testing by not allowing the United States to do any further testing in Canada."

Another very important point about the cruise missile issue now is that the United States has said it's going to abrogate the SALT II Treaty, which has never been officially ratified, but has been kept by both sides. It's not the greatest treaty in the world, but it accomplishes a fair bit and it should be supported. We've got to move forward; we can't move back. The weapon that will be involved in breaking the treaty is the cruise missile, so if Canada wants to say that international arms control treaties should be maintained, our government can say, "We're not going to allow testing in Canada of a weapon that's going to help break that arms control treaty." There are more reasons now than there were initially for the Canadian government to say, "No more cruise missile testing in Canada."

Fred Judson (Canada–Central American Policy Alternatives, Edmonton, Alberta)
We've been told how many freedoms we have here in Canada to protest Canadian nuclear complicity. Would you care to comment on the RCMP's, the Canadian Security Intelligence Service's and Defence Department's surveillance, infiltration and harassment of those involved in the peace movement in this country, such as taking photographs and names of peace marchers, filing reports on people who have public conversations with visitors from the Soviet Union, and carrying out surveillance and harassing those who have visited the peace groups in the Soviet Union?

Penner
In my experience in the peace movement, you find out very quickly that the work for peace sometimes goes hand-in-hand with the work for the extension of our democratic rights. I don't want to be side-tracked to other issues, but I have to agree with you. You do find it inevitable that there are certain democratic rights that we should not take for granted. I was involved with the Cruise Missile Conversion Project several years ago, which was, by the admission of the security service, under heavy surveillance. The telephones of fifteen of our members were tapped, and many members were harassed. There are many other examples. I think that we have to keep our eye on the ball. Our issue is nuclear disarmament, but we do suffer from limitations of the democratic system in Canada in that work and I think that's an important issue for peace activists here.

Philippa Beck (Youth for Peace, Edmonton, Alberta)
I am a member of Youth for Peace and in August 1986 I participated in the House-Senate Joint Commission hearings on Star Wars, where we, along with many other groups, condemned Canadian participation in Star Wars. I would like to know what concrete measures and steps are being taken by the Canadian peace movement to oppose Star Wars. As well, as a young person and a member of Youth for Peace, I'm very concerned about youth participation in the peace movement and youth recognition

from the peace movement. Can you please tell me what is being done to encourage and increase youth participation in the fight against Star Wars—because it's our future that we're fighting for.

Penner

To answer the first question, there is an ongoing campaign against Star Wars that's being organized by the End the Arms Race Coalition in Vancouver and facilitated by the network that I work for, the Canadian Peace Alliance. It's been a modest campaign this year as there have been other issues, but it is an ongoing project. We'll almost certainly see that Star Wars is a key issue in the next federal election. The political parties are divided on this question, both amongst each other and amongst themselves internally in some of the parties. It's important that we seize that opportunity and demand that all the political parties come out with a clear, unequivocal opposition to Star Wars. We've got a year and a half or a little longer to work on that.

You said your second point better than I could. The involvement of younger people in the peace movement is essential. We're not going to achieve our aims in the next year or two. We've got to be around for a long time. We need a broad cross section of people to participate, and over the long haul we certainly need the participation of younger people.

Michael Lancaster (Canadian Caribbean Association, Edmonton, Alberta)
You said that Canada's military policy is tied to our foreign policy. I would like to suggest also that our foreign policy is directly tied to our economic policy and stability. How can Canada completely divorce itself from American programs such as SDI when our economic stability depends to such a large degree on our foreign policy?

Penner

That's an important question, but let's get the issue straight. The United States is doing us no favours by its economic relationship with us. It benefits from that relationship as well. It's not a question of benevolence. The United States has an interest in trading with Canada and would have to take that into consideration when it might consider economic reprisals on Canada for foreign policy decisions we make that they don't like. Certainly the United States carries a lot more weight than we do in economic situations, but it carries a lot more weight than many countries and a lot of countries have stood up to the United States. Nicaragua, for example, isn't getting much U.S. trade. It's not doing too well in its relationship with the United States, but it's surviving as a sovereign country. It's a lot smaller than Canada; its population is smaller than Toronto's. There are a lot of examples. If New Zealand can do it, if Nicaragua can do it, if a lot of other countries can do it, Canada can do it.

Dan Heap (NDP—Spadina, Toronto, Ontario)
As the member of Parliament for Spadina, I'm interested to know well in advance of the next election what the peace movement plans to do in order to make sure that the complaint raised against the Canadian government for supporting a policy of nuclear first-strike, and all that goes with it, is put on the agenda for the next election.

Penner
There's nothing more important that we've done in the last few years than to start preparing for the election. Our organization, the Canadian Peace Alliance, is a coalition of about four hundred Canadian peace groups. Last week we had our convention in Winnipeg where we discussed a strategy for intervening in the next federal election. The Canadian Peace Alliance isn't the organization that will run that campaign. We'll use our structure to help member groups of our organization run the campaign.

Already there are very serious plans underway. We're talking about having committees in every riding in the country. We're talking about having a peace voter pledge campaign, where people would pledge to support only those candidates who take a strong position in favour of concrete Canadian action for nuclear disarmament; this would be done on a riding-by-riding basis so that each individual politician will know how many votes he might lose if he doesn't stand up on the issue of disarmament. We also recognize that policy in Canada isn't made just at the riding level. Canada has a party system, and we're going to put pressure on the national level and on the federal party structures. Plans are already underway for fund-raising activities so that we can make our voice heard on a national scale.

In the last federal election, as many people know, peace and disarmament emerged halfway through the campaign as an important issue. It emerged because so many people across the country were demanding answers to very important questions on the nuclear freeze and other disarmament issues. The campaign that we launched then, with much less lead time, was carried out by a much smaller peace movement with a much smaller organizational base. We now have two years' lead time. We have groups across the country and we have a commitment to intervene. I think you'll see that the peace movement will have a decisive impact in the next federal election.

Notes

1. The "umbrella" agreement was signed February 10, 1983, as the Canada–United States Test and Evaluation Program, permitting testing of various U.S. weapons on Canadian soil. The cruise missile tests were specifically agreed to on July 15, 1983.

2. After an unsuccessful U.S.-backed attempt to oust Castro's communist government, the Soviet Union began building missile launching sites in Cuba. These were detected by U.S. reconnaissance flights, and President Kennedy imposed a naval blockade on Cuba until the Soviet Union agreed to dismantle the sites in exchange for a U.S. promise not to invade Cuba again and to remove its own missiles from sites in Turkey that threatened the Soviet Union.

CHAPTER 8
Canada's External Affairs Policy

RALPH LYSYSHYN

It is a great pleasure for me to participate in this inquiry into Canadian security policy. I hope that I can do my part in what I see as the main task of this seminar, that is, to remove the question mark from the title of this conference (The True North Strong and Free?) and to replace it emphatically with an exclamation point. My sense as a Canadian is that we are strong, we are free and we are true to the values that we cherish. I will focus my comments on arms control and disarmament, but I wish to remind you that defence policy and arms control policy cannot be separated.

First, I will outline Canada's major arms control and disarmament goals. Second, I will give you a candid description of the context of arms control; by that I mean both the opportunities and the limitations in what we can expect arms control to achieve. Third, I will outline briefly how Canada participates in arms control. I will touch on both the constraints and opportunities that we have as a North American nation, as a principal power in the world, as a member of the United Nations and as a member of NATO and NORAD.

Let us turn then to the first element: our arms control policy. In October 1985, Prime Minister Mulroney spelled out the following six Canadian goals in arms control and disarmament:

1. negotiated radical reductions in nuclear forces and the enhancement of strategic stability,
2. maintenance and strengthening of the nuclear non-proliferation regime,
3. negotiation of a global chemical weapons ban,
4. support for a comprehensive test-ban treaty,

Ralph Lysyshyn

5. prevention of an arms race in outer space, and

6. the building of confidence sufficient to facilitate the reduction of military forces in Europe and elsewhere.

The pursuit of these goals is, therefore, our basic arms control policy.

In arms control, as in any journey, setting our destination is the first and often the easiest part. Our goals must be long range because I do not believe it is realistic to expect to get there quickly. This is a judgement based on experience and not a statement of policy. Too often, when those who develop and implement arms control policy urge patience, they are accused of *wanting* to progress very slowly. That's a false accusation. The goal of arms controllers must be to make themselves obsolete. Good arms controllers want to do this sooner rather than later.

The failure to put arms control in its proper context can seriously undermine the arms control process. It can lead to disenchantment with the process and pessimism about the progress. Thus, in considering what we want to achieve in arms control, we should remind ourselves that arms are the result or symptom of international distrust and not the primary cause. Arms control may limit, and perhaps even eliminate, some of the symptoms of international distrust, but it does not address the core issue. We must see arms control as what it really is: a tool in the management of weapons and of East-West competition. It is a support for our security. It is not an end in itself.

The arms control process is at the heart of reducing tensions, increasing confidence and, thus, building security. And while we often say that increased confidence is necessary for arms control agreements, we must not assume that arms control agreements by themselves can be equated with an absence of distrust. Arms control agreements, if they are respected, can control and channel the competition among nations, but they cannot eliminate it.

Indeed, an interesting question is to ask ourselves what the world would be like if sweeping arms control proposals, such as those discussed at Reykjavik, were suddenly agreed to. Some say such agreement would lead to rapid progress in other areas. Others say that lowering the level of nuclear arms would make the "rocks," or basic problems, more evident. Factors such as the conventional weapons imbalance, tensions in places

Ralph Lysyshyn is director of the Disarmament and Arms Control Division of the Department of External Affairs. He has an M.A. in English from the University of Alberta. He has been with the Department of External Affairs since 1972, and his responsibilities have included postings in Moscow, Lagos and Washington. He has also worked in the Privy Council Office in Ottawa.

such as the Middle East and South Africa, and human rights issues would loom larger. I'm not sure which of these possibilities will emerge, but both require serious consideration.

If the arms control process itself is to be evaluated prudently, it is equally important to examine various arms control proposals critically. It is important to take into account a broad range of factors. The first is that East-West rivalry has global dimensions. That means that solutions in international relations and in arms control have to be broadly based and widely applicable.

The second is that there is a deep interrelationship among weapons systems. The more radical the arms control proposal, the broader its implication for other weapons. Progress in one area of arms control or nuclear weapons changes the significance of the remaining weapons. Progress across the whole range of nuclear weapons changes the significance of chemical, biological and conventional weapons.

Finally, we have to realize that weapons and weapons systems generally exist for a variety of reasons. These include economics, technological capability, geography, tactical and strategic decisions, international politics and, on occasion, domestic politics. Thus in formulating our arms control proposals, we have to realize that different weapons systems have different values to different countries. It may, therefore, be impractical to focus exclusively on one particular kind of weapon. For instance, the United States focuses on Soviet land-based intercontinental ballistic missiles (ICBMs) and the Soviet Union focuses on cruise missiles. Directing attention to one weapon won't bring the two sides closer together until they're willing to look at weapons in a broader context.

A responsible approach to arms control—and Canada's approach to arms control is a responsible one—must therefore be a cautious one. Arms control proposals that do not do what they purport to do, that are easily circumvented, or that do not take into account the kind of complex relationships I just mentioned, have to be avoided as unhelpful and misleading and perhaps even as dangerous to our security.

The complexity and interrelationships involved in arms control account for the slow pace of negotiations and also for our disdain for arms control by declaration. Declaratory proposals and quick fixes proliferate in public debates such as this one, but experience has shown us that no meaningful arms control measures have been achieved and sustained outside the negotiating framework.

Let us turn now to Canada's role in arms control and the context in which we find ourselves participating in it. For an increasing number of Canadians, the sense of Canada sitting in a sort of no-man's-land between the superpowers is a powerful image. In the age of strategic weapons and cruise missiles this concept has a very urgent meaning. As neighbours of the United States and as partners in a democratic value system, we inevitably share the threat to the United States and the West. Geography, the power and effect of nuclear weapons, and the manner in which they might be used make it impossible for people who live huddled close to the U.S. border to avoid the threat of nuclear war. To suggest that we can is wishful thinking. Our commitment to democratic values augments the threat and diminishes our ability to avoid it. The fact is, we sit between the superpowers only in the geographical sense.

The threat to Canada gives us the right to be concerned about arms control, but it is a right we share with all mankind. The harsh fact of political life is that, by itself, this threat does not buy us a very significant role in arms control. For, however vividly *we* understand that in a major nuclear war Canada will be a battlefield, this is not a concept that is well understood outside of Canada. Other nations, including our European allies, tend to regard us as living basically out of harm's way, far away from the front line, which they see as being in Europe. The superpowers, which worry about escalation arising from confrontation in Central Europe, from instability in the Middle East or from problems in Central America, also have difficulty seeing Canada as being in the middle.

In today's nuclear terms the concept of living out of harm's way is not real. It is, however, a political perception, one that we must overcome if we are to play an effective role in international politics and arms control.

But this mistaken perception is only one of the impediments to the role we play. There are other factors that limit our voice. It is not Canada's military power that needs to be controlled. We have no nuclear weapons, and our conventional forces are very small. We cannot do very much about this situation; we are not about to undertake a massive rearmament campaign just so we can better participate in arms control!

Canada goes into arms control negotiations with another disadvantage. We are, as I said earlier, a principal power. Located elsewhere in the globe, we would be known as a regional power, but we are a "regional power" without a region. Thus, despite our economic size and power, we do not go into international forums carrying with us the weight of several clients or able to express the views of a region.

Over the years Canada has found that we must consciously work hard to overcome these limitations, and we have done it in a number of ways. The most important of these are (1) practising activist bilateral diplomacy, (2) participating in multilateral alliances and organizations such as NATO, the United Nations and the Conference on Security and Cooperation in Europe (CSCE), and (3) displaying competence, pragmatism and responsibility.

We carry out a large part of our arms control activity in the course of our bilateral foreign policy relations. We have found that our many different relations (even our good relations) with the United States do not always give us the voice we believe we should have in security affairs, but we work at it.

History, geography and shared values with the United States have brought us certain advantages, but the changing U.S. governments and the surprisingly personalized nature of their policy making means that our involvement in arms control must be an ongoing process.

In bilateral terms, our dialogue with the Soviet Union is far less intense. It does not approach the daily dialogue with countries such as the United States, the United Kingdom and West Germany, but it is real and it is growing. We also focus on other countries, particularly those with the potential to become nuclear powers. It is vitally important that we deal with these other countries if we are to prevent the proliferation of nuclear weapons that could damage the already fragile arms control process.

Bilateralism is not enough. Canadian bilateral diplomacy alone gives us no seats at the negotiating table. We must, therefore, creatively participate in alliances and multilateral organizations. We work with like-minded nations to build a stronger voice for Canada. We do this in NATO, which is a privileged confidential forum where we can discuss with our allies all aspects of arms control. Through our participation in NATO we first obtained and now maintain a voice in arms control, not only in NATO forums, but in negotiations such as the CSCE, and the Mutual Balanced Force Reductions (MBFR). This European presence is also essential if we are to participate in any other new arms control forum that may arise in Europe.

There is also the United Nations. We participate in the First Committee, where Ambassador Roche so ably represents us. We participate in the conference on disarmament in Geneva, where a broad range of arms control issues are discussed in great detail. Any chemical weapons ban, for example, is likely to come out of Geneva.

The third means I identified was displaying competence and responsibility. By themselves, these qualities would do little, but without them whatever advantage we gained through our other diplomatic activities would be meaningless. We enhance our voice by ensuring that what we say is consistently worth listening to. We do this by our expertise, and we have chosen verification as one area in which to develop our expertise and make a practical contribution to resolving arms control negotiating problems. Verification has been dismissed as a smoke screen, as a problem that has been solved. I wish that were true. It is continuing to be a problem and it gets larger.

In summary I would stress three points: Canada is committed to arms control; we are actively pursuing it; and it is a difficult process. This is not and must not be seen as a call to pessimism. What we need is patience and perseverance, a strengthening of our efforts, and a true commitment to our freedom and values.

QUESTIONS

Leonard Johnson
It's customary in human affairs to look for results at some point. I would like you to tell us, if you can, what our cautious arms control approach has achieved in the past thirty or forty years. Are there any concrete and specific achievements that you can claim credit for?

Ralph Lysyshyn
I think the major achievement of a cautious approach to arms control has been peace, with no war between East and West superpowers for the last thirty to forty years. We also have a number of arms control agreements. We have agreements that ban the use of chemical weapons. We have agreements that ban the use and production of biological weapons. We have an agreement that limits the number of nuclear weapons. We have an agreement that limits ballistic missile defence systems. We are working cautiously, but we are approaching further agreements in the area of chemical weapons; indeed, we could be very close to a total ban, not just on the use of chemical weapons but on the production and storage of chemical weapons. The progress that was made in Reykjavik also offers some hope for this. Negotiations continue in Geneva and in the bilateral and multilateral forums in New York and in Vienna—these facts are a positive sign and one on which we should build and not simply throw our hands up in despair.

Cynthia Cannizzo
In terms of results, could you please comment on the relative effectiveness of an approach that Trudeau termed "megaphone diplomacy," that is, loud public denunciations of another country's foreign policy, and an approach based on quiet, bilateral, behind-the-scenes diplomacy.

Lysyshyn
Canada uses something of both approaches. If you relied solely on megaphone diplomacy (one of today's speakers once called it "yapping at the heels of the superpowers"), I think you would be dismissed as somebody seeking publicity. On the other hand, you do have an obligation to your own people and to your own alliances to stand up and say what you believe. The government does that; it has done that quite regularly. Joe

Clark, Minister for External Affairs, has spoken in the House at about six-month intervals on our arms control policy. He has stressed the importance Canada attaches to compliance with SALT II. By far, the more important aspect of the quiet diplomacy is our daily conversations with the United States and our other allies. With this approach, there's no chance of having what you say dismissed as playing to the grandstand, so the quiet diplomacy channel is also important and we will continue to use it.

Lois Wilson
You've spoken about NATO, in which membership imposes obligations as well as opportunities, and you indicated that one of the opportunities is a privileged, confidential forum, in which the United States consults with us and advises us on a whole range of nuclear arms control issues. Obviously you believe that the opportunities outweigh the obligations. Many Canadians disagree with you and think that NATO is an outdated tool that Canada should get out of. Could you comment on that.

Lysyshyn
You have basically given the two sides of the coin, and I believe that we gain considerable advantages being in NATO. The first advantage is the ability to consult with the United States in a multilateral forum where we can support the views of our other allies on American policy—or on whoever else's policy, for there are other nuclear nations in NATO as well. It is a forum in which we get a seat at the table in arms control negotiations. We get a seat at the table in the Mutual Balanced Force Reductions. We get a seat at the table in the Conference on Security and Cooperation in Europe. These negotiations are dealing with conventional arms, but we all realize that any conventional war in Europe is likely to escalate very quickly to nuclear war, so we have a stake there. We need to be at the table if we are going to be heard. I just don't believe that you can effectively influence arms control by leaving the table and by standing outside shouting into the wind.

Cannizzo
Mr. Penner argued that the western disarmament movement influenced the Soviet Union to promote a test moratorium. Would you please comment on the equally plausible, in some people's view, explanation that the Soviet Union, having finished a major round of testing, decided that playing to the western disarmament movement would serve the Soviet Union's own long-term interests of splitting people from their governments in the West or splitting the NATO allies and putting additional pressure on the United States.

Lysyshyn

I think the latter description of what happened is true. I think the Soviet Union, as it has done on other occasions with INF missiles[1] in Europe, has seen western public concern and has chosen to play to it. It's interesting that in Reykjavik the Soviet Union basically abandoned its support for the moratorium and started talking seriously with the United States about a step-by-step approach to reducing nuclear tests, which is the approach that Canada has urged them to take.

Don Richards (Lawyers for Social Responsibility, Vancouver, British Columbia)

I would like your comments on how you would reconcile your statements this morning, which I must say sound optimistic and activist in terms of Canada's foreign policy, with the fact that at the United Nations General Assembly, Number 40, in 1985, Canada abstained from voting on thirteen resolutions related to nuclear weapons. These included resolutions calling for the prohibition of nuclear weapons tests. Indeed, Canada opposed twelve resolutions, including resolutions calling for a nuclear arms freeze and non-use of nuclear weapons. And with regard to your comment that Canada is indeed strong and free, I wonder whether you feel it a coincidence that, in our opposition votes that I've referred to, Canada was in a small minority. Also present in that small minority was the United States, and Canada abstained when the United States was opposed.

Lysyshyn

Much as some people would argue otherwise, I find United Nations' resolutions of differing merit. Some of them talk about nuclear tests. Some of them talk about all kinds of different test bans. We did support one resolution for banning nuclear tests—working towards a test-ban treaty. Others we abstained on. I think the explanation is in the wording of the resolutions. In certain cases resolutions are patently partisan, aimed at the policies of one side or the other or criticizing one side or the other. As an example of problems with wording, there are two resolutions on arms control verification. In 1985 Canada successfully sponsored for the first time a resolution that urged countries to pay attention to the verification needs of an agreement. There is another resolution on verification in 1986 that, in the way it was originally worded, suggested that there is no verification problem, and it is still worded to some extent in that way. Obviously we can't vote for a resolution like that. So the whole explanation of why we vote for one resolution or another is that you must look at the resolutions in detail.

I have a bit of trouble with your second question in which you suggest that when the United States votes against certain resolutions and Canada abstains, Canada is not acting freely. If we're voting differently we're taking a somewhat different approach. On the other hand, there is a fairly strong congruence of our votes with the United States' votes because we are countries that share the same values and share the same alliances. General Macnamara spoke about the small minority of countries—twenty per cent—that share or actually practise our democratic values. I think that is reflected in the votes.

Wilson
It's true that we do share many values with the United States, but many Canadians do not like the way those values are expressed in U.S. foreign policies. I think it's important to make that distinction because some of us see that the foreign policy of the United States contradicts some of the values that we thought we shared.

Lysyshyn
My comment was not in absolute terms. Our record of voting with the United States in the UN varies from year to year. The United States has been keeping a scorecard for the last four or five years on the percentage of votes in which ours coincide with theirs. We have ranged fairly consistently somewhere in the sixty-seven to seventy-two per cent range, so there are a number of issues on which we are voting very differently from the United States. Ambassador Roche referred to the Comprehensive Test-Ban Resolution. That is one example, and Canada also recently differed from the United States on the Nicaragua issue. There's a fairly large coincidence, but it is far from one hundred per cent.

Murray Pearson (Edmonton, Alberta)
Concerning accidental nuclear war—the time it takes for a submarine-launched ballistic missile to reach America from a submarine's normal patrolling range is less than ten minutes. Computer errors in NORAD saying that an attack was underway have lasted as long as half an hour. This would seem to make accidental nuclear war a large possibility. Could you please comment on this.

Lysyshyn
I think everybody is aware that there is always a danger of accidents with whatever kind of weapon you have, whether it is a nuclear weapon, whether it is a chemical weapon stored somewhere in Europe, or whether it is a biological weapon such as the kind some people believe the Soviet Union has developed in central Asia. All of these are problems we have to work on. I find there's not that much point in sitting here and wringing

our hands about it. I do think work is being done on it. We are very fortunate that we have not yet had a major accident with nuclear weapons. We have had very few accidents even with nuclear reactors, but I think that the experience of Chernobyl taught us that you can't become complacent. Nobody is being complacent about nuclear weapons, and the danger of accidents is one of the reasons we are seeking to limit them.

Heather Addy (Vegreville, Alberta)
If our goal is security in the nuclear age, instead of concentrating on armaments and on arms limitation, could not Canada have an important role in finding commonalities and ground for cooperation between the two superpowers?

Lysyshyn
My comments were limited to arms control because I had fifteen minutes to talk about Canadian foreign policy. If you have been reading the Green Paper[2] and the response to the Hockin Commission Report that will come out soon, you will see that this is a very broad subject that takes a lot more time than fifteen minutes to discuss.

Canada has not concentrated on arms controls and neglected other international issues. Canada is one of the nations in the world with the highest per capita donation to development projects. We are also very much engaged in peacekeeping, as General Macnamara said. And of course there's the whole aspect of our relations with the East in building confidence and trust. We have recently signed a new exchange agreement with the Soviet Union that will further build trust by promoting human contacts. Those are all things we're very much involved in, and I apologize if I gave the impression in my presentation that we're only interested in arms and arms control. We are interested in all these other things you talked about.

François Roy (Project Ploughshares, Edmonton, Alberta)
You referred to bilateral diplomacy and you also stated that through NATO we can discuss with our allies all aspects of arms control. How can we ensure that our country might make an independent contribution to world peace when our own democratically elected representatives are not allowed access to agreements that our generals and Defence Department officials have made with the U.S. Defense Department?

Lysyshyn
If we ever reach a situation where our ministers are not allowed access to agreements, we're in trouble. The minister of national defence, the mini-

ster of external affairs, and the prime minister, who are our elected representatives, indeed do have access to all of these. During the question period, General Macnamara was asked why our representatives did not have access to the NORAD agreement. The NORAD agreement was signed by the prime minister. It strikes me that this is good evidence that elected representatives do have access.

Jim MacDonald (Veterans Against Nuclear Arms, Ottawa, Ontario)
Surely Canada can remain a member in good standing of NATO and still refuse the U.S. demand to test the cruise missile in Canada and also refuse to permit low-level flights, which violate the rights of our native peoples in the areas concerned.

Lysyshyn
The point at issue is not that Canada would be booted out of NATO if it didn't do certain things. The point is that the Canadian people want the Canadian government to meet its responsibility, I'm sure. We have to do our share in the allied defence. We have chosen to do that in one way: by stationing our troops in Europe. We have chosen to do it in another way: in certain kinds of participation in arms control negotiations. We have chosen to do it in part by testing the cruise missile. This is not a question of having to do this to stay in NATO. It is a question of this being the manner in which we choose to meet our responsibilities and do our share.

Ray Stevenson (Veterans Against Nuclear Arms, Toronto, Ontario)
As a veteran I know that war is the result of bad politics, and some of us found that out in 1939. War is the extension of politics by violent and other means. I am not convinced that all of the initiatives that could have been taken by the Canadian government have been taken. Why does the Canadian government not develop a policy and a program calling for an Arctic conference of all the polar nations, which would lead to the demilitarization of that part of our world instead of the militarization policy that is currently being pursued?

Lysyshyn
I think everybody in the Canadian government shares with you the view that we have not yet done all we can do. We are continuing to work. It is the job of those of us involved in arms control. It is certainly the job of our ministers and people like Doug Roche. We do want to do more. We are looking for good ideas and for good input into the process. Nobody is saying, "We've done enough, we're going home." The Canadian government is committed to doing everything it can in a concrete, responsible manner to promote arms control.

Nabi Ahmadyar (Afghanistan Freedom Society in Canada, Edmonton, Alberta)
In your speech you mentioned regional conflicts and problems. Is it possible to have peace in one part of the world when people in another part of the world are being killed and tortured by the more than one hundred and fifty thousand Soviet troops in Afghanistan?

Lysyshyn
We are all working towards a secure peace and that involves, quite evidently, ensuring peace everywhere. There is always a danger that a local conflict will escalate into the kind of war we want to avoid. We have to look at all these issues. You've mentioned one of the problem areas in the world. There are unfortunately too many others.

Ron Aspinall (Green Party and Canadian Physicians for the Prevention of Nuclear War, Tofino, British Columbia)
You mentioned that nothing can be achieved outside of the arms negotiations talks. I think you're denying some facts: that nuclear-weapons-free zones have been formed around the world—in New Zealand, in the South Pacific and now in places in Canada; that the peace movement was instrumental in pushing for the Soviet test ban; and that the peace movement is growing around the world. How long does your government expect to retain power if it continues to use a façade of so-called arms control to support the production of ever more sophisticated and dangerous weapons?

Lysyshyn
To start with, it's not *my* government; it's *our* government. I'm an official in the government. I didn't say that nothing can be achieved outside of arms control negotiations. Indeed, the whole process of building political will before we go into arms control negotiations, the whole process reflected in research work and in strategic studies programs—this process is most effective sometimes when the peace movements are most active. Good, serious proposals come out of them. We want to sponsor these activities, and the Department of External Affairs, through its verification budget and its disarmament fund, contributes directly to sponsoring such programs. But coming up with a good idea, whether it's from a peace movement or from some institute of research or strategic studies, is only the beginning of the process. We then have to take that idea and negotiate it into a meaningful arms control agreement that will then have the force of international law. I'm far from saying that nothing comes out of the good idea, but in order for us to make good use of it, it must be worked into a treaty and gain international acceptance.

Don McKinnon (Lawyers for Social Responsibility, and Ploughshares, Saskatoon, Saskatchewan)
You have pointed out the six stated goals of Canadian disarmament policy. Those goals include Canada's alleged support for a comprehensive test ban. Why has Canada not placed on the public record its support for the Soviet testing moratorium, which has been enforced since August 1985? And why has Canada not strongly urged the United States administration to abandon its categorical rejection of a comprehensive test ban and to accept a moratorium on nuclear testing?

Lysyshyn
There's an element in your first question of a point that was made earlier—that somehow Canada thinks it's a bad idea that the Soviet Union has stopped nuclear testing. That's not the issue. The issue is the one that you have raised in your second question. Why has Canada chosen not to pressure the United States to join in that moratorium? In any kind of diplomatic activity you have to decide if certain exercises constitute bashing your head against a brick wall. The United States rejected the Soviet moratorium proposal, and our judgement was that pursuing this would have constituted bashing our head against the wall. So we decided to look for some other way to work towards our objective. And so we said, "Let's try it step-by-step." The initial reaction from both superpowers was negative, for different reasons. However, when President Reagan spoke at the UN, he then came forward with a step-by-step proposal, reiterating previous offers to begin negotiations on verification of the Threshold Test-Ban Treaty[3] and the Peaceful Nuclear Explosions Treaty,[4] but adding to that an offer to start negotiating reductions in tests as the number of weapons decreased. We noted that in Reykjavik the Soviet Union had indicated to the United States that it was also willing to take that approach. Instead of bashing our head against the brick wall, we decided to work in an area where there might be a possibility for progress.

Bruce Torrie (Canadian Bar Association, Special Committee on Nuclear Arms, Vancouver, British Columbia)
Canada regularly allows United States ships carrying nuclear weapons to use our coastal waters and harbours. In 1986, the International Year of Peace, over sixty of these ships visited the port of Vancouver. I have three quick questions and I would very much appreciate answers. What is the government's policy with respect to these visits? What plans exist to deal with a fire aboard a visiting warship? And where does the government of Canada intend to relocate the population now living in the Fraser Valley after a nuclear disaster occurs?

Lysyshyn
Canada has been fairly clear in its policy of allowing nuclear ships to visit. The United States neither confirms nor denies the presence of nuclear weapons on any particular vessel. We believe that is a wise policy in terms of defending your deterrent, and Canada is part of an alliance that depends on that deterrence for its security.

Torrie [*interrupting*]
Admiral Robert Falls has confirmed that all ships that are capable of carrying nuclear arms *do* carry nuclear arms. He's the former Chief of Canadian Defence Staff. Sir, that's not an answer.

Lysyshyn
Sorry.

Barry Vall (Camrose, Alberta)
How can Canada be seen as a trustworthy nation, one that attempts to encourage trust among nations in the world, when our country and our communities allow new businesses such as CFV Industries in Camrose, which is to build 525 replicas of Russian planes per month to sell on the open market? Does not the attitude that we are open for business in arms sales increase mistrust, further the arms race and destroy our credibility as a peaceful nation searching for peaceful solutions to war?

Lysyshyn
In other times, a policy such as you are describing has been dismissed as appeasement, since there is a consistency between maintaining your defence and working to create the conditions in which these defences will no longer be necessary. Until we get there, we can't give up every aspect of working for and building our defence. Canada's policy on the export of weapons and defence products is a very restrictive one, and I think it belies the claim that we are "open for business."

Gera Schneider (Canadian Physicians for the Prevention of Nuclear War, Ottawa, Ontario)
The moral and ethical dilemma of our nuclear involvement has not been mentioned this morning and my question arises out of the Nuremberg Trials. Would Canada support, under the euphemism of "deterrence" or "defence," the construction of components for gas ovens and support their use under given circumstances? What is the difference between this and supporting the first use of nuclear weapons in Europe and the construction and testing of components of nuclear weapons systems, know-

ing that their use would result not only in local genocide, but global genocide?

Lysyshyn

I take it that was a speech, not a question, and I see no point in answering it.

Notes

1. Intermediate-Range Nuclear Forces (cruise, Pershing II and SS-20 missiles).
2. "Competitiveness and Security: Directions for Canada's International Relations" (Ottawa: Secretary of State for External Affairs, 1985).
3. This treaty between the United States and the Soviet Union deals with underground weapons tests. It limits the yield to 150 kilotons and requires both sides to provide relevant data on the test sites (such as geological formations).
4. The treaty between the United States and the Soviet Union covers underground nuclear explosions for peaceful purposes.

CHAPTER 9
Canada's Agreements with the United States and Her Role in the Strategic Defense Initiative

WILLIAM M. ARKIN

In the two years that I've been a close observer of Canadian defence (and I should remind you that I'm an American), I've watched a number of debates. First there were the American plans for deployment of nuclear depth bombs at Canadian naval bases. Then there were revelations about the testing of enhanced radiation artillery shells at Canadian ranges. Then there were disclosures dealing with the dispersal of B-52 bombers to Canadian air bases. Then came the exposure of hundreds of secret agreements on U.S.–Canadian defence cooperation. This was followed by an active public debate about the potential dangers of the North Warning System and the renewal of the NORAD agreement.

Throughout this period, Canadians have fretted about cruise missile testing, sovereignty of the Arctic and its territorial waters, and the growing militarization of the North. There have been warnings about covert Canadian involvement in U.S. nuclear war planning and calls for Canada to establish itself as a nuclear-weapons-free zone. And there have been constant deceptions about Canada's involvement in the Strategic Defense Initiative (SDI).

Early last year, I was the person instrumental in revealing the existence of U.S. authorizations for the deployment of nuclear weapons to Canada. Throughout the debate on nuclear depth bombs, Canadian government officials told me that I just didn't understand sensitive arrangements and consultations, that I just didn't understand how things really worked.

When I testified before the Standing Committee on External Affairs and National Defence (SCEAND) last December, I presented a document called "Canada–U.S. Arrangements in Regard to Defence, Defence Production, Defence Sharing." This, to me, was the centrepiece of those ar-

William M. Arkin

rangements and consultation procedures, but eight arrangements had been deleted by the Canadian government from a similar list given to the committee. And why were these eight arrangements censored from the committee's list? It's obvious. They were too politically sensitive to be shared with the public. Four of them dealt with nuclear weapons cooperation, including one on the conditions under which nuclear depth bombs could be brought to Canadian soil. Two revealed secret supplements to open treaties, the May 5, 1955, DEW Line agreement and the March 11, 1981, NORAD agreement.

The implication of these secret agreements was clear to me. The Canadian government was trying to hide ties with the United States that they weren't proud of, that contradicted Canadian policy and that couldn't be publicly acknowledged. After the experience with these secret agreements, one would have to be a simpleton not to realize that a secret supplement to the North Warning System agreement also exists. One would have to be a fool not to realize that a secret supplement to the NORAD agreement also exists. And one would have to be a moron not to realize that secret links are being forged between Canada and SDI.

As I was preparing for this conference, I put on my Canadian thinking cap and I began to spot bits of new information in documents that were coming across my desk. Under the Freedom of Information Act I received the report for the U.S. military exercise that is held in Alaska every year, an exercise called Brim Frost. Well, I thought, that certainly applies to Canada. And there Canada was mentioned: "The Canadian–United States Land Operations Plan provides for the exchange of liaison at the REDCOM[1] Forces Mobile Command Level." In English, that means that the joint U.S.–Canadian plan for the defence of North America requires Canadian military presence at the highest headquarters. Canada did send a battalion to run around in the Alaskan snow during the Brim Frost exercise, but when it came to having Canadians actually present in the com-

William Arkin is the director of the Arms Race and Nuclear Weapons Research Project at the Institute for Policy Studies, Washington, D.C. He is the author of numerous articles and books and a contributing editor to the Bulletin of the Atomic Scientists. *In the last two years, he has revealed secret U.S. plans to place nuclear depth bombs on Canadian soil, the testing of the neutron bomb components and other nuclear-related systems at Canadian bases, and the planned crisis dispersal of strategic bombers to Canadian airfields. Testifying before the Standing Committee on External Affairs and National Defence, he revealed the existence of secret agreements between the United States and Canada relating to nuclear weapons cooperation.*

mand post, the report commented dryly, "This exchange was simulated."

Another document, also released under the Freedom of Information Act, deals with the Strategic Air Command's annual exercise called Global Shield, which practises implementation of its nuclear war plans. The report also mentions Canada.

> No nuclear weapons will be taken airborne or dispersed off-base except for normal transportation to and from weapon storage areas. Sorties simulating nuclear missions will not be flown in foreign air space except for Canada, Greenland and Japan.

There seems to be a lot of simulating going on when it comes to Canada! If the Pentagon simulates Canadian involvement in decision making for its exercises, it is only appropriate that the use of Canadian air space be simulated for waging nuclear war. Of course, the Canadian government will assure you that nothing would happen that would affect Canada without Canadian permission, but maybe after many years of practice that permission would be simulated as well.

Canadian consultation being on my mind, I read with interest a statement by the parlimentary secretary to the secretary of state for External Affairs. He stated that Canada could not be a nuclear-weapons-free zone because nuclear weapons cannot be disinvented. There would be blackmail, the bogeyman and other horrors too unmentionable. But here's what Mr. Weiner really said: "Would Canada's voice be listened to more seriously and would our words carry greater weight in the corridors of power around the world if Canada were made into a nuclear-free-zone?"

How much is Canada listened to? How much weight does Canada's voice carry in the corridors of power? Has Canada's milling about in the corridors of power influenced American strategies? I don't think so. I think the answer to that last question is no.

The Canadian government decided in September 1985 that Canada would not officially participate in the Strategic Defense Initiative. Canada's refusal is very interesting. It doesn't sound like the kind of decision that a government concerned about having access to the corridors of power would make. But don't worry, Canada's non-participation in SDI would be forgiven by the United States because Canada was going to be involved in the Strategic Defense Architecture 2000 study. According to U.S. congressional documents, "Strategic Defense Architecture 2000 is intended to develop an integrated defense architecture that will include air, space and ballistic missile defense." General Theriault, the chief of the defence staff, welcomed the opportunity in August 1985 for Canada to walk down those corridors of power, right down to the room where Phase II of SDA 2000 was being prepared. By being an equal partner in the SDA 2000 study, Canada would know exactly what the United States was planning.

So what happened? Brigadier-General Terry Liston, the director general of information for the Department of National Defence, told the *Toronto Star* on October 21, 1985, "I believe the Americans just went ahead and finished their study. We were not invited to participate. We never received a formal invitation and therefore never turned it down."

Baloney! When General Harries, the commander of NORAD, testified before SCEAND, he invited Canada to participate in the SDA 2000 study. The fact of the matter is that a telephone call or a memo won't get Canada involved in a real way.

Even without Canada's involvement in SDA 2000, its integration into SDI is well underway. Canada and the United States will increase their cooperation on space-based surveillance technologies, which will particularly investigate the ability to detect cruise missiles from satellites. In fact, air-launched cruise missile tests over Canada will provide cooperative air vehicle targets for the satellite tests.

Moreover, the Canadian government followed up on its SDI decision with a NORAD renewal, keeping its eyes closed about the connections between NORAD and SDI. U.S. Defense Secretary Caspar Weinberger and American generals are making the connection as they run around the United States and testify before Congress. They're the ones that are using the "house without walls" analogy—you can't have SDI without having continental defence. But the Canadian government remains silent.

Now the U.S. Air Force has even created its own mini—Star Wars called the Air Defense Initiative, or ADI, and it combines programs relating to cruise missile surveillance and air defence battle management. It's a new acronym and let's remember, it's only one letter away from being SDI.

Canadian refusal to participate on a government-to-government basis in SDI is a weak protest from a powerless government. Britain, Japan and West Germany are scrambling to figure out how they can fit under the space shield and how they can profit from the new technology. But Canadian territory will be used for SDI whether the Canadian government likes it or not. The fact that the majority of Canadians oppose involvement in SDI influenced the Mulroney government's decision not to participate.

Of course, the Canadian refusal to officially participate in SDI was accepted in the Pentagon as a sanctioned dissent. The U.S. government expressed perfunctory disappointment at Canada's decision, but in the corridors of power it understood that, for purposes of manipulating public opinion, Prime Minister Mulroney had to follow the contradictory policy even though he didn't believe it himself. Until Canadian territory is actually needed for the deployment of SDI, the SDI scientists will simulate its use. Until then, the Canadian government can continue to show no backbone when it comes to defence. When it comes to defence, the Canadian government can't even simulate a backbone.

QUESTIONS

Cynthia Cannizzo
Woodrow Wilson, the American president in the early part of the twentieth century, was the champion of what he called "open covenants," that is, agreements openly arrived at. In the end he had to acknowledge that, because of the realities of politics and international relations and the hope of getting results with other countries, some things were not to be made public. Do you not believe that there are some agreements that should not be open? That national security can be a legitimate reason for secrecy? And do you think that the evidence that you have presented this morning in terms of building a case of conspiracy or a case of implication against Canada and the United States would stand up in a court of law?

William Arkin
I don't think there's any secret about the extent of U.S.–Canadian defence integration. In fact, there's no secret about these agreements. There's no secret about Canada and where its loyalties lie. The only secret is the details of the agreements and the extent of the integration that's being kept from the Canadian people. The Soviet Union, even if we had a system of perfect secrecy, would assume that Canada and the United States were fully integrated. The Soviet Union would have to assume that Canadian air bases or Canadian ports or Canadian communication facilities would be utilized in wartime. And the dangers for Canada would therefore be the same as if all of those agreements were public and could be publicly debated. So I think the answer to your question is really quite simple. No, I don't believe that there are some agreements that should be secret.

I think that secret agreements are an illusion. First of all, in the American system, they'll be found out sooner or later. Second of all, it's not the agreements that should be secret. It's the details of the war plans or the details of the sources of intelligence information that should be secret. Should the fact that the United States and Canada cooperate on intelligence collection be secret? Of course not. Should what it does to collect intelligence be secret? Of course. But the Canadian people should have the ability to decide whether or not they want the United States and Canada to cooperate on intelligence collection or on nuclear matters. Then, and only then, will they have confidence that the secrets the government is keeping are legitimate and are being safeguarded in their interests. And that's not the situation that exists today. Today we have a situation where people perceive that secrets are being kept in the interests of the bureaucracy and in the interests of the government, not in the interests of the people.

On your second point about a court of law, would the evidence that Canada is integrated into U.S. nuclear war planning hold up in a court of law? Yes. Would the NORAD agreement and the Strategic Defense Architecture 2000 study and implementation show that Canada is intrinsically tied to SDI? Would the evidence hold up in a court of law? Yes. Is there documentary evidence to show the extent to which the United States is moving in the direction of a strategic defence that integrates all aspects of defence, not just ballistic missile defence, but air defence, space defence and anti-submarine warfare? Yes. Would the evidence hold up in a court of law? Yes, I believe it would. Does it mean that there is a conspiracy? No. Did I mention conspiracy? No. Did I talk of conspiracy? No. Conspiracy is a ridiculous term. We're talking about people. We're talking about institutions. We're talking about our own foibles, the mistakes that I might make in my research, the mistakes that a general in the Department of National Defence might make in his. We're talking about the way people work, not a conspiracy. I don't have anything against the people in the Canadian military. I'm sure that they believe that what they are doing is the best thing to do. I don't question that for a minute. The thing is, they're wrong.

Lois Wilson

You seem to be suggesting that Canada has no backbone, or at least that we've lost a few vertebrae here or there. I think from what you said, we don't do anything because we don't know of some of these secret agreements, and even if we did, we might not have the vertebrae to do anything. So I'd be interested in your comments about our strategy in this area.

Arkin

Clearly that's a much bigger debate and it is beyond the time and the philosophical direction that we have here today and tomorrow. But Defence Minister Perrin Beatty, describing the White Paper, said: "We're going to look at Canadian defence from the bottom to the top. Everything is open for grabs except for NATO and NORAD." Essentially what that says to me is that nothing is open for grabs. What is lacking in this country is a sense of what Canadian interests are. It was very interesting this morning that General Macnamara, in his wonderful, concise description of deterrence and alliance, which are two of the pillars of American post-war foreign policy, put Canada's interest in preventing a superpower nuclear war above Canada's vital interests. He said that Canada's primary concern was preventing a superpower nuclear war and the second concern was protecting Canadian vital interests. I think that he's got it backwards. There first has to be a concept of what is in Canada's vital interests. When the United States moves in the direction of nuclear war-fighting policy, and when the United States moves in the direction of a ridiculously counter-productive Third World strategy, and when the United States moves in the direction of covert operations that undermine its own ability to influence governments in the Third World, then it's time for its allies to say, "You've got it wrong!"

Leonard Johnson
What you have described is a country that is totally under the domination and control of its neighbour to the south. I'd like you to tell us the source of that U.S. control over Canadian policy. What are the channels and mechanisms of influence, and what would you do about it if you were a Canadian citizen?

Arkin
First of all, let me say that I'm not pessimistic. I'm not pessimistic, because I see five thousand people here today. I'm not pessimistic, because I think the Canadian debate right now is much more interesting and much more lively on some fundamental questions relating to defence than it is in the United States. Canada has finite interests. It's not a superpower, and therefore it can define much more clearly, within those finite interests, what Canada wants and what's best for Canada.

So let me give a philosophical answer to your question, Why does this domination exist? I think it exists because we're playing out the last years of the nuclear era, and the nuclear era has brought about permanent Cold War and total hegemony by the nuclear powers over their allies. The nuclear era has brought about an infrastructure of preparedness for waging nuclear war, an infrastructure we call deterrence, which necessitates constant guard, which necessitates constant preparedness, which necessitates secrecy, which necessitates subordinating vital interests to nuclear interests. I hope that we are playing out the death throes of the nuclear arms race.

What Canada is realizing and what the nuclear "allergy" is showing all over the world—in New Zealand, in Greece, in Iceland, in Scandinavia, in Spain, in the South Pacific with the Rarotonga Treaty—is that people are realizing what a negative impact nuclear weapons have had on the development of politics and the development of accommodation and the development of co-existence on the planet. And so what Canada is facing, because it is so close to the United States and so closely integrated with it, is the biggest problem of all. On the one hand, Canada is fully integrated with the United States and realizes, as the nuclear consensus starts to drop off, that it has to do something; on the other hand, and this is why I'm not pessimistic, Canada is the only country that can have any influence over what happens with SDI. I don't care what happens in West Germany or in the United Kingdom, the United States cannot have its Strategic Defense Initiative without Canadian territory and Canadian help.

Sara Johnson (Spruce Grove, Alberta)
It is a pleasure to direct this question to such a realist as Mr. Arkin. Since the first rule of defence for both the Soviet Union and the United States is to kill Canada first before the missiles reach themselves, do you not think that the development of a system to reverse the trajectory of all missiles entering our airspace would do more to make Canada strong and free than any number of reasonable arguments, since the prospect of eating their own missiles would be a powerful suppressant for their appetite to kill other people?

Arkin
I don't believe that the United States and the Soviet Union desire to fight a nuclear war on Canadian soil. I think that that is ascribing a motivation that is too evil. The fact is that the United States will eat Soviet missiles and the Soviet Union will eat American missiles and at that rate it doesn't matter whether the plutonium is made in Moscow or made in Washington. Your boomerang is a very good strategy, and you accomplish it by making sure that those missiles never take off in the first place.

The key question we have to ask ourselves through all the rhetoric that we hear is, Are we focusing our attention on the question of preventing nuclear war? Are we really putting our mind to that issue or are we just preparing for nuclear war, preparing for the inevitable? Isn't SDI, in many ways, just a statement of the fact that we believe nuclear war is going to take place and we have to defend ourselves when that inevitability occurs? We are not spending our time and energy trying to prevent nuclear war. We're spending our time and energy trying to prepare for it, and it is when we stop doing this that your boomerang will be very effective.

Colin McKinley (Calgary, Alberta)
Last year I published a novel, *Marjorie's Missile,* about a secret preliminary cruise missile that runs afoul in 1983. Now in some aspects it is no longer fiction. Just two nights ago in a farm near Kamsack, Saskatchewan, east of Saskatoon, in the heartland of Canada, I got a signa-

ture from a woman who, on September 1, 1983, looked up from her breakfast table and through her kitchen window saw what she describes as being a cruise missile pass at tree-top level between her house and her barn. Sounds funny, but this is not a stunt. I've gathered the signatures of three additional eye witnesses from three different neighbouring households who claim that two missiles shot through their community that morning, one at eight o'clock and the second at ten o'clock. Many more eye witnesses, I was told, are available in that area. I have hastily created a map of the witnessed trajectory, and I was given a clipping from a small-town paper that touched on the event of September 1, 1983.

My question is, Can you tell us about any secret cruise tests that have taken place in Canada?

Arkin
You're obviously much smarter than I am, so obviously you know much more than I do. I shouldn't respond at all, but let me say something about people seeing things. People see things when they're afraid. People see things when they feel helpless. People see things when they're hysterical. I get letters all the time, as I'm sure the Department of National Defence does, from people who believe they've seen things, or believe they've heard things, or believe that the system in some way is out to get them. I believe that it's manifested because those people feel so frightened and so helpless. I think that's probably what's happening here as well.

Anthony Halls (Franciscans of Western Canada)
We have discussed the effects of nuclear war. We've discussed arms control and foreign policy. These are issues in an East-West dialogue. Meanwhile, one person in the Northern Hemisphere uses four hundred times as much of the earth's resources throughout his or her life as a person in the Third World, and we are spending billions of dollars on nuclear arms, whilst thousands and millions starve to death. Where does the issue of North-South dialogue fit into this conference?

Arkin
I'm not an organizer of this conference and don't speak for it. I'm afraid that's a misdirected question.

Bishop Remi De Roo
I'm sure the executive will hear that question. Possibly the panel will make a note of it and see that the matter is dealt with at some point. I don't think it would be fair to ask our speaker to respond to that question. However, we will hold the question and get back to it.

Don Scott (NDP—MLA, Inkster, Manitoba)
I would like you to give us further information on the linkage of the North
Warning System to Star Wars. Also I would like to know, given the arrangements between Canada and the United States, if it is possible for Canadians to turn the North Warning System into a system that could warn
both sides, and the whole world, of approaching missiles.

Arkin
That's a very good question, but it also smacks of a lot of misunderstand-
ing of both what the North Warning System is and what the connections
between air defence and SDI are. First of all, the North Warning System
doesn't have anything to do with the detection of missiles. It has to do
with the detection of aircraft. The North Warning System is a part of SDI
because you cannot have a system to shoot down ballistic missiles without having a system to shoot down aircraft and cruise missiles as well.
The Canadian Parliament through SCEAND heard plenty of testimony in
the context of its investigation that made this connection between the
North Warning System and SDI, but the Canadian government chose to
ignore that connection in March 1986 when it signed a memorandum of
understanding about the North Warning System.

I believe that the North Warning System is dangerous and detrimental
to Canadian interests only if it is seen in a broader context of American
nuclear strategy and SDI. It is only when you understand that American
nuclear strategy is moving more and more in the direction of fighting war;
that the United States is deploying weapons systems like the B-1 and the
MX missile and the Trident II; and that the United States has deployed
weapons systems capable of counterforce, such as the Pershing II, the
ground-launched cruise missile and the sea-launched cruise missile—only
then do you realize that the North Warning System might be seen by the
other side as part of a comprehensive system capable of impeding retalia-
tion to a nuclear strike. And just remember, the Pentagon has been telling
us for the last thirty-five years that we need to have retaliatory capability
in order to maintain deterrence. Now SDI comes along and continental air
defence comes, both trying to stop the enemy's ability to retaliate. I think
the only way that you can look at it is to say that it is part of a dangerous
offensive move.

What can Canada do about this situation? What changes can Canada
make? First of all, what I suggest may seem peculiar, but I do not think
that the Soviet Union really desires to send bombers to the United States
or to North America, so we don't need a North Warning System at all. If
the Soviet Union ever wanted to attack North America with bombers, it
could use thirty ballistic missile warheads to destroy the very radars that

are intended to detect those bombers coming in. The North Warning System is sitting there asking to be destroyed, so the justification for having a fixed radar no longer holds up. If Canada really wanted to maintain its sovereignty and wanted to have a system that made sense, it would invest its money either in something like an AWACS[2] plane or in something that would be less connected to American strategic policy. But that's not what Canada is doing, so it gets the North Warning System and with it, it gets American strategic nuclear offensive policy and SDI.

Notes

1. Readiness Command, Unified Command Headquarters (MacDill Air Force Base, Florida).
2. Airborne Warning and Control System. This highly sophisticated U.S. detection and communications system is carried on specially modified aircraft.

CHAPTER 10

The Economic Implications of Canadian Industry and Arms Production

ERNIE REGEHR

My remarks will address the political implications of Canadian military production. In a sense this speech is really a response to the question of why Canada acts as it does and why there is the extensive integration and dependence that William Arkin has just described for us. It is a response, too, to what contributes to the loss of those vertebrae that Lois Wilson mentioned in her question to Mr. Arkin and what contributes to Canada's reluctance to say to our friends, "You've got it wrong."

My premise is that the way in which we organize our military production influences Canadian defence and foreign policy towards support for or acquiescence in American policy, even when that policy is recognized by political leaders in Canada as reckless and dangerous.

First, a brief overview of military production in Canada. The central political fact is that Canadian military production is not intended to respond to Canadian defence needs. Our arms industry serves the American defence market. We produce about three billion dollars worth of military commodities annually, about two thirds of which are exported. About eighty per cent of those exports go to the United States, about ten per cent to Europe and about ten per cent to the Third World. And these exports are concentrated particularly in the aerospace and electronics industries. If the Canadian defence industry were to lose access to the U.S. military market, it would literally be finished. So the industry depends on a single market for its survival—the Pentagon.

Within the United States there is not universal joy that Canada–U.S. Defence Production Sharing Arrangements give Canadian industry the opportunity to compete directly with American industry for U.S. defence contracts. The White House and the Pentagon traditionally support the ar-

Ernie Regehr

rangement because they know and believe that the integration of Canada's military industry with that of the United States encourages defence policy integration as well. Successive U.S. administrations have been champions of Canadian military sales to the United States, but the White House and the Pentagon frequently, as is currently the case, find themselves in direct conflict with the protectionist Congress.

The Defence Production Sharing Arrangements are not guaranteed by any treaty obligations. As ad hoc arrangements, they require constant vigilance and, this is the important thing, political protection. Hence, the Defence Production Sharing Arrangements are an important element of the Canada–U.S. defence relationship. I want to suggest five ways in which they serve integration and undermine Canadian independence.

First, these arrangements spell political vulnerability for Canada. The industry has always openly assumed that access to the U.S. military market has a political price. During the nuclear weapons debate of the early 1960s, the Aerospace Industries Association of Canada argued in favour of accepting nuclear weapons on the grounds that this would solidify access to the U.S. market. "We cannot," said the association's president at the time, "go on expecting Washington to take politically difficult decisions like allowing us an equal break in their defence market, while we refuse to take politically difficult decisions that face us. If we don't take nuclear arms, we must be prepared to face the consequences." And by the consequences, he meant lost military markets in the United States. In the fall of 1986, the Aerospace Industries Association complained again that the failure of the government to pursue government-to-government involvement in SDI has locked Canada out of the U.S. market. The Pentagon, the association said, is bitter and has closed the door on Canadian SDI contracts.

Canada's two billion dollars' worth of military exports, coming mainly from Toronto and Montreal, require political support of U.S. policy within a spirit of continental defence cooperation. What might happen if Canada were to send a strong signal of non-cooperation, such as refusing to test the cruise missile? You may, at the very least, be sure that the U.S. administration would be rather less enthusiastic about keeping con-

Ernie Regehr has a B.A. in English. He worked as a journalist from 1968 to 1973, as a parliamentary research assistant from 1970 to 1974 and as a writer-researcher in South Africa from 1974 to 1976. Since 1976 he has been a researcher for Project Ploughshares and Conrad Grebel College. He is the author of several books on Canada and the nuclear arms race, most recently Arms Canada: The Deadly Business of Military Exports *(Toronto: Lorimer, 1987).*

gressional protectionism at bay. This is not a suggestion that Canada is or need be the victim of blackmail. This does, however, suggest that the vulnerability of Canada's military industry contributes to a predisposition in Ottawa to act cooperatively with the Pentagon, even in the face of strong domestic opposition and even when our political leaders may know better.

My second point about how the Defence Production Sharing Arrangements serve integration is that they have an impact on Canadian defence procurement. Another relevant political fact about Canadian military exports to the United States is that they must be matched by Canadian military imports from the United States. A 1963 oral agreement concluded that the defence trade between the two countries should be kept in rough balance, so if we want to sell to the Americans, we have to buy from them. In April 1963, for example, when Canada was in the market for a military transport aircraft, the question was whether Canada would buy Canadian-built aircraft or cheaper American-built aircraft. The president of the Treasury Board at that time argued that Canada should buy American aircraft in order to facilitate Canadian production of components for an American fighter aircraft. In effect, he said that if we don't buy U.S. planes, the willingness of the United States to have us share in the production of its military equipment would be seriously prejudiced.

A decade later, after Canada had built up a Vietnam-induced military trade surplus with the United States, Canada appeared to have very little choice but to buy American goods when it came time to acquire new long-range patrol and fighter aircraft. In fact, the purchase of these patrol aircraft from the United States represented our support of alliance policies and of anti-submarine warfare at a time when Canada's official defence policy had actually downgraded alliance roles in favour of greater emphasis on sovereignty roles. This purchase went through in spite of the fact that Prime Minister Trudeau expressed serious concerns that strategic anti-submarine warfare was a dangerous and destabilizing activity. This U.S. pressure on Canada to buy American aircraft is well documented, and it was effective partly because the Canadian industry's vulnerability provided the United States with a lever with which to influence Canadian procurement. Canada at the time, after all, was doing more than purchasing American maritime patrol aircraft. It was also buying a market for the Canadian aerospace industry, a market that was available only in the United States.

The extent to which the United States can influence Canadian military procurement has important implications for Canadian defence policy, and—this is my third point—it also has an effect on Canada's perception of threat and on our assessment of our own interests. Military equipment comes with defence policy effectively built into it. It really even comes with a built-in world view. The maritime patrol aircraft are a case in point. If you buy a U.S. anti-submarine warfare aircraft whose usefulness is entirely dependent upon fitting into a much larger American anti-submarine warfare system, you have obviously bought a pretty specific defence policy along with that aircraft. The world view built into that aircraft is that of a world dominated by East-West rivalries in which the most urgent task for Canadians is to locate and threaten Soviet weapons. In Ottawa, where these weapons systems must ultimately be justified or rationalized, it encourages the propagation of a view of the world that accords with the weapons systems purchased. In other words, as consumers of the U.S. weapons systems, are we not also consumers of U.S. perceptions of threat?

Similarly, such weapons systems have an impact on military assumptions about what represents a significant military role for Canada. Analysts have suggested a developing sense in members of the Canadian Forces that to reach the pinnacle of professional soldiering, they have to be playing in the big game. Professionalism as a soldier is related to the extent to which one is engaged in roles and with weapons in the main military action in the world. I suggest that this tends to lower the level of enthusiasm for strictly Canadian roles such as sovereignty patrol or even peacekeeping operations.

The fourth point is that Canadian military production for the U.S. market also means production for the nuclear arms race. Canadian industry participates in U.S. military production without apparent regard for the particular weapons systems or military functions which such production supports. This includes participation in the full range of systems from, for example, the cruise missile and the Trident nuclear submarine to tactical nuclear weapons systems and nuclear-capable and conventional weapons systems.

What is the nature of Canada's responsibility for the weapons systems in which it permits Canadian industries to participate? Canadian firms must obtain permits for selling military commodities to any country but the United States. Essentially, the government grants Canadian firms a blanket permit to sell any military commodity to the United States. But what distinctions should be made between different weapons systems?

During his peace initiative, former Prime Minister Pierre Trudeau made the comment in the House of Commons that "there are nuclear weapons that deter, and there are nuclear weapons that threaten us all." Surely, at the very least, Canadian industry should be required to distinguish between those two classes of weapons. If there are weapons that threaten to destroy us all, as Trudeau said, should Canadian firms not be prevented from participating in their construction? Surely the minimum that we can ask is that this distinction be made, even if Canadian firms are permitted to participate in the production of weapons that deter. But Canada makes no distinction between such weapons in our military production activity. By failing to meet the responsibilities of a sovereign state to make independent decisions, the Canadian government undermines our contribution to a more stable strategic environment.

My final point is this. In an effort to reduce dependence on the American market, Canada has developed a growing interest in selling military commodities to the Third World; in other words, Canada now has a stake in the international arms trade. However, that is a very competitive market, and in an effort to compete more effectively, most military exporters are tempted to slacken the guidelines regulating such sales. This means relaxing and reinterpreting Canadian military guidelines to allow Canadian exporters a wider latitude in search of world markets. There is now, for example, no absolute prohibition on Canadian military exports to gross and systematic violators of human rights. There is only a prohibition on selling those specific weapons that are likely to be directly used for repression and human rights violations.

Canada does not yet have a major economic stake in military exports to the Third World, but there are determined efforts underway to increase our stake in the international arms trade. The value of this trade is already noticeable, with military exports to the Third World now exceeding all types of Canadian exports to Africa and the Caribbean combined. When the trade reaches economically more significant levels, there will be a fundamental conflict between our interests in promoting exports and our interests in active pursuit of arms trade control. This trade effort is carried out in the strictest secrecy, away from public and parliamentary scrutiny. Since it is widely acknowledged that full public disclosure tends to have a restraining effect on arms sales, secrecy implies a lack of restraint.

In conclusion, Canadian military production, as it is now arranged, contributes to Canadian political and economic vulnerability to U.S. pressures. It distorts the military procurement process. It prejudices our collective perception of the real threat to our nation, and it engages us in nuclear and conventional arms races against our own best interests, and the world's as well.

CHAPTER 11
Can Canada Afford an Outbreak of Peace?

SHIRLEY CARR

Can Canada afford an outbreak of peace? I certainly think we can. I think it's time somebody had an outbreak of peace. Many people have forgotten what the word "peace" means. There's something that I share with some people in this room, and that is that people who talk about Canada and the sovereignty of this nation are called "raging nationalists." I guess five thousand people in here are "raging nationalists."

I should tell you first of all that the Canadian Labour Congress represents 2,200,000 workers in this country, and I am speaking to you on their behalf. There are 2,200,000 workers out there who think the way I think about the topic of my speech. That's one point. The other point is that it's time now that we talked about people. I certainly am not a scientist; I'm not a lawyer; I don't come from the military. So I want to talk to you about human things. I want to let you know, too, that the Canadian Labour Congress at its last convention mandated a full-time peace coordinator and I have appointed a coordinator as my first job as president of the Canadian Labour Congress.

So I want you to know that we are moving. It's sad that we can't be out there talking publicly, on the streets, anywhere we want to, about peace and the sovereignty of this country. Some of us are too frightened to do that, but if we could have more forums like this, the message, surely, would get to the Canadian government. Somebody said it was our government. Let me tell you, it may be the government of Canada, but it's not necessarily our government.

I know how difficult it is to arrange for so many Canadians from all across this country to be in one place at one time, so I certainly want to congratulate the organizers of this forum. It is appropriate and it's critical

Shirley Carr

at this time in the life of our country to provoke constructive public debate on Canada's defence policies and on Canada's potential as a peacemaker.

During the First World War, Georges Clemenceau, France's leading statesman and politician, declared that war was too important to be left to generals. I believe that. I hope that now, in the post–Iceland summit era, generals and prime ministers and presidents will agree that peace is also too important to be left to politicians. Perhaps this conference will symbolize the reality that the pursuit of peace has to involve us all—politicians, generals and the workers—just as it must involve all nations, big, small or, like our own, mid-sized.

The most recent Canadian government Green Paper[1] on foreign policy questions underscored an important reality. The Special Joint Committee of the Senate and the House of Commons received 1232 written submissions and heard 461 witnesses and 331 public participants, so there can be no doubt that the issues of foreign policy in general, and peace and security issues in particular, are very much public issues. We have an absolute and defined right to speak about them and to be involved in them. There is a growing perception among Canadians that an energetic public can, and certainly must, insist on the primacy of the call for human survival and human dignity.

If Canada is to play a stronger role in the pursuit of peace, our politicians will need to offer the kind of policies and leadership that will disarm people in terms of their mental attitudes. This will require dialogue, not rhetoric; new thinking, not old prejudices. Perhaps Albert Einstein put it best when he said after the explosion of the first atomic bomb in 1945, "Everything has changed but our mode of reasoning and so we drift toward unparalleled disaster." We as Canadians must understand that the pursuit of peace does not inevitably imply the erosion of security, and security is not just a matter of weaponry and the will to use it.

Nuclear weapons threaten all life on this planet, and as Einstein said,

Shirley Carr is president of the Canadian Labour Congress. She first became active in the labour movement in 1960 in the Canadian Union of Public Employees and served in various capacities at the local, provincial and national levels. In May 1986, she was unanimously elected president of the Canadian Labour Congress by the 2800 delegates at the Sixteenth Biennial Convention, thereby becoming the first woman ever elected as leader of a national labour body. Shirley Carr is a graduate of Stamford Collegiate Vocational Institute and School of Labour Studies, Niagara College of Applied Arts and Technology. She has an honorary doctorate from Brock University and from Acadia University.

they have changed everything but our attitudes. Governments continue to cling to the illusion that they can achieve security by increasing their nuclear and conventional forces. Certainly, I would agree that a condition of peace means that nations should be able to defend their own sovereignty, their values, their way of life, their culture. But I do not believe that such defence requirements, under any circumstances, justify the arms race. The Canadian Labour Congress will not stand by and witness a drift to disaster. We will play our part and we challenge others, politicians and generals alike, to play theirs in the name of peace and in the name of security and in the name of human rights.

The coordinators of this event have asked me to address three specific questions. Two of these questions deal with the impact of arms production and defence spending on the labour force. The third question asks for labour's view on the issues of peace, security and disarmament. I want you to know, without going into greater detail, that if we continue to pursue free trade, as the United States government and the Canadian government want us to, we will have sold our country to the United States, letting the United States have Canada as its own territory in which to operate.

I have already begun to express labour's general views of peace and defence. I would like to state the principles that guide the labour movement of this country as we work for a more peaceful, just and secure world.

First, we see the issues of peace, freedom and economic and social justice as completely interrelated. We believe that the major causes of tension and war in the world stem from unemployment, hunger, poverty, greed, a lack of respect for human freedoms and a lack of respect for national sovereignty.

Second, we believe that the arms race involves a shameful waste of precious human, natural and capital resources. We believe that these resources should be used to meet the basic needs of the hundreds of millions of people living in dire poverty throughout the world and the two and a half million to three million people in Canada who have no jobs.

Third, we believe in the right of nations to defend themselves, but not as a justification for the arms race or as a pretext for the forcible occupation of territory that is not theirs.

And finally, we believe that every possible effort must be made by all nations to make internationalism work. We believe that multilateral mechanisms, particularly the United Nations, must be vigorously pursued to eliminate the sources of tension, to give fresh impetus to confidence-building measures, to strengthen the machinery for resolving conflicts peacefully, and to assure global collective security.

If you have followed public events in Canada, you will know that the Canadian Labour Congress has played an instrumental and even a pivotal role in bringing like-minded people together through efforts like the Peace Petition Caravan and the Canadian Peace Alliance. You must also be aware of the role the Canadian Labour Congress has played internationally; we are aware of what goes on in the peace-loving nations and in those nations that are out to destroy other nations by taking over their political sovereignty. Yes, we know all about that, but the Canadian Labour Congress is not ever invited to go into the hierarchy of secrecy, and do you know why? Because I personally will not take an oath of secrecy on this matter. Why should I?

Our program for peace, security and disarmament calls for the immediate cessation of nuclear weapons production and testing, including the cruise missile, and the rejection of the militarization of space whether it be through Star Wars or through the United States and Soviet anti-satellite programs. We have also demanded effective national and international control of the arms trade, especially Canada's part in it, and have worked for the creation and progressive enlargement of nuclear-free zones, beginning with Canada. In condemning the reliance on nuclear weapons and the buildup of conventional arms, the Canadian Labour Congress has demanded that Canada seriously consider a program of conversion and retraining as part of its contribution towards a better world climate for disarmament negotiations and agreements.

This final point leads me directly to the question dealing with arms and jobs. As you know, much of the information on the extent of arms sales is cloaked in secrecy. It is known, however, that military activities and the manufacture of armaments employ more than sixty million people throughout this world. Half of those are in industry and the other half are in the armed forces. It is also known that Canada's share in the arms market is approximately 1.5 billion dollars annually and that Canada spends nearly nine billion dollars a year on defence. Yet we have three million people unemployed in this country and five million who are illiterate. Little consensus exists among specialists on the overall socioeconomic impact of military spending. There is, however, growing evidence to suggest that because of the Defence Production Sharing Arrangements with the United States and because of public subsidies to foreign-owned arms producers in Canada, Canadian military expenditure actually costs jobs to the Canadian economy.

For many years the Canadian labour movement has pressed for an end to the arms race. At the same time, unions have rightly felt the obligation to defend and protect their members' jobs in every sector of the economy, including defence industries. We think economic conversion may offer a way to combine a commitment to peace with the provision of job security for union members currently employed in defence-related industries in both public and private sectors of the economy.

The idea of conversion is to shift defence production to socially needed civilian products and services, using the same skills and knowledge possessed by workers in defence-related productions to create alternative industries and services. Under this scheme, research and development funds and investment capital now devoted to the military would be used instead to rebuild our manufacturing industries and strengthen our economy.

While the labour movement's research is still incomplete, there are several findings that need to be publicized as a way of dispelling the myth that military spending is crucial to jobs. First, the arms industry is increasingly substituting capital for labour at a rate much faster than any other industry, thus creating a loss of job security.

Second, because the arms industry in Canada is largely foreign-owned, the secondary jobs go abroad, as do the profits and the jobs that might have come with those profits had they been reinvested in Canada.

Third, defence contracts are very unstable because specific defence technology can quickly become obsolete and because production and sales are subject to political influence, both domestically and internationally, as we have seen with the CF-18 affair.[2] These factors combine to make the arms industry in Canada one of the most unstable and insecure job producers. In addition, there are poor economics in paying two or three times as much to create a job in the military sector as to create a job in the personal consumption industry or in public education.

I am not suggesting that Canada should cut its military spending altogether, but I am suggesting that Canada should consider a serious program of conversion in some of those industries that produce armaments—as a way of demonstrating Canada's commitment to ending the arms race. Canadian workers will continue to demand their right to secure jobs and they will not accept unrealistic sacrifices. Economic conversion must mean sensible and realistic employment alternatives, with full consultation and agreement with the workers involved.

Recently, a provincial delegation from British Columbia travelled to Ottawa to lobby the federal government. The group, which included trade unionists, hoped to persuade the government to place a multi-million dollar contract in their province. The delegation wanted the promised Polar Class 8 icebreaker built on the west coast.[3] I recall that when the United States icebreaker *Polar Sea* sailed unwanted through our Northwest Passage in 1985, there were reports (denied, of course) that the intruder would be conducting anti-submarine warfare research in the area. I am sure that the *Polar Sea* affair finally moved our government to commit itself to building a polar icebreaker as part of a belated recognition of the widespread concern for our Arctic sovereignty.

The workers in British Columbia, like those elsewhere, are concerned about Arctic sovereignty and about jobs. I think they may also be concerned about reports that the new icebreaker might serve as a naval listening post to monitor Soviet submarines under the Arctic ice cap.

Questions about the nature of the arms race are being directed by the coordinators of this conference to other speakers, but I cannot resist a little speculation. It has been argued that if the Strategic Defense Initiative is ever put in place, there would be an increase in the use of Canadian waters first for Soviet submarine deployment and then for a western response. I cannot emphasize enough the Canadian Labour Congress's opposition to Star Wars.

I was heartened last summer when a report from Spar Aerospace was leaked, pouring Arctic water on the notion that Canadian participation in Star Wars would bring major economic benefits (including jobs) to Canada. The Spar report thought that fewer than one thousand jobs would be created and these would mostly be in specialized fields already crying for workers.

When the Canadian Labour Congress appeared before the special parliamentary committee in the summer of 1985, we said we would oppose Star Wars however many jobs it might create. Not much of a gamble there, but a statement, I am glad to say, that was repeated by respondents in an opinion poll taken not long after. As published in the *Globe and Mail,* the poll showed that even when told that SDI promised jobs to Canadians, one in four people opposed SDI—a position, I might add, taken by a large number of women.

I am speaking not only as a woman, not only as a trade union leader, but also as a very concerned Canadian who wants the North, our country, to remain strong and free and true to its ideals. I hope the government of Canada gets that message from the people here today.

Notes

1. "Competitiveness and Security: Directions for Canada's International Relations" (Ottawa: Secretary of State for External Affairs, 1985).

2. In October 1986, Canadair of Montreal was awarded the contract for maintenance of the new CF-18 jet fighters. Bristol Aerospace of Winnipeg had also bid on the contract. In technical assessments by government experts and in cost, the Bristol Aerospace bid was better. However, Prime Minister Mulroney stated that Canadair could better use "technology transfers" (something not mentioned in the tendering) and he cited "national interest" as the deciding factor in giving the contract to Canadair.

3. In August 1987, Versatile Pacific Shipyards of North Vancouver signed a letter of intent to proceed with design of the Polar 8 icebreaker.

CHAPTER 12
Question Session

ERNIE REGEHR AND SHIRLEY CARR

Leonard Johnson
Ernie Regehr, I wonder if you could say something about the adequacy of Canadian controls on the export of nuclear materials and technology.

Ernie Regehr
I will speak specifically about nuclear technology as it relates to military issues. There is no control of the export of Canadian technology that is directly related or not related to nuclear weapons systems. The Canadian government makes no distinction between conventional and nuclear weapons systems in its treatment of the export of military commodities from Canada. Nor does it make any distinctions between weapons systems that are deemed by Canada to be stabilizing and deterrent weapons systems and those that are understood by Canada to be destabilizing and threatening. Canada does not take the state's sovereign responsibility to make precisely those distinctions.

Lois Wilson
Ernie Regehr, could you tell us something about the extent and effectiveness of the business and military lobby in Ottawa for arms production.

Regehr
There is a lobby in support of increased military production in Canada and increased military exports from Canada. But it is not only a business and military lobby; it is a lobby advanced by Canadian political leaders because of the notion that there are major economic benefits to be had from the production and export of military commodities. The CF-18 is a

great example of that. The whole focus of the debate is, Who gets the economic benefits?—and they don't even put quotation marks around "benefits." There is an assumption that military commodities bring prosperity—that we can have a militarized prosperity. Interestingly, within the government there is a kind of alliance among several groups: departments of government that are there to expand trade and are supportive of increased military exports; departments that are concerned with regional and technological development and promote the increase of military production for export because they believe it will bring benefits to their sectors; the Defence Department, which obviously has an enduring interest in the increase in military production and expenditure; and private industry, which is an organized lobby in support of such programs.

I don't think that we can say that Canada is in the grip of a military-industrial complex that has control of the Canadian budget and decides how much will be spent, but I believe that we have, within the government and in industry, a group of people who, when it comes time to make decisions between social spending and military spending, choose the latter because it furthers the interests of their particular department. When we talk about social spending we talk about a social "net" that keeps people from falling. The image of a social net creates an impression of a burden and heaviness on society, as opposed to military spending, which is equated with technical advancements and high technology spin-offs.

Cynthia Cannizzo

Shirley Carr, you noted that the arms race is wasteful and that money that is spent and currently wasted on the arms race should go to help poverty and unemployment. Yet you also implied that the root causes of poverty and unemployment, which are in turn causes of conflict and war, are in attitudes and human nature—greed, lack of respect for people, lack of respect for sovereignty. Is the historical record of aid very encouraging in seeing aid as a way to peace? For example, in Ethiopia food donations were used for political and personal gain—exactly your point concerning attitudes and human foibles. How will increased aid cure basic problems and defects in human nature and political attitudes?

Shirley Carr

First of all, if people are employed and they have a decent standard of living, they have something that they can be doing. I think that they are then more encouraged by a number of things. Obviously, we have to assist people with aid. There's no question about that. It will not happen overnight that the people in Ethiopia are going to be able to think on a number of subjects, let alone about peace or war. They're trying to survive as human beings.

The attitude of the Canadian Labour Congress is that, as far as the government is concerned, there has to be a will. But there is no will in the government's mind to stop using all of the money now allocated to military expenditures and to use it instead to help the poor in *this* country, let alone anywhere else, even though we do help the poor in other countries. If a country declares itself a nuclear-weapons-free zone, there obviously is a change of attitude. When a country treats people with equality and dignity, already attitudes have changed. We as a nation have a potential contribution to make to other countries that could assist in bringing the parties together.

In view of the summit in Reykjavik and the breakdown in discussions, I think that Canada can play a major role in bringing the superpowers together. I can assure you that the trade union movement internationally is going to make every effort to talk to those two superpowers, to President Reagan and Soviet leader Gorbachev. But we will do that as an international trade union movement, not through the trade unions within our own countries.

You have to change the attitude of people. Everybody wants peace and nobody wants to be in a holocaust. But when you have the wealthy and politically powerful people making decisions that affect the poor and underprivileged, then there is a tremendous difference of attitudes to be taken into account.

Jean Hodgkinson (Edmonton, Alberta)
I'm very concerned about the social and moral issues. Investment of Canadian money in war-related, defence-related products promotes world disharmony. A consulting firm recently published an article in a Canadian financial magazine about investing only in companies that pursue peaceful endeavours, enterprises and products. Will a sound propaganda program that emphasizes moral issues promote peace and can it influence politicians to redirect the thrust of where Canada's money goes?

Regehr
I think a prerequisite to a full and open discussion of the moral, political and economic implications of military production is full disclosure of the nature of that military production and its destination. Canada is distinguished as a country that operates in particular secrecy when it comes to military production. Canada does not disclose what is produced and where it goes, and there will not be an effective debate of that issue as long as we are, in a sense, whistling in the dark. We don't know the nature and full extent of Canadian involvement in the arms trade. I think that a primary element of freedom is the right to know, and we therefore have the right to know where the efforts of Canadian labour and capital

are going. I would like to put in a strong plug for the pursuit of full disclosure of Canadian military exports.

Sheridan Milner (Edmonton, Alberta)
Mr. Regehr, you called for Canadian responsibility with respect to military buildup and economic gain in marketing arms to the Third World, which indeed does stimulate the Canadian economy to the benefit of some Canadians. But there has been little mention here today of similar intentions of the Soviet Union, our competitors in the Third World. Do you propose that Canada become a so-called peacekeeping nation or nuclear-free zone and dissolve our military and economic friendship with the United States when these actions would put Canada on the same level as other countries with less military strength than the Soviet Union? Are Canadians to be foolish and expect the Soviet Union to respect our borders when it has already invaded or influenced so many other countries?

Regehr
The export of Canadian military commodities to the Third World is not a means of dealing with the Soviet threat. In fact, Canada does not export military commodities to the Third World for strategic objectives. It doesn't have a plan in mind. It doesn't say that the Soviet Union has too much influence in the Persian Gulf and so we had better sell someone else some armoured vehicles in order to hold the Soviet Union at bay. There are no strategic objectives to Canadian military exports. There could be no strategic objectives to Canadian military exports; they aren't large enough to make that kind of impact. There are only economic objectives to Canadian military exports. The problem is that there are economic, political and health consequences as a result of Canadian and other military exports to other parts of the world. And I put it to you that there is not a moral or strategic basis upon which to justify a commercial industry devoted to the export of military commodities. Canada ought to put its effort into the pursuit of diplomatic remedies for the international arms trade.

Marion MacIntyre (Psychologists for Peace, Edmonton, Alberta)
Shirley Carr, you mentioned that the pursuit of peace has to involve us all. In your view, how can this be done? How can we arrive at this new way of thinking, discover this new type of security, and truly evoke an outbreak of peace?

Carr
I think this forum is a good beginning. This is not the first forum on this whole question, but it's probably the one forum I have attended where the

press has been given legitimate information and has printed it as such. I think it's critically important that Canadians stand up and talk about our concerns. There's a government in power, regardless of which government it is, and its first priority is to protect this nation and the people in it. The second priority is to make sure that there's peace and to assist other nations to achieve that goal. Not enough Canadians spoke out against the cruise missile testing. Cruise missiles have no place crossing our Canadian land, absolutely no place at all, and yet it still happened.

I have concerns about what happened in the Northwest Passage. Some daring Canadians from British Columbia were going to parachute onto that American ship since the Canadian government did not seem willing to do anything about it, and then the Canadian government parachuted somebody from the military onto the ship to make the passage through our waters legal.[1]

We Canadians have a massive country of wealth and a massive country of people who want to make sure there is peace around the world. Canadians are respected around the world, but, unfortunately, in some countries Canadians are looked upon as being in bed with the United States and Ronald Reagan and his Star Wars. We have to stand up and be truly independent Canadians.

Wilson

I just want to make a brief comment because I think that Marion MacIntyre raised a very important question. How can we arrive at a new way of thinking? There hasn't been much said yet in this symposium on the whole culture of violence, which is increasingly unacceptable in Canada, from the domestic battering of women to the battering of humanity in the nuclear arms race. So I think it's a deceptive question. It seems to be very simple, but in fact it really is asking, How are we going to transform the whole culture of violence on which so much in our society is based?

Darren Kelly (Students' Union President, Ross Sheppard High School, Edmonton, Alberta)

It gives me great pleasure to talk to you, people closely tied to my future and the future of this country. Throughout today's discussion there has been an overwhelming consensus that Canada should play an active role towards achieving a nuclear-weapons-free world. But to play out this role successfully Canada must convince the two superpowers to cooperate with each other and share a mutual trust. It has been brilliantly demonstrated in recent years that neither the American government nor the Soviet government can be trusted. Chernobyl, Afghanistan and Nicaragua verify this undeniably. This lack of trust is the real reason for insecurity in Canada's quest for world peace. How can Canada referee the nuclear game when the players don't play by the rules?

Johnson
The short answer to that is that, despite all of the facts that you've said, we don't have to be compliant in preparations for our own destruction. We can withdraw cooperation from the arms race and from preparations for our annihilation.

Carr
I'm very pleased that a student has asked a question, because the future is his. The future is my grandchildren's too, and their grandchildren's. I want to suggest to my young friend and all of your colleagues that your teachers have to play a role to make sure that you have an open and frank debate in your classrooms about these subjects, so that you can understand the issues. The next point is that you, being the future of this country, have to make sure that your political friends understand exactly where you stand as Canadians and that you're prepared to play your role as up-and-coming voters to make sure that the future of this country and the world is safe enough for you to bring up your children and your grandchildren.

Ann MacInnis (Strategic Studies Program, University of Calgary, Alberta)
Shirley Carr, how do you propose to keep the Canadian North "strong and free" if you object to Canada having any capability to protect our territorial integrity against American and Soviet submarine incursions?

Carr
I did not say that I was against Canada making sure that we have sufficient protection of our country as a sovereign nation. I totally agree with that objective, otherwise where would we be? What I have said, though, is that no country has the right to invade our waters, but that is exactly what happened when the American ship went through the Northwest Passage until somebody suddenly got the bright idea to make Canada do something about it. We need to make sure that our government understands that there has to be a will and a way to make sure that we can, in fact, show other people that we have the determination to save our country and keep it. We do not have the right, though, to produce arms to send off to other countries to destroy still other countries for someone else's political benefit.

Cannizzo

What objective criteria can we use to determine how much is enough for our defence and how much we need to spend to defend our sovereignty in the North? Can we then apply those criteria to the question of whether icebreakers or submarines capable of operating in the polar cap would be better for both sovereignty assertion and sovereignty protection, that is, for the maintenance of our territorial integrity?

Carr

Canada has allowed its ship-building capacity to lapse, and it's going to be very difficult for us to get it back. And if you talk about creating jobs, there are thousands of jobs that could be created for peaceful purposes to meet the needs of our country alone. How much is enough to assert our sovereignty? One never knows. There's so much secrecy. We may have enough. One never knows what's underneath that sea. What I am suggesting to you is that there is something we can do to maintain our own sovereignty, and the only way we can achieve this is for our government to be more open with us and for us to have the political will to take the necessary steps. And, in fact, we can do it. There are other countries around this world that are nuclear-free zones. There are other countries around this world that are peace-loving nations, and certainly we can benefit from their example.

Cannizzo

I don't feel the question was answered. I asked what criteria you and the Canadian Labour Congress would use to determine the best means to assert our sovereignty in the North. You don't need to know what the government is doing to make an objective analysis on your own as to how much is enough and what you think we should have as a defence.

Carr

The Canadian Labour Congress is not privy to all of that technical information, and we would certainly be happy to be involved in it.

Joanne Oldring Sydiaha (Women in Peace and Interhelp, Saskatoon, Saskatchewan)

It has been common belief that uranium from Saskatchewan and other parts of Canada is used only for peaceful purposes, not military purposes. What do both of you have to say about the contribution of the export of Saskatchewan's uranium, or other Canadian uranium, to the nuclear threat? In particular, how does the nuclear energy industry contribute to the nuclear threat?

Regehr

I have not myself investigated the export of uranium and nuclear technology, but I do have one comment. It is clear that uranium and nuclear fissionable materials go into an international reservoir that people draw from for both weapons and non-weapons uses. I think it's very difficult for the Canadian government to claim that it can control the ultimate destiny of Canadian fissionable materials. We also have to be aware that when we export nuclear materials and nuclear technology into an international environment we are exporting them into an environment filled with many incentives to use those materials and that technology for weapons.

Carr

I really don't think I can add much to that except one comment about the radiation problems that resulted from the accident at Chernobyl. A delegation of the Canadian Labour Congress met with the Atomic Energy Board two weeks ago about protecting the workers from radiation. We asked that the regulations and laws guarantee protection for anyone involved in the radiation field who felt compelled to leave the job if it seemed dangerous. We were told that it takes nine steps to get amendments to any of those pieces of legislation. They have to proceed through those nine steps before one piece can be changed, and if there's a change in one of those nine steps then it goes back to step one. So there will be nothing there protecting the workers that deal in radiation until 1988 or 1989. That's how concerned the Canadian government is and that's how slowly it moves! People involved in this kind of work are not going to be protected on the job and neither will the people in the surrounding communities. That's where you come in. You have to put the pressure on.

Suzette Montreuil (Nuclear Free North, Yellowknife, Northwest Territories)

We are discussing the economic gains that Canadians receive from the arms industry or the economic losses that we might endure with a decrease in the arms race. I wonder if Lois Wilson, or anyone else, could comment on the economic, social, cultural and physical suffering that the Inuit of Labrador are presently enduring with the low-level military flights.[2]

Wilson

I think I should defer to others. I'm not very well equipped to comment on that.

Carr

There seems to be some hesitation about talking about this problem, but I can assure you that they are suffering tremendously there. These are the kinds of things that we should be lobbying about too, if anyone is concerned about the culture of the North. And we should also be concerned about women in this country. There's no question that women are suffering the most and will suffer the most if we have this kind of violence in this nation. Human rights and the dignity of all are dependent on the things we've been talking about today. So that's an area we have to talk about too.

Cannizzo

When the government is considering new routes for low-level bombing flights and so forth, there are public notices letting contracts for environmental impact studies and for social impact studies, and that is a place at which people could have input into the policy-making process. In fact, you could even get the routes changed in some places if you could prove there would be damage to the environment or damage to a community.

Wilson

I don't know whether the Inuit know they're supposed to submit these things for environmental impact studies. They're probably more aware that the animals they used to hunt are being scattered, with the result that the Inuit haven't got an economic base anymore. And there have been numerous objections to this procedure. Although I acknowledge what you're saying, I don't think the procedure is adequate for dealing in any negotiation with Inuit people.

Cannizzo

That's right. There's an educational problem there.

Notes

1. In the summer of 1985, the United States gave advance notice that it would be sending a U.S. Coast Guard icebreaker through the Northwest Passage, but it did not ask Canada's permission. When the *Polar Sea* entered Canadian waters on August 2, 1985, two Canadian Coast Guard captains boarded it and remained with the vessel. However, their status was disputed: the Americans welcomed them as "observers"; the Canadian government represented them as "government officials." On August 8, two members of the Council of Canadians and two Inuit dropped a cannister of Canadian flags on board the ship from a small plane and then went on to erect Canadian flags on islands where they would be visible to the *Polar Sea*. On August 21, External Affairs Minister Joe Clark rejected calls to take the affair to the International Court of Justice. The *Polar Sea* incident is generally seen as a challenge to Canada's historical control of the Arctic waters.

2. Labrador is used for military exercises for the United States and other NATO allies. From 1986 on, very low-level flights were flown, thought to be in preparation for the new U.S. "deep strike" mode of warfare. The rural people of Labrador were not consulted (indeed, one document described their land as "uninhabited"); however, many residents appreciate the income the military exercises bring.

Gwynne Dyer

CHAPTER 13
The Possibility of Canadian Neutrality

GWYNNE DYER

The subject of neutrality for Canada was, I suspect, not discussed in polite society just three or four years ago. Canadians knew where we belonged, and we had always been allied to the greatest power of the time—Britain in the nineteenth century and then the United States (after Britain ceased to be the world's greatest superpower). We fought in all the wars, on the right side of course, and that was our place.

When Tina Viljoen and I began doing a television series on the defence of Canada about two-and-a-half years ago, we were well aware that we were moving towards wanting Canada to disentangle itself from the responsibility for preparing for a nuclear war and to give some sort of lead towards the gradual depolarization of the world—the dismantling of the alliances—but we didn't honestly think it was feasible.

Over a couple of years we had a lot of time to think about this goal, and we came to the conclusion that it was possible, if Canadians had the polit-

Gwynne Dyer was born in Newfoundland and entered the Canadian navy when he was seventeen. He earned a B.A. from Memorial University, an M.A. from Rice University and a Ph.D. in war studies from the University of London. Gwynne Dyer served in the Canadian, American and British navies and taught at Sandhurst in England. He played a major role in the creation, writing and presentation of the seven-part National Film Board television series "War," and more recently, in collaboration with NFB director Tina Viljoen, he co-wrote the three-part television series "The Defence of Canada." Dyer writes a syndicated column that appears in more than 150 newspapers throughout the world.

ical will to do it. So I'd like to talk about neutrality, or perhaps I should say non-alignment, for Canada. Neutrality is what you do in wartime. Non-alignment is what you do in peacetime.[1]

First of all, is non-alignment for Canada desirable? Is it good for us? Would it be good for the world? And if it is desirable, then is it feasible? Could we do it even if we should?

I'll start with what Geoff Pearson stated to be the priority I think we all share. Does this action, does any action we as Canadians take, aid in making nuclear war less likely? That is our priority. Obviously, non-alignment, or neutrality, could not save Canada from destruction if nuclear war comes. There is nothing on earth that would save this country. We could be aligned, non-aligned, left-handed, right-handed—it would make no difference. Our geography means that we will be destroyed in a nuclear war, so the question of whether non-alignment is desirable for Canada is a question of whether it will help to *prevent* that war. You won't survive it if it happens. Indeed, all of our defence and foreign policy is essentially about preventing that war. We know there is no point in having policies for surviving it, once it occurs.

The danger of war (especially nuclear war, given the existence of nuclear weapons) arises mainly from the perception of each side that the other side is a threat, rather than from the intention of either side to attack the other, seize its territory and conquer it—all the traditional motives for which wars were fought before the modern era. I do not believe, and I don't think many people in this hall believe, that the United States intends to conquer the Soviet Union or that the Soviet Union intends to conquer the United States. The danger of war arises from perceptions that the other side is a menace, and those threats are confirmed in our minds by two phenomena: (1) the other side has a lot of weapons aimed at us that will kill us and our children if they go off; and (2) the other side has been organized into military alliances that define us as the enemy. We, of course, have done the same, so the other alliance sees us as a threat.

The priority, therefore, in making nuclear war less likely is to lower that perception of threat on both sides, to make ourselves look less menacing to the other side in the reasonable expectation that such initiatives would elicit a favourable response.

There are two ways to lower the perception of threat. One is to lower the level of the weapons that you're aiming at the other side. You pursue arms control and disarmament measures, which I wholeheartedly support. I think they're excellent, necessary, vital. In the case of nuclear arms, there is not, however, a great deal that we as Canadians can do directly about facilitating that process, other than to deny our own territory to nuclear weapons. The other way to lower the perception of threat is to start taking apart the alliances that confirm in everybody's mind on the other side the fact that we are ganging up on them—we start dismantling them slowly and carefully. We've had these alliances for forty years, and it's about time we rethought them.

As presently constituted, the alliances have two very bad effects. First, they bring the superpowers into direct contact in a wide variety of areas all over the Northern Hemisphere, thus creating many points at which the clashes between the superpower forces, the alliance forces, could begin and escalate into a more serious war—the more countries in the alliances, the more areas of the world where the superpowers can clash directly. Second, the alliances give moral support to a bipolar, crusading view of the world, in which our purpose is to stop the wicked other side from ravishing our maidens and generally doing nasty things to us.

Leaving its alliances, if Canada were to do so, would be useful in both of those contexts. We are the space between the superpowers. The removal of a superpower's military influence from our territory and from as much of the North as possible, including Scandinavia, would create a useful buffer zone between the superpowers. Its military effect might be less important than its psychological effect, but both are relevant. Second, and maybe more importantly, if we were to leave our alliances and become non-aligned, we would be the first large industrial country to reject that alliance-oriented, polarized view of the world. I think that this action could have a very powerful influence and even exert an exemplary influence on other members of our own alliances and, indeed, on the other side.

In withdrawing from our alliances, we would withdraw our ratification of the polarized view of the world that accepts the preparation of nuclear war as a necessary adjunct to our security. The more non-aligned countries there are in the world, the better, from my point of view. There is strength in numbers. We are now at the end of a period of forty years in which there has been a sustained propaganda campaign in our part of the world against non-alignment, neutrality and not being onside. Frankly, it's time we started to offer a little counter-propaganda. The more non-aligned countries there are, the more credible that posture, that analysis, that refusal to accept a bipolar view of the world, becomes.

If it is desirable for Canada to become non-aligned, however, is it feasible? Can we do it? It does involve pulling up our roots in the sense that we would reject our traditional behaviour, which has been that of a loyal alliance partner in every major war of this century. It also involves re-examining our traditions and adopting an analysis of the world entirely different from the orthodox view in Canada for the last generation and a half.

I think the answer to that, without going into any detail, is that if the political will were present in Canada, it would be possible for us to be non-aligned; however, it would be necessary to be quite determined, because pressures would certainly be brought upon us if we sought to become non-aligned. Yes, it is practically possible for Canada to be non-aligned.

A non-aligned Canada would not and could not be, in the initial stages, a disarmed Canada. Neutrality, alas, does not equal disarmament. Non-alignment is an intermediate step to improve world security in a world that remains, on the whole, armed and polarized, and we, as non-aligned Canadians, would still have to consider the security interests of our neighbours, especially the United States. We would have to provide them with guarantees that our non-alignment did not seriously damage their own security or even their own perception of their security.

But neutrality for Canada would not necessarily imply a huge military burden. You often hear that we couldn't afford to be non-aligned and neutral. People say: "Look at the Swiss. Everybody's in the army. We'd have to have conscription." That's nonsense. We are not in Switzerland. We are Canadians. Conscription of a large army is not one of the consequences that Canada would have to consider in becoming non-aligned. Nobody is going to march across our territory to attack the United States, so we don't have to stop them.

Neither, I think, would it require a vastly larger defence budget than we now have in order to maintain the commitments we would have under a non-aligned policy, though we probably wouldn't get away with a very much smaller one. Effectively, as a non-aligned country, we would need to control our own airspace and sea space and their approaches in order to stop intrusions into those spaces and to provide advance warning to the United States if we were unable to stop such intrusions. We would not be required, under any conceivable extension of non-alignment, to be able to stop the entire Soviet air force from attacking the United States if it chose to do so, but then the United States doesn't even try to do that itself at the moment. But we would be required to maintain control of our own airspace and sea space, and that is mainly where we would have to put our defence budget as a non-aligned country. It would be expensive.

On the other hand, as a non-aligned country we would no longer have large forces committed to Europe, which collectively account for about half of our present defence budget. So there would be money to spare, which could be transferred to the different defence tasks a non-aligned Canada would have to undertake.

The last question about the feasibility of Canadian neutrality is, Would the Americans let us do it? I don't know for sure, and I don't think anybody can predict for sure, but they would have no legitimate reason to protest, provided we gave guarantees that they would not be left unprotected and unwarned against attacks coming at them across our territory.

They would certainly be very cross, and they might try to punish us economically. I think you have to reckon with that, although I'm not as certain as many people are that we could not survive such economic pressures if they came. But if we're serious about our own survival, I think it's worth trying non-alignment even if it does cost us quite a lot.

I would end by offering an analogy that some people find a bit difficult to take, but I think is relevant. There is a country that has such a policy already, a neighbour to the other superpower. Finland is a neighbour of the Soviet Union. Its territory is of strategic importance to Soviet defence, but Finland does not belong to the Soviet alliance system. It's a non-aligned country. Finland guarantees the Soviet Union that it will prevent anybody else from crossing its territory to attack the Soviet Union. Realistically, Finland knows there might be circumstances in which it could not stop everything NATO might send across Finland to attack the Soviet Union, and it accepts that under those circumstances the Soviet Union would come in and help. That's simply realistic. Certainly a non-aligned Canada would have to face the prospect that in a war the United States would want to come in and help, but as I said, when you get to war, everything's over anyway. And as far as peacetime is concerned, if the Soviet Union is willing to extend that kind of tolerance to Finnish non-alignment, is it unreasonable to expect the United States to grant Canada the same kind of freedom?

QUESTIONS

Cynthia Cannizzo
First of all, I've been having a bit of trouble with your terminology, since you seem to be using *neutrality* and *non-alignment* almost interchangeably, which is not technically correct. Non-alignment deals with political values, culture, trade patterns, social patterns and economic kinds of things, as a matter of history, not as a matter of political will. Sweden and Switzerland, for example, are not non-aligned in this political sense; they are neutral. Neutrality is a legal position that obligates the neutral country to prevent the use of its territory, as you indicated. This means that a neutral country must be prepared to prevent all comers from using its territory for strategic purposes. Thus, it's not just a question of control and surveillance of our airspace. It's a question of preventing incursions and physically preventing the use of our territory by either of the superpowers. Therefore, cost really is a consideration. If we compare Canada's current defence spending, which is about 2.1 per cent of its Gross National Product (less than or equal to many of the neutral countries in Europe, which are much smaller than Canada), there really is a question

of cost involved. Given what we've heard so far in this conference about military spending and the cost, other than economic, of military spending, don't we have to address that question? On the alignment question, Canadians consistently support membership in NATO by about seventy per cent so you're talking about going against majority public opinion. Would you please address that issue as well.

Gwynne Dyer

I think there are three questions, really. One is non-alignment versus neutrality, the second is cost, and the third is public opinion.

The Swedish say that they are "non-aligned in peace"—this is the phrase they use themselves all the time—in the hope that they may be "neutral in war." And they're very realistic, even though they may be unable to preserve their neutrality because either the Soviet Union or the United States may decide to use their territory. They don't worry a great deal about that, because they know very well that if it gets to that stage, most bets are off anyway. War in northern Europe would be about as bad as war in North America.

I'm not going to quibble about *neutrality* versus *non-alignment*. Effectively, we're talking about the same thing either way. I prefer the term *non-alignment* because it is related to my view that the main reason to take this position is to reject the alliance view of the world that says we must be aligned on one side and against the other. But I don't object if you would rather use the word *neutrality* all the time.

On the question of cost. Each neutral country has an obligation to prevent its territory from being used by any attacker against any of its neighbours. The cost of that depends very much on where the territory is and how it might be used by an attacker. In our case, for example, there is virtually no need to have land defences, because nobody's going to march across the Arctic tundra to the United States. If the United States ever decides to invade, there's not much point in having defences. We are gone. But the air and sea defences that we would need in order to maintain both surveillance and defensive capabilities are quite extensive. It is not an obligation of a neutral nation that you be able to stop single-handedly anything that anybody might throw at you. It is an obligation to be able to put up serious resistance to incursions and to try very hard to prevent your territory from being used against a neighbour by an attacker; and that, I think, is within Canada's capacity. The kinds of costs that we're talking about are in a sense hypothetical because we haven't defined precisely what the requirements are. Think in terms of the ten billion dollars that we now spend annually on defence, of which approximately half goes to our European commitments, if you include all of the logistical backup that we maintain for those commitments. If Canada became non-aligned and pulled out of Europe, we would have five billion dollars a year with which to acquire the surveillance and defence capabilities needed to maintain sovereignty in a non-aligned role.

The final question concerns public opinion. It is certainly true that Canadians traditionally have been allies. They have been loyal junior partners in every alliance they have joined. Not only is it my perception that public opinion is shifting, but there has been a considerable amount of evidence recently that the proportion of Canadians who now are convinced of the necessity of remaining in the alliances is not nearly as overwhelmingly large as it was in the past, while the proportion who are prepared to consider other policies, specifically neutrality, is rising. In fact, there was a Gallup poll last spring, which, leaving out the "don't knows," found that two thirds of respondents preferred alignment and one third preferred non-alignment for Canada. That's still a two-to-one majority in favour of alignment, but you're in a ball game when opinions are that close in a changing situation.

Leonard Johnson

We don't hear very much original thinking on defence in this country and I find your thoughts very refreshing indeed. Non-alignment is a concept that is emerging, of course, and it requires a great deal of discussion and analysis and refinement and then it has to be sold to the public, but I suggest that one of the reasons that support for NATO has been so high in this country is that our people have been consistently told that there's no alternative to it. Now you've provided us with one.

I wonder if you've considered the possibility of extending this concept somewhat and making Canada part of, say, a northern nuclear-weapons-free zone, or a demilitarized zone, and placing it under international surveillance and control.

Dyer

I'd very much like to see things move in that direction, and I think there would be very considerable support for that approach in the other northern countries, the Scandinavian countries, some of which are now themselves enmeshed in alliances, as the Norwegians, the Danes and the Icelanders are.

The defence production burden that we would face as a non-aligned country would be greatly eased if we were collaborating with other non-aligned countries, particularly those in the North. Also, the virtue of creating a buffer zone in the North, plus the virtue of the power of example of Canada going non-aligned, would be greatly enhanced if other northern countries were to do the same thing. I think that there is a very substantial possibility that other northern countries would be interested in doing the same thing if, by going non-aligned, we help to create a context in which they could comfortably fit. Sweden is neutral. Finland is as neutral as it can be. If Canada were also non-aligned, the possibility of all the North fitting into that non-aligned "bloc," if you like, would be greatly enhanced and it would ease everybody's task. First of all, working with other countries helps in defence production sharing, the sort of thing we'd have to do to keep costs down. It would also help politically. If we do come under pressure, it's nice to have other people around who agree with us, rather than being the lone dissenter who is vilified.

Lois Wilson
You've made a very risky and astonishingly bold proposal. The main thing you've done is to say we should re-examine our traditions. What I'd like to hear from you is not what alliances we should get out of, but what traditions Canadians should be re-examining.

Dyer
We have a tradition of belonging to alliances. That comes from our history. We have belonged to alliances or have been militarily tied to the English-speaking great powers, first the British and then the United States, for two hundred years, even before Confederation. And we have traditionally fought in our allies' wars. We had various rationales for doing so at the time, most of which are now lost in the past. It's hard to remember why we went off to the Boer war in 1899, but we did, and the tradition persists that the way we keep ourselves safe is by sending our troops off to kill people overseas. This belief has not been true, since the Second World War, because there has not been any possibility that enemies overseas could attack us. We were contributing to various great powers' attempts to swing the balance of power in their favour in the kinds of alliance wars that are the traditional ways of changing the international system. But we have this justification in our minds: that we make ourselves safe by deploying forces overseas and keeping unnamed enemies at bay who would otherwise be in Edmonton.

Rather more subtly, we feel we have a debt to our past and cannot re-examine this behaviour because to do so would be to reject the sacrifice of those who died for it in the past. A hundred thousand Canadians died in this century in wars overseas. We feel a debt to them, and so we should. They did it for us. But we also, therefore, feel that we ought not examine why Canada went into those wars and that we ought not to change our behaviour in a radical way that would seem to discredit their sacrifice. I don't think that rethinking the way we behave towards the rest of the world does discredit their sacrifice or devalue it in any way. I don't think our dead, if you could ask them, would demand that we forever continue to do what got them killed. But there is a strong reluctance among Canadians to open that can of worms, because it does involve looking at a lot of our past behaviour with a very critical eye.

Cannizzo
You have raised the analogy with Finland and suggested that it might be a model for Canada. Is it not true that Finland did not freely choose to be neutral but that a neutral status was imposed upon it by the Soviet Union in 1948 after Finland was defeated in a war by that country?

Dyer
Finland chose to be neutral rather than be a member of the Warsaw Pact. I'm suggesting we choose to be neutral rather than be a member of NATO and NORAD. I'm not suggesting that the model is exact. Models are not exact for different countries. I think Finland is relevant as an example of how one can be a neighbour to a superpower, a neighbour that is strategically important to that superpower, and yet not be a member of the superpower's alliance.

Cannizzo
Finland fought a war to make that point.

Unidentified Member of the Audience
I'd like to ask about those forty-year-old multilateral alliances that you referred to on several occasions. The thesis has been put to us several times by previous speakers that by being members of those alliances we are in a far better position to influence Britain, France, the United States and other members of the western nuclear club, quite apart from questions of sovereignty for ourselves. As they have explained, by being within the alliances we are in a better position to use quiet diplomacy, as the phrase went, and hallway meetings to influence the major nations of the world and move them towards nuclear disarmament. Would dropping out of NATO, NORAD and those commitments prevent us from operating in that sort of fashion?

Dyer
If that sort of approach actually worked, I suppose it would be a more difficult question to answer, but, in fact, the quiet diplomacy has invisible results. There is a Canadian tendency (part of what used to be a national inferiority complex) to want to be allowed in to play with the big boys — the tickets to the high tables, seats at the council of the mighty — so that we would know what's going on and so that they might listen to us occasionally. I am not convinced that this policy's record of achievement over

the past thirty-five or forty years has been very impressive. Rather than being consulted about major developments, we tend to get them dumped in our laps; and the putative influence that we might lose by leaving our alliances I am sure would be more than compensated for by the influence that we would gain as an exemplary case. People might call this "megaphone diplomacy." Is Canada, within its alliances, a more influential country than Sweden, a country a third our size? I don't think so. I think that as a major industrial power that has drawn certain conclusions about the present alliance system and become non-aligned, we would have an enormous influence even within the alliances, especially within NATO, which something close to half the members would quite cheerfully leave tomorrow if they had the nerve.

Robin Clewley (Edmonton, Alberta)
When William Fox introduced the term *superpower* in 1944, he suggested that there were three: the United States, the Soviet Union and Britain. Clearly, Britain is no longer a superpower. Would you care to speculate on the consequences for nuclear stability if, in the future, a genuine rival to the current two superpowers were to arise? Would a tripolar world be better or worse than the current bipolar world?

Dyer
I honestly don't know the answer to that. My instinct would be that probably three-party games are less manageable than two-party games, so a third major player in the game would destabilize the system. But, on the whole, I don't regard the system as all that stable anyway, so I'm already quite worried. The idea that we have been kept safe for years by a bipolar system, an alliance that freezes everybody in place, and by nuclear weapons to enforce the freeze—this is a pretty unprovable assumption. There hasn't been a nuclear war, but that doesn't prove that we're preventing one. I rather think what we're doing is preparing for it. That certainly is what it looks like when I look at our defence policy. An additional player in the game would make things less predictable and more dangerous. I would like to see us solve this problem long before we have to worry about new players.

Notes

1. The distinction between *neutrality* and *non-alignment* is further discussed on page 127.

PART II

The Alternatives

Panelists Cynthia Cannizzo, Major-General (Ret.) Leonard Johnson, and Lois Wilson participated in question sessions in the following chapters: 15, 16, 17, 18, 19 and 22.

Jean B. Forest

CHAPTER 14
Moderator's Introductory Remarks

JEAN B. FOREST

Good morning, and welcome back to the second day of our conference, all you hardy souls! You may be much hardier than I, for with the True North's first icy blast I caught such a cold that my most fervent prayer at this morning's ecumenical service was simply, "Dear God, may my voice hold out for the day!"

After yesterday's marvellous beginning, today simply must bear fruit. For those who were not here yesterday, I will recap, from my perspective, a few of the highlights.

One of the speakers suggested that, in future, we should not be so tentative. We should be more emphatic. We should replace the question mark in "The True North Strong and Free?" with an exclamation mark. I think you may already have done that! By registering in such unexpected numbers and then showing up in spite of such awful weather and road

Jean Forest served as a trustee to the Edmonton Catholic School Board from 1968 to 1977 (three years as chairperson) and as president of the Alberta Catholic School Trustees Association. In 1972 she was elected to the Senate of the University of Alberta and shortly thereafter was elected senate representative on the Board of Governors. After six years she was elected chancellor of the University of Alberta and served from 1978 to 1982. She currently serves on the Advisory Councils of the Faculty of Business and Faculté St. Jean and is chairperson of the Senate of St. Stephen's College (United Church). Jean Forest's contribution to the community has been recognized by a number of awards, an honorary degree and the Order of Canada.

conditions—just by arriving, you have produced an exclamation mark in the minds of many Canadians.

For me, it is both an honour and a privilege to participate in a conference that may well prove to be a watershed in the history of discussions on defence and nuclear arms. It is always a privilege to work with Bishop Remi De Roo, and I thank him for having started off the conference on such a positive note and, with your cooperation, maintaining it throughout the day. Amazingly, he still had the energy and enthusiasm to celebrate a beautiful Mass last evening and the stamina to participate in the ecumenical prayer service at seven this morning. I very much appreciated his reminder that, in the midst of all our work for peace, peace is, after all, a gift of God.

Yesterday Cynthia Cannizzo commented that, as an American, she was amazed that Canadians did not show more pride in their country, seeming to be less nationalistic than their neighbours to the south. In response, I mentioned to Cynthia last evening that many Canadians came home really proud to be Canadian only after having been away from Canada for a time.

For my part, I have always been an unabashed flag-waving Canadian, and especially so since we adopted our beautiful, distinctive maple leaf flag. However, as Ambassador Roche so eloquently pointed out in his opening remarks yesterday, it is not just as citizens of Canada but as citizens of the world that we must address the issues before us at this conference if we are to be successful in our search for world peace.

In this context—this search for world peace—I was delighted to see so many ranking officers of Canada's armed forces here to participate in the dialogue. As a daughter of a veteran of the First World War and later the wife of a naval veteran of the Second World War, as well as one who lost a number of school chums in that war, I could relate in a very personal way to General Macnamara's comments about the contribution members of Canada's armed forces have made in the cause of freedom and world peace—a cause that must continue to be the basis for their mandate.

As a woman, I felt very proud yesterday when Mel Hurtig singled out Irene Clay and Lois Hammond, the conference coordinators, for their work, adding that without it the conference could not have been held. With their visionary dedication and their day-by-day work, women the world over have given a real impetus to the peace movement. Today I thank them all for their participation this weekend and I urge them to continue their efforts.

As a mother, a grandmother and a former teacher, I was also delighted to see so many young people here yesterday, many of them accompanied by their teachers. I commend them for coming and for expressing in such an articulate way their concerns, their hopes and their fears for the future.

As I recollect my own teenage years, I realize that my most vivid memories are of that awful day when war was declared and that wonderful day when peace was announced. In between, there were many days of anxiety, relief and grief as friends were reported missing, located or dead. Realizing that the tragedy and devastation caused by that war pales in comparison to what might be expected in a nuclear war, we who remember do well to contemplate the alternatives, to listen to the concerns of our young people, and to work with them in addressing those concerns and preventing a nuclear holocaust in the future.

Each one of us, young or old, man or woman, rich or poor, powerful or seemingly powerless, has his or her own stake in the future. Our democratic way of life allows us the freedom to enjoy our rights, but it also imposes upon us the responsibility to preserve that freedom, not just for ourselves but for others as well. So each one of us must use his or her own unique talents, abilities and special gifts for the good of all. We must pool our individual resources and together make use of that most precious of all resources, human energy. As we begin this second and final day of our conference, let us keep this in mind.

John Lamb

CHAPTER 15
Towards Peaceful Canadian-American Defence Policies

JOHN LAMB

The title suggested by the conference organizers for my remarks—Towards Peaceful Canadian-American Defence Policies—is a bit of a misnomer: although strong common security interests will continue to dominate Canadian-American defence relations, I believe that certain divergences in perceived security interests could lead to serious friction between our two countries over the coming years. This friction will be an outgrowth of changes that have been taking place in military technology and nuclear arms control—changes that threaten to exert a direct and adverse effect on Canadian security interests.

Paradoxically, one particularly critical source of tension in Canadian-American defence relations will be Soviet cruise missiles targeted against North America and the need to defend against them. Surprisingly, the Canadian government, the academic policy community and the peace movement alike appear to have overlooked addressing this problem through

John Lamb is the founder and executive director of the Canadian Centre for Arms Control and Disarmament in Ottawa. Educated in political science at the University of Toronto and Columbia University, he has conducted research on arms limitation for the Department of National Defence and co-authored a report on verification, which became a prominent Canadian submission to the disarmament negotiations in Geneva. He has attended international conferences, published numerous articles and papers on arms control issues, and participated in the Canadian Consultative Group on Disarmament and Arms Control Affairs of the Department of External Affairs.

arms control. We need to begin considering that possibility now.

For the past thirty years, Canada's air defence requirements have been predicated on the assumption that the threat to Canada would be only a modest Soviet bomber force and that there would be no serious threat from Soviet air- or sea-launched cruise missiles. Therefore, air defence under NORAD has been confined to early warning technology and the maintenance of only very limited interception capabilities, designed to deny Soviet bombers a free ride into the North American heartland.

Now, however, American defence and arms control policies are threatening to push Moscow into a significant expansion of its cruise missile force. Were that to occur, the threat posed to Canada by these missiles, and the burden of defending North American airspace against them, would grow enormously. I'd like to make three points in this connection.

First, the renewed American effort to develop an effective strategic defence against ballistic missiles, through Star Wars, could well convince the Soviet leadership of the need to place greater emphasis on the production and deployment of cruise missiles capable of skimming in beneath a Star Wars shield. Reflecting the seriousness of this danger, U.S. military planners have already begun to study how to form a comprehensive shield by combining Star Wars defences against ballistic missiles with enhanced active air defences against Soviet bombers and cruise missiles.

Second, successive U.S. administrations have recognized the quite appreciable lead enjoyed by the United States in cruise missile technologies and the comparative Soviet advantage in the number of large ballistic missiles. The United States has therefore sought through its arms control policies to achieve deep cuts in strategic ballistic missiles, while minimizing the constraints placed on air-launched cruise missiles and avoiding altogether the limitation of sea-launched cruise missiles.

Third, at the Reykjavik summit in October 1986, President Reagan proposed that each side reduce its strategic nuclear warheads by half, down to a total of six thousand. The American proposal also, however, contained limits on ballistic missiles, thus creating an incentive for each side to increase the proportion of air-launched cruise missiles contained in its overall force structure. Under this framework, each side could deploy at least twelve hundred cruise missiles.

In addition, the Americans proposed that no limits whatsoever be placed on sea-launched cruise missiles. The threat to Canada could come in the form of a significant expansion in the number of Soviet long-range sea-launched cruise missiles. Today, the Soviets have only about two dozen of these sea-launched nuclear missiles. Recent estimates, however, suggest that the Soviets could deploy up to fifteen hundred of them by 1995. That's a huge increase. Not all of these new Soviet air- and sea-launched cruise missiles, of course, would be targeted against Canada or fly over Canadian territory. Nevertheless, those that would do so pose a threat to Canada that could grow considerably and increase the requirement for extensive new air defence and anti-submarine warfare capabilities.

We would all agree, I am sure, that balanced, verifiable reductions in ballistic missiles are an important objective. With their short flight times, increasing accuracy and multiple warheads, strategic ballistic missiles pose a growing threat to stability and peace.

At the same time, if cruise missile numbers are permitted to multiply as ballistic missile numbers decline, stability will clearly not be enhanced. The American proposal would, in effect, simply divert the arms race onto a track where the United States has a technological advantage. That is a dead end.

Some people would argue that cruise missiles, although accurate, are slow flying and cannot therefore really be regarded as surprise-attack, first-strike weapons. Such complacency, though, is misplaced. Within just a few years, the next generation of air- and sea-launched cruise missiles will be deployed. These will be more accurate than the current models, be able to fly at supersonic speeds and be equipped with "stealth" technology, designed to help them evade enemy air defences. Such advanced cruise missiles could be just as dangerous as today's ballistic missiles.

In Alberta, cruise missiles have a special significance. Across the country, the controversy over cruise missile testing has helped to raise the consciousness of many Canadians about the nuclear arms race. It is time, though, that Canadians also became aware of the larger significance of cruise missiles for Canada, namely, the danger that widespread deployments of air- and sea-launched cruise missiles by the superpowers will involve this country in a massive air defence buildup. Were that to occur—and it surely will if current trends continue—Canada would face an unpalatable choice. On the one hand, we could join with the United States in developing the huge complex of radars, interceptors, ground and space communications links, and so on, that would be required for an extensive active air defence system. We would also have to increase dramatically our anti-submarine warfare capabilities to hunt down submarines that might be carrying cruise missiles in or near our coastal waters.

Such participation would be exceedingly expensive for Canada but would at least help ensure that Canada had a major hand in the defence of North America. Or, on the other hand, we could just let the Americans do the job for us. That would be much cheaper. It would also, however, cost us dearly in terms of our sovereignty.

There is another way, a way that would enhance Canadian and global security and avoid the necessity and expense of building large-scale air defence systems or enhanced anti-submarine warfare capabilities. That way would involve the strict limitation of cruise missiles through arms control, a route that has apparently been completely ignored thus far by most Canadians.

In June 1986, the Special Joint Parliamentary Committee on Canada's International Relations stated in its final report that Canadian "arms control and disarmament policy, on the one hand, and Canadian defence policy, on the other, should move in tandem." That wise counsel needs to be heeded in the present context. The question is how.

I have argued that cruise missiles could pose a serious threat to Canadian security. We can do either of two things to address this threat. We can wait for the threat to materialize and then be forced to engage in an expensive defence buildup, or we can begin to address it now through arms control.

Canada's European allies have not shrunk from the task of clearly assessing the implications of superpower military deployments for their own national security, nor have they hesitated to press the United States to take Western Europe's interests into account in the development of U.S. arms control policies.

Canadians, though, have not recognized that strategic arms control can affect Canada's own national security interests in very immediate and specific ways. Viewing the benefits of arms control as remote, as somehow "out there," we have paid little heed to the capacity of arms control to help solve our national defence problems.

This was clearly reflected in two recent reports by parliamentary committees studying Canada's territorial air defence and NORAD commitments, which failed even to consider the possibility of Canada's seeking an arms control solution to the threat that could be posed by Soviet cruise missiles.[1] Both reports simply accepted the inevitability of a buildup of cruise missiles by the superpowers and the necessity of expanding our air defence. Nor is there any evidence — in the public record at least — to suggest that the present or any previous Canadian government has even asked the United States to address the cruise missile problem through its arms control proposals.

This apparent Canadian silence on cruise missiles is largely attributable, I would argue, to the Canadian belief that nuclear arms control is essentially a superpower responsibility. That belief, unfortunately, has led us to defer to the judgement of our alliance leader on this problem.

Can Canada afford to take such an approach? In the case of cruise missiles, current American strategic preferences clearly run counter to Canadian security interests. If we are to avoid being forced either to engage in an expensive air defence buildup or to abdicate our sovereign responsibility to defend Canada, we must endeavour to convince the United States to negotiate with the Soviet Union to achieve strict limits on air-launched cruise missiles and a mutual ban on the production and deployment of long-range nuclear sea-launched cruise missiles.

For its part, the Soviet Union has proposed a complete ban on all long-range nuclear cruise missiles. It's time for us to see whether Moscow is willing to negotiate seriously on this issue. Granted, significant verification problems remain to be worked out. These should not, however, be permitted to impede negotiations on the limits of cruise missiles. Recent studies suggest that these verification problems may not be as unsolvable as has been thought.[2]

Going along with U.S. strategic preferences is certainly one way of ensuring that Canadian-American defence relations remain peaceful. In the current context, however, such a peace would be won only at the expense of Canada's security. A better guide for Canadian policy would be the achievement of well-managed defence relations in which Canada's security interests are recognized and taken seriously into account by the United States.

Current government policy on arms control includes, among its six priority areas, the negotiation of radical reductions in nuclear forces consistent with the enhancement of strategic stability. To date, however, the government has not made clear what kinds of cuts it would like the superpowers to achieve.

In the interest of elevating Canada's national security debate, the government should move to put some meat on the bare bones of its policy on nuclear force reductions. As I have argued, it needs, in particular, to explore seriously the arms control options pertaining to Canada's cruise missile problem. Of course, this does not imply that the limitation of cruise missiles should be approached in isolation. If both ballistic and cruise missiles were being significantly reduced, there would be a pressing need to rectify conventional force imbalances as well, especially in Europe.

The government has indicated its intention to issue a new White Paper on defence sometime next spring.[3] Those preparing that document should be encouraged by Canadians to address this cruise missile issue.

Canada's willingness to stand up for the incorporation of cruise missile limitations in the West's arms control proposals—limitations that directly reflect Canada's national security interests—will be a critical test of our ability to protect those interests. It is up to all of us to see that Canada passes that test with distinction.

QUESTIONS

Cynthia Cannizzo
You have given us an excellent worst-case threat analysis, something any government could be proud of. I believe you overestimate, however, Canada's complacency regarding the arms control policies of the United States. Although it is rarely reported in the media, Canada works closely with European allies on nuclear arms control issues in order to put pressure on the United States. That we have not seen shifts in U.S. policy does not mean that Canada and the Europeans have not tried. Your suggestions basically imply that we need to fundamentally alter American arms control and, in some cases, defence policy. How do you propose to do that?

John Lamb
Let me address the first part of your question first. I wasn't suggesting that Canada and the European allies haven't sought to influence American arms control and defence policy. What I did suggest was that they don't seem to have done that in the case of cruise missile limits. And I must say, without mentioning any names, that I have talked to Canadian officials about that and have had it indirectly confirmed.

With regard to the latter part of your question, we need to do more thinking about how to alter American policy and I would not claim to have all the answers for intermediate-range forces. The Europeans, for example, made their interests and perceptions of the problem of intermediate-range missiles clear to the Americans and said that they wanted to do something about this through arms control. Helmut Schmidt was referring to that in 1977, when he said that from his country's point of view, this is a problem. The alliance then went ahead to consider how it could rectify the problem. Canada has not yet done that in the case of cruise missiles, and we really need to do that.

Cannizzo
So you would strongly urge Canada to work through NATO?

Lamb
Yes.

Leonard Johnson
This discussion has brought out one of the problems with arms control that we've seen before in the case of the Multiple Independently-targetable Re-entry Vehicles (MIRVs);[4] that is, negotiations had failed to take account of all the weapons, sometimes capping one category of

weapons but opening the door to others. Would you care to comment about the process generally and how this happened in the case of the SALT I treaty (1972) and the cruise missile. Previous opportunities have existed to put restraints on cruise missiles, but they have not been included in the category of weapons under negotiations.

Lamb

In the case of MIRVs, the original idea was that these would be so-called bargaining chips. Then they acquired a certain appeal to certain interests, and they didn't end up getting bargained away. That is one of the problems of the arms race.

Richard Stollery (Alberta Nurses for Nuclear Disarmament, Edmonton, Alberta)

A common concern most people have with the issue of bilateral, verifiable, nuclear weapons disarmament is the subsequent issue of whether or not the conventional weapons forces of the Warsaw Pact would outnumber those of NATO and be thought of as more threatening to the NATO countries. Would you please comment as to whether or not this is the case, and if so, what steps would you feel need to be taken to resolve this apparent imbalance?

Lamb

I'm not a specialist on all defence issues, but it's my understanding that there is an imbalance in favour of the Warsaw Pact in Europe, and I think that there is a need to deal with that, particularly as the number of missiles, both the ballistic and cruise missile types, declines. I think that the conventional imbalance can be dealt with to some extent unilaterally by NATO by restructuring its forces. There are certainly many strong advocates of that in the defence community in the West. I think, though, that the Soviet Union must recognize that this is a problem for Western Europe, and if it wants to achieve the kinds of reductions in missiles that it seems to want, it is going to have to be more forthcoming in addressing the western concern about the conventional imbalance.

Johnson

I'd like to make a comment on that one if I could. It seems to me that there's no way that we can achieve nuclear disarmament in Europe without first addressing the conventional balance. I believe that the key to nuclear disarmament is the reduction, the disengagement and the restructuring of the conventional forces in Western Europe for purely defensive purposes, leading to (or accompanied by) political reconciliation between East and West. This is not to argue that reductions in nuclear forces should not be made, particularly with respect to tactical weapons and the short time of flight weapons, which are reducing the decision-making time available in the event of the outbreak of war. The question of the balance itself is contentious, in my opinion.

I've spent a couple of years trying to find out about this alleged overwhelming Soviet conventional superiority. As I read the publications of the International Institute of Strategic Studies (their most recent analysis of the military balance was released last week and reported in the *Globe and Mail*), the reports of the Stockholm International Peace Research Institute, the Center for Defense Information, World Policy Institute and other sources, I think you have to be very, very careful to find out what's being counted before you make assertions that the balance is skewed in favour of the other side.

Lamb

Just a very quick comment about how to deal with the conventional imbalance in Europe in the context of declining missile numbers. One gets the sense from the speeches of some West European leaders that if we're going to reduce missile numbers we're going to have to build up on the conventional side. I don't think that is the way to go. Instead, one ought to be trying to get both sides to reduce and, in the process, achieve a more equitable balance.

Shannon Enns (Edmonton, Alberta)

If the United States ever began total disarmament or NATO pulled out of Europe completely, do you think the Soviet Union would attack northern Europe or try to invade the United States if the Soviets didn't initiate their own disarmament?

Lamb

Basically, the answer is no. I don't think that the Soviet Union or its allies are interested in conquering Western Europe. I don't think that there are many people anywhere who really believe that, even national leaders who insist on maintaining military forces. I don't really think that they consider that much of a threat. I think they wonder what the Soviet Union would do with Western Europe if it had it, much less the United States. Nevertheless, I'd say one thing. I think it's a generally correct rule or understanding in international relations that vacuums are not a good idea. They tempt various powers to dominate, if not invade, and I think that there is a case to be made for adequate defences while we develop the institutions required to deal with our differences through more peaceful means.

146

Cannizzo

Maybe we should talk about the various kinds of arms control forums that are available for discussing conventional arms control. The first is the Conference on Disarmament in Europe (CDE), its short name being the Stockholm Convention, an outgrowth of the Conference on Security and Cooperation in Europe. The second is Mutual Balanced Force Reductions (MBFR) talks in Vienna, and there have been periodic calls by the Soviet Union for yet a third forum, which would blend the two together. The French have occasionally asked for a conference, although they seem for the moment to be content with CDE. Do you think that either or both of these current forums have the potential to bring about reductions in conventional armaments in Europe? We'll assume away the nuclear side for now.

Lamb

I think that there was an agreement reached a few months ago in Stockholm, a very important agreement, basically creating confidence-building measures that will be used in Europe to help both sides feel less of a threat from the other side.[5] I believe that improving confidence-building measures is a prerequisite to achieving real force reductions in Europe. There's too much suspicion for either side to give up its conventional forces very easily, so I think we've seen a major step, and I should mention that Canada took a large part in the achievement of that agreement.

Personally, I have some sympathy for combining the confidence-building measures forum with the MBFR talks, which have been going on for some thirteen years. It doesn't make a whole lot of sense to me to have two parallel forums both dealing with force reductions in Europe, and perhaps if the confidence-building measures component were brought together with the force reductions component, we would have a mix that would would be superior. There are problems with it. There'd be many more countries involved. It's not an easy way to go, but I think it should be explored; actually, I think it is being explored at the high-level group on conventional forces that NATO has been convening for some time.

Murray Pearson (Edmonton, Alberta)

Although MIRVs were originally intended as a disarming tool, they ended up as an escalating tool because of the fact that one missile could knock out as many as five silos or targets. Could you please comment on this.

Lamb

You're basically correct. This has become one of the major problems through the 1970s and now into the 1980s. There's a basic calculation made by specialists that in order to, as they put it, "take out" a ground-based missile you need to attack it with two missiles. If the missile you're attacking has ten missiles, then you've got a ratio which favours the attacker; you can take out more warheads than you're using. That is a very unstable situation. In a time of crisis, when both sides are feeling quite anxious that the other side might attack them, that arrangement creates an incentive to "get the other guy before he gets you." That is why there has been considerable interest in recent years in moving away from multiple warhead missiles to single warhead missiles; the example in the United States is the Midgetman missile.[6] Personally, I look with some favour on that as a means of getting away from the unstable situation that you described. Unfortunately, some people in the U.S. military are now looking at making the Midgetman missile a multiple warhead missile. They somehow can't resist doing that.

Peter Quilly (Edmonton, Alberta)
I have a question about the Canadian government's efforts at verification for a comprehensive test-ban treaty. What do you think the benefits of such a treaty are, and what do you think of the chances of achieving success in verification efforts?

Lamb
You've got a whole lot of questions wrapped up there. Basically I think a comprehensive test ban, a negotiated one, is a good thing and could contribute significantly to winding down the arms race. I was pleased with the Soviet moratorium; I understand, and I guess I support, the Canadian government's response to that. That will probably surprise some of you. It's my reading that the Reagan administration is simply not about to go along with the moratorium. If Canada stood up and said, "We want you to reciprocate the Soviet moratorium," knowing full well that that wasn't about to happen, I think that this stand would simply reduce Canada's credibility and, in effect, block what may be some rather more practical measures that Canada could take. The one that I favour (and at some point I would be interested in hearing the Canadian government address this, since it talks about step-by-step progress) is a quota agreement. This is one of the most important steps that Canada could advance with both sides. Each side would agree to some limited number of tests per year that would be scheduled to decline over the number of years. That would gradually (and it wouldn't have to be all that gradual) constrict each side's ability to use tests to modernize its force. It would give each side a chance to get used to the idea of less modernization. It seems to me that that would be a useful step. I'm not all that convinced that the United States

would go along with it easily, but it does conform much more to what some of their statements have suggested.

Jeff Coby (Seminar on the United Nations and International Affairs)
In an earlier answer, you referred to the belief that adequate defence is needed to keep a vacuum from forming in Western Europe. How far do Europeans feel they should go to keep this vacuum from forming, and what are your feelings on how far Canada should go to support this?

Lamb
When I talked about vacuums, I was referring to a general feature—a vacuum in Southeast Asia or parts of Africa would be no less comforting. We haven't reached a situation internationally where we have the kinds of institutions and negotiating methods that allow any country to give up the defensive part of looking after its sovereignty. We still need to rely on defences, and I'm for adequate, but not overwhelming, defences while in the process of building the institutions that would allow us to deal with our differences through negotiation and arbitration. That's going to take a long time. I don't see giving up forces—in other words, disarmament—happening while we've got urban blight and hunger and pornography and all those things. I think we're going through a process of maturation here and that's one of the reasons arms control is so important. It buys us the time to develop the institutions that will allow us to deal with our differences peacefully.

Quentin Miciak (Edmonton, Alberta)
Could you please give us more detailed information on the new technology for verification of cruise missiles, since many people regard them right now as a destabilizing weapon, and what role, if any, can Canada play in developing and using this technology?

Lamb
That's a really good question. It involves more technological discussion than we can probably have here now. Limits on air-launched cruise missiles are verifiable through counting rules that were developed under the SALT II arrangement. To give you an example, certain kinds of bombers capable of carrying a certain number of cruise missiles would simply be counted as carrying that number, whether or not they did. I think that is feasible. The much more difficult problem has always been sea-launched cruise missiles. Those kinds of missiles can be carried either on surface ships or submarines and you could put one on a trawler or an aircraft carrier or whatever. But there have been some recent studies suggesting that certain arrangements could allow the monitoring of even sea-launched

cruise missiles, admittedly with a lot of intrusive measures, that is, each side getting to look very closely at what the other side is doing—on-site inspection.[7] The reason that may not be as far out as it sounds is that the Soviet Union, which has always been most resistant to on-site inspection, has been pushing hardest for cruise missile limits, so it may, in fact, have a strong incentive to go along with on-site inspections when it comes to the limitation of sea-launched cruise missiles. That's something that we should push very quickly because I know we're running out of time. Canada has a verification research unit in the Department of External Affairs. It has done work on all sorts of arms control issues. I think that this might be an issue that this unit could get into. Maybe Canada can make a contribution in this very difficult area.

Notes

1. "Canada's Territorial Air Defence," Report of the Special Committee of the Senate on National Defence (Ottawa, 1985); and "NORAD, 1986," Report of the Standing Committee on External Affairs and National Defence (Ottawa, 1986).

2. See, for instance, James P. Rubin, "Sea-Launched Cruise Missiles: Facing Up to the Arms Control Challenge," *Arms Control Today* (April 1986): 2–9; and Herbert Lin, "Technology for Cooperative Verification of Nuclear Weapons," *Arms Control Today* (April 1986): 10–11.

3. "Challenge and Commitment: A Defence Policy for Canada" (Ottawa, 1987) did make some reference to the Soviet cruise missile threat, but only in military terms, not in the context of negotiating limits or a freeze, as John Lamb was suggesting.

4. A MIVR is a single missile, or booster, equipped with several nuclear warheads that can be armed separately and sent against different targets.

5. See page 40.

6. For a good discussion of this issue, see Jonathon Medalia, "Midgetman Small ICBM: Issues Facing Congress in 1986," Report No. 86-58F, Congressional Research Service (Washington, D.C., 1986).

7. See Rubin, op. cit.

CHAPTER 16
Alternative Strategies for Peace and Security

GEORGE IGNATIEFF

In being invited to address the question of human survival, I feel rather as Hamlet's father's ghost might have felt if he had come upon Hamlet saying, "To be or not to be" — integrated or disintegrated. I say this because I began to investigate what the defence of Canada should be back in 1944, when I was brought back from overseas to be secretary of the Post-Hostilities Planning Committee, and my concern with this topic continued in the 1950s and 1960s. Those who have come up with various solutions, including the one that we should leave NATO, should bear in mind that this was thoroughly investigated in the 1950s and 1960s. As Gwynne Dyer mentioned, one of the unsolved quandaries is how Canada, without a tremendous outlay in modern weaponry, could assure the United States that we would not provide a platform for invasion of the United States. The United States assured Canada in the darkest days of 1940 that it would not stand idly by if we were invaded. That was looked into during the transitions from Louis St. Laurent's regime to John Diefenbaker's and from Lester B. Pearson's to Pierre Trudeau's. It was found to be more practical and much less expensive for Canada to pay an insurance policy towards collective security through NATO.

Some people have suggested that Canada is somehow spineless and complacent. I'd reckon that the Canadian Physicians for the Prevention of Nuclear War can look after the spineless problem. But I do remember this and I think every Canadian should also. There was a time in 1940, and I was a witness to this, when Canada was the only ally that was undefeated in Europe when Britain was standing up to the threat of Nazi domination of this world. As we approached November 11th, it was the Canadian armed forces that provided the defence of Britain while the British army

George Ignatieff

was being reorganized after Dunkirk. It was the Royal Canadian Air Force that fought alongside the British in the Battle of Britain, and it was the Royal Canadian Navy that provided the essential supplies to keep Britain going against the submarine threat. And thousands paid with their lives. I don't buy the idea that we are spineless or unable to take a position that is not in the Canadian interest in relation to defence.

The problem that I wish to address is rather different. I'd like to focus on a problem that is basic to this whole discussion on what we do about Canada's security, because we have to think anew in the face of the nuclear threat and the complexity of the types of weapons coming onstream. In the nineteenth century, or in even preparing for the last war, governments knew that it was the military that was going to fight the military on some battlefield, so it was left to the military to decide what the battle plan would be, what the weapons would be and when and how the weapons would be used. It was a delegation of authority. That situation has totally changed.

In World War I, the proportion of victims, civilian to military, was something like ten to ninety. In the last war, what with the Holocaust and the bombings in Britain, Japan and Germany, that proportion was overturned. There were far more civilian casualties than there were military. And in the next war, and this is the whole point, it is you and I who are going to be the victims. Therefore, the very first question that we have to address is the political and economic implications of applying modern technology to war. There is no simple technological fix. This is why I approach this public inquiry as a hopeful move. Public opinion, not just here in Edmonton but in the whole world, is being aroused by this issue.

I don't believe Canada can isolate itself in trying to resolve this issue. Particularly because of our strategic location between the two nuclear superpowers, we have to look for security in a collective security system, but that does not mean that we need to consider abdicating control of our

George Ignatieff is a former ambassador to NATO and a former ambassador for disarmament and is now president of Science for Peace. Born in St. Petersburg, Russia, George Ignatieff left with his family for England and eventually settled in Canada in 1928. He has served his adopted country as Canadian ambassador to Yugoslavia and the North Atlantic Council. He represented Canada on the United Nations Security Council and at the Geneva Disarmament Conference. He participated in tense negotiations over most of the world's hot spots in the 1950s and 1960s: the Middle East, Suez, Korea, Czechoslovakia, Cyprus. He has received much recognition for his work, including eight honorary degrees, the Order of Canada and the Pearson Peace Medal (1984).

destiny to the superpower-oriented world view of the United States. We have to stand up for Canada's vital interests.

Having represented Canada for four years at NATO, I can tell you that the discussions in the North Atlantic Council,[1] both at an administerial and permanent representative level, address the very kind of questions we are discussing here today. You need not assume that a lot of patsies just sit there and accept whatever the military people say. The whole question of arms control and the balance between arms control and deterrence are constantly under discussion. But here is the absolutely crucial question that we have to face—NORAD is an integrated command structure in which there is an element of dangerous automation that could, by accident, precipitate us into a nuclear world war.[2] I say this with the full knowledge of what responsibility is involved in facing that issue. I was representing Canada at the time of the Cuban missile crisis in 1962, and there was a nuclear alert issued in NORAD. In the North Atlantic Council, there was a discussion of what kind of alert should be issued. But NORAD immediately declared a nuclear alert, which extended into Canada and would have given permission to the military for nuclear deployment in Canada. Prime Minister Diefenbaker refused to accept that NORAD alert. It took four out of six days of the crisis to make a decision as to whether or not we'd go on any kind of alert. I didn't know what to say on behalf of the Canadian government. Now, is this a situation in which we dealt with the political implications of nuclear weapons? I say it is not.

NORAD has to be placed under responsible, political control. For that reason, we have to say clearly to our allies that either NORAD comes under the North Atlantic Council and its political control at the ministerial and other levels, or we leave NORAD.

This is not "copping out." It's a question of facing the political implication that we cannot delegate the power of life and death of us all to a military decision alone. Shirley Carr said that the question of survival should not be left either to generals or to politicians, but the implications are not fully understood and that is why we are assembled. That is why in many cities the people are saying that we cannot go on with the accumulation of automated weapons systems that could destroy not only our civilization but also life on this planet. And this is not just on one side. People suggest that the peace movement is somehow oriented towards the sympathies of the Soviet Union. I have been to the Soviet Union, and the Soviet Union is facing exactly the same kind of problems we are facing here. And indeed, this was the basis of the proposal made at Reykjavik—that all nuclear weapons and other weapons of mass destruction should be eliminated by the turn of the century. Somehow or other this came as too much of a shock, I take it, for President Reagan. He and

Soviet leader Gorbachev did agree on a proposition from which we cannot let them move; namely, nuclear war cannot be won and must not be fought. This means that war cannot settle the differences between the Soviet Union and the United States, and this is the beginning of the thinking anew that is required by governments and by us.

How does the public ensure that this thinking anew takes place? We've heard a lot about brick walls and not being able to change, and I found exactly the same situation while visiting the Soviet Union. The bureaucracy doesn't want to change (and bureaucracies anywhere never like to change from the status quo), but we are facing a totally new, different problem of accountability from the decision-makers to us, the potential victims. As I've said many times, there can be no incineration without representation.

What specifically do we do? First and foremost, NORAD must be brought under proper civilian control for the declaration of nuclear alerts or any other decision, as with every other military command in NATO. Second, it is necessary in the nuclear age to increase democratic participation in the discussions of the whole strategy of survival. For that purpose, we should do something that has been done in the United States. We get most of our information about nuclear weapons through the United States and the hearings of the congressional committees. With the help of the Veterans Against Nuclear Arms, we should establish a centre for defence information, which will give out as much information about the implications of nuclear weapons and the various developments of new weapons systems as does the Center for Defense Information in Washington. This information should be for the education of the public and should be available regularly to everyone in the peace movement.

There must also be a crisis management centre that would be manned continuously as long as we have these weapons and until they are reduced and eliminated. This would be manned continuously by American and Soviet civil and military authorities. And why shouldn't it be in Canada, because we are situated between the two countries, and over Canada is the shortest distance for missiles to fly en route to their targets.

I believe in improvisation in a crisis. One of the marvels of modern technology is what can be done in communications in a crisis. I have seen this in action, not only at the time of the Cuban missile crisis, but at the time of the crisis in 1967, when I was on the UN Security Council. The Soviet Union used the marvels of satellite communications to communicate with the White House and resolve the crisis that arose over the possible action in Syria. A confrontation between the United States and the Soviet Union nearly took place when Israel defeated all its Arab enemies in six days. I think the communication system should be used to provide not just one hot line, but a continuously manned crisis centre as long as we have these dangerous weapons.

One point that the Canadian government has stood by, and I think should be absolutely insisted upon, is that existing agreements must be respected while we are negotiating arms control to try to reduce and eliminate these weapons. Mention was made about the cruise missile and its dangers, and I quite agree with what John Lamb said, but I'd go further. If President Reagan insists that the restraints of SALT II are to be no longer respected, this will result in more B-52 bombers, which carry air-launched cruise missiles of the type being tested in Canada.[3] In that case, we should stop all cruise missile testing in Canada.

Finally, I think that we should return to the strategy that was launched on behalf of Canada at the 1978 Special Session of the United Nations General Assembly—the strategy of suffocation. The essential point is that you cannot get any control over this runaway technology of destruction, which threatens life on this planet as well as our civilization, unless you put a stop to the constant flow of new devices for destruction. The strategy of suffocation included the ending of all testing. We've got to stop somewhere; why not a moratorium? On this I disagree with John Lamb. I believe that Canada should insist on a moratorium and not take this line of "little by little." If we continue new testing little by little, there will be innovations and each one will be destabilizing and countered by the other side. This approach will only continue the arms race.

One more point that gives me great hope is that the cost of the arms race has been escalating just as much as the dangers, when you consider that even the repair and maintenance costs of these CF-18 planes that we just received are something like two billion dollars and the cost of *each* plane or new device is in the millions. This is the reason why the Congress of the United States is now trying to cope with a deficit of approximately a hundred billion dollars, and the Soviet economy, as I witnessed in a visit just a few weeks ago, is faced with unresolvable problems unless that country finds some way of curbing the arms race. Therefore, there is an important economic implication in the escalation of the new weapons systems, as well as the political one of mass destruction, implications that move us in the direction of facing up to thinking anew about curbing the dangers of war. War itself has to be abolished, and this is the direction in which we have to work.

QUESTIONS

Lois Wilson

You've mentioned the importance of increasing democratic representation in the discussions on strategies, and it seems to me that one of the ways in which many Canadians receive their information is through the media, through the electronic media. Could you comment on the capabilities or the responsibilities of both radio and television in terms of what you're talking about.

George Ignatieff
If it weren't for the media, we would be talking only to ourselves in this hall. Television and radio are the essential tools, not only for public participation in the decisions that bear on our survival, but also for our production of new ideas, new thinking, particularly through the use of public programming such as TV Ontario in producing discussions that can be used in schools, adult education, programs and public forums. I think it is an absolutely essential part of developing a strategy of peace.

Wilson
Do you have any comments on the recent cuts at the CBC?

Ignatieff
Well, I think that these cuts are quite counter-productive. I think we should have cut some of the maintenance costs of the aircraft instead.

Cynthia Cannizzo
Things have changed a lot in NORAD since 1963 because of the Cuban missile crisis, which you described. Each country does have control of its own armed forces within NORAD, and forces in NORAD are integrated; that is, they are separate pieces working together. They are not unified. Moreover, no offensive forces are attached to NORAD. Those forces are part of a U.S. chain of command, a separate chain of command from NORAD. For a NORAD alert to lead to a missile launch (may that never occur) several human decisions would be required; thus there is positive political control. NORAD is affiliated with NATO through the U.S.– Canada regional grouping. Would not putting NORAD as a formal NATO command simply be adding another layer of unnecessary bureaucracy, and second, do the Europeans want NORAD as a formal NATO command?

Ignatieff
As far as the relations between NORAD and NATO are concerned, in my experience this is purely a relationship on paper. It's called the North American Regional Planning Group, and there was a new report submitted. Whereas, in relation to all the other commands—the Central Strategic Command, the southern and northern flanks—the North Atlantic Council considered in detail precisely what contingency plans were available in relation to the various types of threat. But there was no such report from NORAD as long as I was in NATO. My understanding is that

NORAD can still declare an alert based on input from the early northern warning systems and a nuclear alert can be declared by the authority of the president of the United States. The prime minister of Canada would then be faced with making a decision in a few minutes. The whole movement of modern weapons is in the direction of launch-on-warning, where decision making takes place in a matter of minutes. I'm suggesting that there should be proper political control through the North Atlantic Council administrators meeting; and before activating any kind of launch-on-warning that might lead us into a nuclear holocaust, our elected representatives should have a chance to make a considered decision. I know this is apparently more and more difficult, and that is one of the reasons that I say that the resolution of any kind of conflict by nuclear weapons is becoming absolutely impossible.

John Guy (United Nations Association and Project Ploughshares, Calgary, Alberta)
The ultimate goal of the United Nations in the matter of disarmament is general and complete disarmament, namely, phased, balanced, monitored and controlled disarmament of both nuclear and conventional weapons so as to reduce national standing armies to the lowest possible level. This disarmament goal of the United Nations has been reaffirmed many, many times. Why does the government of Canada support general and complete disarmament at the United Nations and yet never talk about it at home or explain it to Canadian citizens? How can this disarmament be started and accomplished?

Ignatieff
The basic predicament that we find ourselves in is that the Canadian government has two strategies. This is not unique to the present government, but it has been a persistent problem and that is why defence papers are so difficult to produce. One strategy is the international, multilateral approach, including arms control, peacekeeping and negotiation in the multilateral forums for our collective security; the other is the bilateral, continental commitments between Canada and the United States, some of which are secret (and this secrecy is one of the problems). We need to recognize that if the leaders of the free world and the non-free world are agreed that nuclear war must never be fought and cannot be won, then we should move from the two main alliances to a common security that recognizes (and this has now been admitted at least on the side of our adversary) that there is no way in which the security of one country can be bought at the expense of another. We are all interdependent and we have to work towards a system of collective security and of resolution of our differences by negotiation. The United Nations experience has shown

how even so-called localized wars, such as those witnessed in Afghanistan, Vietnam, Iran, Iraq and Lebanon, produce this phenomenon, fundamental to this conference's agenda, namely, that the victims are mainly civilians, not the military.

Michele Demers (Change for Children, Edmonton, Alberta)
In these last two days, there have been several references to our war dead, our war heroes as we call them, which always manage to elicit enthusiastic response. Along this same line, when the issue of the U.S. icebreaker in the Northwest Passage was brought up, there was a definite feeling of anger here. Isn't it precisely this attitude of reverence and glory that we instil into the military, this primitive violence within ourselves, and the generally un-Christian attitude that we have even towards other Canadians that makes world peace impossible and this conference nothing more than empty rhetoric? If we can't even achieve domestic peace, how can we ever dream of international peace?

Ignatieff
You've touched on the essential question of what constitutes peace, and I agree fundamentally with what Bishop De Roo said, that it starts with each one of us. This is why conferences such as this are important. We cannot pass the buck in a situation where we face the accumulation of nuclear destructive technologies and where we can all die in a holocaust. Prime Minister Mulroney said that the quest for peace is the greatest and highest priority of every Canadian and that it's a personal responsibility.

As to the honour that we do to the dead, it is a fact that people have died for a cause in which they believed, one that we all believed to be just; namely, we faced in the last world war a threat of domination by an appalling, cruel dictatorship that was responsible for such horrors as the Holocaust. Canadians went into war to fight that threat and were prepared to sacrifice their lives, and I think it's only right that a country protect itself against such horrors. What I'm saying is that we have to find new ways, while honouring those who have stood up and protected us in the past. The people who are thinking with us and joining the dialogue are the people who have been through the experience of war. I think those who have known war are less inclined to be trigger-happy about launching a new war.

Wilson
While I agree that peace starts with each one of us, what has been raised in the last question is the culture of violence. Increasing numbers of people are saying that violence is no longer an acceptable way of settling differences, so I think that peace is not only a personal but a corporate responsibility as well.

Garnet Thomas (Project Ploughshares, Edmonton, Alberta)
Dr. Ignatieff, I ask you as head of Science for Peace, should we or can we challenge scientists in this nuclear age to take an oath similar to the physicians' Hippocratic oath, an oath to work to preserve life and to refuse to work on research that appears to be headed towards weapons development?

Ignatieff
Science for Peace started from a world movement of concerned scientists and it's a very rapidly growing organization on every campus from Halifax to Victoria. The objective is twofold: one is that the scientists who join this organization, while they don't go through any particular oath taking, pledge themselves not to engage in being experts in producing new weapons; the second is to work for the solution of the problems created by science and technology. There is a lot of commitment of science and technology and research to the new methods of destruction, as well as to bringing welfare to the peoples of the world. There's no question, as I'm sure that our friend Dr. Suzuki will tell us, of what science and technology have done for the benefit of mankind, and I don't deny the benefits. Science for Peace is an organization aimed at doing two things: one is to keep scientists pledged to working for the benefit and not for the destruction of mankind, and the second is to try to help bring and maintain peace through methods such as arms control, verification and new technologies of communication.

Notes

1. The North Atlantic Council is the principal authority in NATO and is composed of the foreign ministers of the member states. It meets continually through permanent representatives, of which the author was one.

2. NORAD is an integrated command of air defence of North America established by bilateral agreement in 1957. Although North America is part of the NATO area under the North Atlantic Treaty, NORAD is the only military command that does not come under the authority of the North Atlantic Council. This is because the United States does not wish to share control over nuclear decisions affecting American security (while accepting consultation over nuclear weapons deployed in Europe).

3. In May 1986, President Reagan said that the United States would no longer be bound by the terms of SALT II. The outcry from NATO allies and critics in the United States was so great that the administration decided to re-evaluate this decision. However, on November 28, the equipping of a further B-52 bomber with cruise missiles went over the agreed limit, breaking the treaty. This was the first time either side had clearly done so.

CHAPTER 17

Three-Party Debate: Can Canada Really Be an Effective Peacekeeping Middle Power?

LLOYD AXWORTHY, M.P., PAULINE
JEWETT, M.P., AND TOM HOCKIN, M.P.

Lloyd Axworthy

The three of us have been asked to discuss whether Canada can be an effective middle power. I think we should start by getting rid of the name *middle power*. I don't think Canadians want Canada to be a middle power. I think they want Canada to stand for something. If you talk about *middle* it has the aura of a musty museum piece where you're talking about being Mr. Fix-It, the honest broker, the international boy scout. As I travelled across the country for public hearings with a committee that included Tom Hockin and Pauline Jewett, I heard views similar to those expressed at this conference: Canadians do not want Canada to straddle the fence. They want Canada to take a stand very clearly on the side of those who are against nuclear insanity and to make sure there is no equivocation on this issue. We can't be a middle power; we have to be something else.

The public needs and demands a vision of where Canada should go. I think the vision Canadians want is one that would get rid of the kind of ad hoc, capricious, step-by-step way to do business that we heard from the External Affairs spokesman [Ralph Lysyshyn] and others. I really believe that a different role for Canada is one that is against the kind of superpower flouting of international rules and laws that we see in Nicaragua or Afghanistan. There is a demand that we end the kind of inconsistency where our government says it believes in a policy to control nuclear weapons but then refuses to take a clear stand on the Strategic Defense Initiative. There is a clear demand for the defence of human rights, and then the government tolerates the kinds of things that we see happening in Nicaragua. We've heard many different recommendations and proposals at this conference, but we have to be clear about one thing if we're going

The Honourable Lloyd Axworthy, M.P.

to have a new vision for Canada and if there's to be a new foreign policy role: these things can only come about if Canada is an independent country. There's no point talking about all the alternative strategies and all the new thoughts if, at the same time, through a very clear and conscious decision, we are allowing ourselves to be integrated into a North American security and economic system that will limit our freedom to choose what that foreign policy will be.

The issue that Canadians face right now is that we have, by a deliberate policy choice, accepted integration with the United States into its new defence security system for North America. You have heard it described in a variety of ways, but the fact of the matter is that strategy for North America has been substantially and fundamentally changed by the Americans and we are, step by step, accepting that change without posing an alternative. We have to ask ourselves if it is really possible for Canada to be a mature nation and a peaceful power if we have already become integrated into a new defence system that doesn't give us the freedom to choose.

Equally, we have to look at the major linkage between defence and the trade issue. We talk a lot about free trade in this country, but we've never talked about its relation to defence and security. How can we have freedom to choose where we want to go as a country if, at the same time, we have decided to totally integrate our defence industry with the defence industry of the United States? How can we possibly have freedom to choose if, at the same time, we have harmonized our policy on services and communications and culture? If we are going to have a new vision of foreign policy in this country, we must retain and enhance our ability to choose the options that are in front of us. And that means that we must say no to the defence system that's being developed, and we must say no to free

Lloyd Axworthy has been the Liberal member of Parliament for the Winnipeg-Fort Garry riding in Manitoba since 1979. He has an M.A. in political science from United College in Winnipeg, and an M.A. and Ph.D. from Princeton University. He taught political science at the University of Manitoba from 1965 to 1979. He has served as an executive assistant to John Turner and Paul Hellyer, and before entering federal politics represented Fort Rouge in the Legislative Assembly of Manitoba. As a member of Parliament, he has served on a number of committees, including Foreign and External Affairs. He has been Minister of Employment and Immigration and Minister of Transport. He is currently the deputy critic for External Affairs for the Official Opposition, as well as Trade and Wheat Board critic.

Pauline Jewett, M.P.

trade. Then we must decide what kind of independent country we want to be.

Pauline Jewett

I'm delighted to speak about New Democratic Party policies on these matters, which happen to coincide with my own views. We feel that Canada could indeed have been an effective peacekeeping power if not only had Canada refused to be a nuclear power itself, which is of course laudable, but had it also declined to manufacture components of nuclear weapons; had it declined to test the cruise missile; had it declined to get involved in the defence production arrangements with the United States and, in the post-war period, to almost totally integrate its economy with the U.S. war economy; had it declined to go into NORAD; had it said no to the latest renewal of NORAD; had it objected to the first use of nuclear weapons in NATO (and, indeed, if it would only speak out and remove itself from NORAD and NATO); had it had an honourable ports policy; had it supported the nuclear freeze and the Comprehensive Test-Ban Treaty at the United Nations; had it joined Nordic and Arctic nations in the development of a demilitarized northern zone; had it spoken out strongly against Star Wars, saying why Star Wars was both technologically unfeasible and strategically undesirable; had it admitted that in recent years the United States has been the driving force in the nuclear arms race; had it stopped its highly questionable arms sales and its complicity in the global war economy; had it not backed down from the targets set many years ago for international development assistance; had it continued to address North-South issues. Had Canada done even any of these things, Canada could have been and could still be an effective power for peace in the world.

We could lead in setting the debate on an entirely new level. The problem in this country is that we won't face and talk about the alternatives to being tied into the military economy and the strategic doctrines of our

Pauline Jewett has been the New Democrat member of Parliament for the New Westminster–Coquitlam riding in British Columbia since 1979. She has a Ph.D. in government from Harvard University and has completed post-doctoral studies at the London School of Economics. She has served as a Liberal member of Parliament, director of the Institute of Canadian Studies, president of Simon Fraser University, and first president of the Canadian Research Institute for Advancement of Women. Pauline Jewett has been the New Democratic critic for External Affairs and Post-Secondary Education. As a member of the External Affairs and National Defence Committee, she helped create the minority report on security and disarmament in 1982. She has written extensively on Canadian, international, socialist and women's affairs.

The Honourable Tom Hockin, M.P.

great neighbour. We won't look at what kind of world we might have if we didn't have superpower-dominated military blocs. We might analyse the difference we could make in the world if we were not tied into NORAD and tied into NATO and if we did not have all these nuclear-related defence agreements with the United States.

The New Democratic Party wants to move the debate to that level, and it is shocking to us to discover, for example, that the Arms Control and Disarmament Consultative Committee to the government is required to give advice "in the context of our military alliances." We must get out of that context. Only then can we have a productive debate about what more powerful initiatives we as Canadians can take.

Tom Hockin

I congratulate the Council of Canadians and the Canadian Physicians for the Prevention of Nuclear War for putting on perhaps one of the largest and most interesting conferences of its type in the last decade. This is an impressive show of concern and of knowledge.

I speak to you as a former co-chairman of the Special Joint Parliamentary Committee on Canada's International Relations, on which I served with Pauline Jewett, Lloyd Axworthy, other members of Parliament and senators. My comments this morning will be based more on that experience than as a government minister, because now my portfolio is not foreign affairs but finance. In my answers I'll try to reflect not only my own and the committee's thoughts in its report,[1] but also government thinking.

My theme is this: Canadians are unique internationally in their emphasis on what I like to call voluntarism. We believe that Canada has an obligation to help with world stability and world peace. Canada has an obligation to elevate international relations to more civilized and more peaceful standards. This has been a tradition of this country for over fifty years, and any government, be it Liberal, New Democratic or Progressive Conservative, that ignores the voluntarist instinct and tradition of Canadians

Tom Hockin is Minister of State (Finance), and the Progressive Conservative member of Parliament for London West. He has served on the standing committees on External Affairs and National Defence and on National Health and Welfare. In July 1985 he was elected co-chairman of the Special Joint Committee on Canada's International Relations, which recommended over one hundred foreign policy initiatives for Canada. Almost all have since been adopted. Tom Hockin was a founding director of the Canadian Centre for Creative Technology and the Canadian Centre for Arms Control and Disarmament. He has published a number of articles and books on the Canadian government and on Canadian foreign policy.

is in peril. And the present Conservative government, of which I am proud to be a member, is very aware of these instincts and has carried on a number of initiatives to focus them and take them still further.

First of all, peacekeeping. Canada is now playing a major role in the Sinai and in Cyprus. Canada is giving strenuous leadership on the South African issue within the Commonwealth context; it stands ready to help in Namibia. All of those proposals and initiatives are profoundly important to this government and they respond to the voluntarist instincts of Canadians.

Second, I read a newspaper report about the first part of this conference, stating that you're concerned about the government of Canada speaking out. Let me remind you that the government of Canada is profoundly disturbed by any possibility of a rejection of SALT II, and it has said so. The government of Canada believes in a strict interpretation of the Anti-Ballistic Missile Treaty, and has said so frequently. There has been correspondence between Prime Minister Mulroney and President Reagan and between External Affairs Minister Joe Clark and U.S. Secretary of State George Schultz on specific proposals for weapons cuts and specific proposals for decreasing the level of weapons systems. We are speaking out.

We also have carried our views to the Soviet Union, an action that is equally important. Canada's position on Nicaragua is not necessarily that of the United States. Canada's position on South Africa speaks strongly in keeping with our traditions in international relations. In the First Committee on Disarmament in the United Nations, of forty-four votes in 1985, Canada voted twenty-two times with the United States and twenty-two times on the other side. We speak out. We have an independent view of what leads to peace and security. It responds to the voluntarist tradition and to the initiatives that Canada believes need to be taken in these troubled times.

In international relations generally, there's another whole set of consultations where this government is taking initiatives, but especially in the Arctic; and since this is a conference on the True North Strong and Free, I hope I can share with you some of the many initiatives that are being taken in the Arctic as well. I look forward to your questions.

Axworthy
Let me take issue with what Tom Hockin said about speaking out on all the issues. The problem is that the government often speaks out from both sides of its mouth and, therefore, people don't know what the government stands for. You can't say, on the one hand, that we are against SDI when Joe Clark, at the NATO meetings after the Reykjavik conference, refused

to condemn the United States for not putting SDI research on the agenda for negotiation so that there might have been a breakthrough. The government refused to do that. You can't have it both ways.

At the same time, you can't say that we took an action against American initiatives in Nicaragua when Prime Minister Mulroney says on an American public affairs show that Nicaragua is a client state of the Soviet Union. That's not the way to establish that kind of position; you can't do those kinds of things. I think that is what the public of Canada is rebelling against. Canadians are saying that Canada must demonstrate not only a series of ad hoc reactions but a coherent statement of principles and initiatives.

And just one final point. Tom Hockin says we have to talk about the Arctic. I agree, and it was a major issue of our committee's hearings, but we know full well that the Canadian northern frontier is becoming one of the central action centres of the Cold War (and I don't mean that as a pun). There is major submarine activity on both sides. Both the Soviet Union and the United States are now using the Canadian North as a major staging area for strategic exchange and interaction. This government has said nothing about that, nor has it taken any action to internationalize our Arctic waters and to bring in other northern powers and say, "Let's have a nuclear freeze up north."

Jewett

It may surprise you to hear that I agree with everything Lloyd Axworthy has said, but this is a three-party panel and my concern is that the Liberals, when they were in power, did not do those kinds of things. This is a very genuine concern. It may be because the defence and external establishments are dominating our foreign policy. But I believe there is also the capacity, if the political will is there, to dominate them and to provide leadership and say where we really are going to go as a government. I see no indication that either a Liberal or Conservative government is likely to pursue the policies that the New Democratic Party has in its platform and would pursue when we come to power. I think that's terribly important. The present Conservative government, like the former Liberal government, gives lip service to an independent Canadian foreign policy, gives lip service to an independent assessment of the nature of the threats around us. We've got to start making that independent assessment and judgement, and we can't do it as long as our military alliances and our defence production arrangements are totally linked to the global war economy and to arms sales to the Third World. We cannot do it unless we put a party in power that is prepared for the kind of approach that I have suggested to you this morning.

Hockin

The position Canada has taken in Nicaragua is not lip service. The leadership that Canada has shown within the Commonwealth on South Africa is not lip service. The position that Canada takes in the First Committee on Disarmament in the United Nations is not lip service. The position that Canada takes within the General Agreement on Tariffs and Trade (GATT) to put together a new negotiating round on agricultural matters without reference to the United States is not lip service. Example after example of independent Canadian foreign policy occurs every week in this country, and these are actions. It's not lip service.

I'm not surprised that Pauline Jewett and Lloyd Axworthy agree on so many matters, because both of them underestimate the importance of the NATO alliance for the defence of freedom. Just as we should take part in the Geneva conference on agricultural reform through GATT, just as we should be taking part in other forums to help with environmental matters, just as we should be concerned with freedom, so we should participate in the forum of NATO for the defence of freedom. We are not participating in NATO because the United States wants us to. We're not participating in NATO because of geography. We're participating in NATO because we believe in the defence of freedom. Because of that, I am going to have to disagree with Pauline and Lloyd on the question of cooperation with allies in certain contexts. In some contexts, we must work with our allies in the defence of freedom.

Axworthy

I think the most successful part of this conference has been holding three politicians to five minutes each. Talk about conflict resolution—that's a real example. Pauline got her shots off about the Liberals. I'll remind you that it was former Liberal Prime Minister Pierre Trudeau who started peace initiatives that awoke a lot of people in this country and around the world to the fact that we have to ask some serious questions about the kind of world we live in.

I also want to say that the tradition that goes back as far as former Prime Minister Pearson and the peacekeeping days, a tradition of standing up against the United States over the Vietnam War has clearly demonstrated that we hold no candle to which party can establish the right foreign policy. Of course I don't agree with the NDP foreign policy; neither do most Canadians. That's why the NDP has never formed the government of this country. We are facing a new future, and to spend your time hacking over the old wounds and the old anecdotes doesn't get you very far. Right now the key foreign policy issue for Canada is in North America. Because of the major changes in the defence system and the trade system, we're about to lose our independence. Canadians of all parties should be united to fight against that.

Jewett

"Hacking over," or whatever that phrase was! On the contrary, only if we understand what we have done in the past can we correct it and behave differently in the future. I was one of those who applauded former Prime Minister Trudeau's peace initiative. It just came fourteen years too late and wasn't really able to get off the ground. Tom Hockin says that we are participating in NATO for the defence of freedom: it's that kind of sentiment that does not really analyse either what we mean by freedom or what we mean by the common security. I know I don't have long enough to get into this now, but the most fascinating discussion we could have would be on the question Tom has raised. He has stated what he thinks is a defence of freedom, and I guess he has to accept the idea that the nuclear umbrella is also a defence of freedom. I don't accept that. I think a lot of people reject that. The greatest threat to us all is the nuclear arms race itself.

Hockin

On Lloyd Axworthy's point about Canadian independence let me say this. The government of Canada believes that through negotiations with the United States, where eighty per cent of our trade is now conducted, our lines of trade with the United States are in peril. Every day in the House of Commons, Mr. Axworthy mentions threats from the United States and the relationship with Canada. Through these negotiations, we want to secure our access to the U.S. market; that's what it's all about. We want to secure it, tie it down and, if possible, put up a few more runs on the scoreboard by enhancing it somewhat. We have a strategy, therefore, for dealing with this enormous protectionist wave that's sweeping the United States. That's what these free trade negotiations are all about, nothing grander than that. By securing our access, we will have the wealth and the ability to be independent in international events.

With regard to the nuclear umbrella, I agree with Pauline Jewett and Lloyd Axworthy when they say the nuclear umbrella is not the preferred way to bring peace. What we must do as a government and as a country is to make sure that the nuclear umbrella is made unnecessary through disarmament, through proper arms control, through a sense of security, through compliance and inspection that everybody can feel comfortable with. Therefore, the goal is to do away with the nuclear umbrella. To do it unilaterally, without proper inspection measures and without proper compliance measures, is a great danger. All countries should move together.

Finally, a word about Canadian independence. I don't want Canada to be a Finland. I don't believe that we're the same as Finland. I believe we've got enormous resources for good in the world by working with our allies as well as by working multilaterally, and I do not want to see that stopped by "Finlandization" of the Canadian foreign policy.

QUESTIONS

Leonard Johnson

Mr. Hockin, in 1984, when the Conservative Party was campaigning for office, one of its promises was that defence and foreign policy reviews would be held. We've seen the foreign policy review process that our three members of Parliament here participated in, and we saw that it was a very successful effort. Canada is much indebted to you for it. I would like to know why you didn't go ahead with the defence review, why it was decided there would be no Green Paper, why we haven't had a White Paper yet, why we keep hearing that it's set back six months at a time, and why, if the case for being in NATO and NORAD is as strong as you say it is, your government has discouraged any debate on membership in the alliances.

Tom Hockin

We are operating in Canada with the last defence policy review entitled "Defence in the Seventies." I think it was published in 1971. That's the last comprehensive review of Canadian defence policy. The present government was elected in 1984. No comprehensive review occurred in those intervening thirteen years. We took power and committed ourselves to a thorough review of defence policy. When the parliamentary committee that the three of us served on did its review across the country we, in fact, were looking at issues that touched on defence. I think the Department of National Defence wanted to review that report. The Department of Finance seems to be putting the Department of National Defence through strict budgetary examination and therefore it has decided to produce the White Paper this spring, not earlier. In 1987 the White Paper on defence will be revealed.[2] Don't blame us for being six months late when the previous Liberal government took thirteen years without doing anything.

Lois Wilson

I wish to tell you that the missing vertebrae have been discovered and returned, so I'm very grateful now to have the opportunity to test the strength of the backbone.[3] My question is addressed to Tom Hockin. If the United States breaks the limits on SALT II, what assurance have we that the Canadian government will review its decision on cruise missile testing in Canada?

Hockin

If the United States hasn't heard, it should read the speeches again and read the statements again. We have said in the clearest possible way that the government of Canada would be profoundly disturbed by any break out of SALT II. That's our position and it remains our position.

Lloyd Axworthy

Can I just make one comment? I asked External Affairs Minister Joe Clark that question in the House of Commons about three or four weeks ago and the answer was that he doesn't see the connection between the two. We asked very clearly, "Will you stop cruise missile testing if the United States breaks SALT II?" And he said it was a hypothetical question. It's not a hypothetical question. That's the stand we should be taking.

Cynthia Cannizzo

Lloyd Axworthy and Pauline Jewett, Canadian foreign and defence policy is not a choice between independence and alliances but between domination and alliances because of the relative power of the United States. Traditionally, only with formal alliances that put restrictions on the United States and with coalitions with the Europeans through NATO has Canada been able to redress that balance of power in any way at all. What would you substitute for the alliances if we were to withdraw from them in order to redress that relative imbalance of power?

Pauline Jewett

As far as I know, the New Democratic Party is the only party that advocates the withdrawal from the alliances. Certainly when Parliament had the NORAD review a few months ago, both the other parties agreed to a five-year extension of the NORAD agreement, despite a great deal of broad-based public concern that the agreement should be renewed, if at all, for a much shorter period of time. I would be delighted if Canadians would start talking about our defence policies in the absence of these military alliances. We have done a fair bit of work within the NDP. At the party congress in 1985, we discussed the ways in which we would spend our defence dollars; the kind of passive defence we would be involved in; what kinds of reconnaissance and surveillance—some of it costly—we would need to have, particularly in the Arctic, but also on our two coasts; what kind of an arrangement we might be able to enter into with the northern countries in a common agreement to demilitarize the Arctic. There are a number of areas in the development of mobile forces that we are sympathetic to and would like to pursue. We would like to see the role that we play in the United Nations made stronger. And so there are a number of both independent and multilateral routes in developing the common security that the NDP would pursue.

Axworthy

To gain a much better level of independence for Canada to choose our own security policy, we have to see a major restructuring of NATO. Obviously, one of the first requirements is to substantially transfer the resources that we now commit to the ground and air brigades in Europe and bring them back into Canada so that we can establish our own independent surveillance system in the Canadian North and not be dependent upon the U.S. system for information and detection. That is a very clear necessity, but I think you can still do that within the alliance policy. I think that it's time for a major modernization of that policy, and as George Ignatieff said earlier, NATO could be used to hold accountable a lot of the other superpower initiatives that we now deal with. I don't think you necessarily throw NATO away, as Pauline Jewett has recommended, if you can turn it to your proper use, which is to provide adequate checks and balances on the role of the United States rather than allowing the United States to proceed with its present North American defence system. That's what I'd prefer to see—the restructuring and refocusing of that alliance so that we can make much better use of it in terms of an independent northern policy.

Hockin

Cynthia, just a quick further response to your question. I worry that the NDP defence policy would give us a very quick phone call that an invasion was at hand, but once we got the phone call we would have nothing to respond to it with. That's my concern with the NDP defence policy. Lloyd Axworthy essentially is suggesting that we unilaterally withdraw NATO brigades from Europe and put them to the task of defending Canada. That unilateral action would be very bad for the alliance. I agree with Lloyd on this point: we have to get NATO to look at the Arctic as part of the defence of freedom, and Canada will have to devote more resources to the Arctic. This doesn't mean militarization of the Arctic, but it means that the Arctic and our obligations there must be recognized by NATO. We should continue a dialogue within NATO on these matters, but not act unilaterally.

Cannizzo

With regard to the Arctic, I have a series of three questions, all of which have the same answer. Which country has a major submarine base in the Arctic? Which country has a major military base and major military installations, including half of its fleets, in the Arctic? And which Arctic country consistently puts forward nuclear-weapons-free zone proposals but also consistently refuses to include its own territory in such a nuclear-weapons-free zone?

Axworthy

Well, that's easy. It's called a three-part question: one, two, three. It's the Soviet Union, but let's also remember that in 1982, the United States put forward a new maritime attack strategy called the Forward Maritime Strategy, where the United States clearly enunciated that it would use its attack submarines to trace Soviet ballistic missile submarines and cruise-launch submarines into their home waters. For all we know, those attack submarines are there now, but we don't know because we have no way of finding out at the present moment. Because of the interaction between the two superpowers, the Canadian waters are becoming one of the most dangerous potential areas of conflict between them—it's happening in our territory. We've said in the report that the committee put forward (and I wanted to go much further in the report) that we can't simply talk about sovereignty by building an icebreaker. It's not going to get us anywhere. We've got to put the proper surveillance systems under the water and in the skies, and most importantly, we're going to have to internationalize that system by a proper international legal document so that all countries will make sure the superpowers respect the right of free, peaceful passage in the Arctic and not use it as an area for the Cold War.

Jewett

Canadians pay far too little attention to U.S. naval policy. There is simply too little discussion about what the United States' basic, fundamental policy is—this thrust of trying to push the Soviet Union back in and back in. People in the Center for Defense Information in the United States, for example, have done some excellent studies of the errors in U.S. naval policy, including U.S. strategy in the Pacific. I really would like to stretch our minds to include the study of the policies of both superpowers in the Arctic and in the Pacific. We are too Euro-centric, and we must start looking at what is happening elsewhere because it affects Canada. So I would agree that we've got to study more, analysing more what the superpowers' naval policies are. I'm extremely concerned about what is happening in our oceans—the militarization of our oceans and the nuclearization of our oceans. I think Canada has got to become much more knowledgeable and concerned, whether it's about the United States or the Soviet Union.

Hockin

The largest nuclear submarine base in the world is at Murmansk. The

Soviet Union has awesome power in the Arctic. We must remember that. We don't know if the Soviet Union is penetrating Canada's Arctic or not, but the possibility is there. The same with the United States. We cannot properly prevent this penetration or have proper surveillance, in my view, unless we have submarines that can do that surveillance, and we said this in the report of the special joint committee. I commend this report to you. We made it very clear that it is a *sine qua non* of our sovereignty in the North to have those submarines, along with drawing straight base lines. International lawyers and Canadians from all walks of life have been arguing that we should declare our sovereignty in the North, and in September 1985, the Conservative government declared those base lines, something the Liberal government had never done. The United States doesn't like that action, but we've done it and now the United States must come to Canada rather than us to the U.S. This government's position on protecting our integrity and enhancing our control over the Arctic is profound and detailed, and it's outlined in part in this report.

Gerry Harle (Edmonton, Alberta)
Before asking my question I would like to make a short comment. I don't think there's a person in this room who is not thoroughly disgusted, dismayed and frustrated with the mutually-assured-destruction policy of the two superpowers. Peter C. Newman, who wrote *True North: NOT Strong and Free* (Toronto: McClelland & Stewart, 1983)—and I'm dismayed that he is not here—says that in exchange for making Canada nuclear free, we must pay a price, that is, to take more responsibility for our own defence in order to maintain our national credibility. Do you agree?

Jewett
Yes.

Axworthy
Yes.

Harle
Then why don't you get off your collective political duffs and do something about it?

Jewett
The NDP is trying to. Vote for us.

Jill Metcalfe (Canmore, Alberta)
Having come recently from Britain, where we have vigorously campaigned against the stationing of the U.S. cruise missiles on British soil, I would like to know if this inquiry can initiate a similar commitment towards the ban on testing and stationing of cruise missiles on or over Canadian soil?

Jewett

I would hope that the inquiry that has been conducted these two days will do exactly that, among many many other things.

Isabelle George (Arcola, Saskatchewan)

Mr. Hockin, we're being asked to accept that the West has a genuine fear of Soviet conventional, chemical and biological weapons as well as of their nuclear weapons, and the Soviet Union would seem to have a genuine fear of the West's nuclear weapons as well as the development of SDI. Yet, we don't hear the Americans and the Soviets talking about negotiating away these fears, and I'm wondering why we as Canadians are not calling them to task on this. Why aren't we telling them that they should be saying, "I'll give you SDI if you'll give me a verifiable treaty on significant reductions of all arsenals."

Hockin

I think that's a question that's on everybody's mind. What kind of trade-offs should exist between SDI and other weaponry? First of all, in June 1986 the Soviet Union made it quite clear that certain kinds of research related to anti-ballistic missiles (ABM) and SDI were permissible from its point of view because, of course, the Soviet Union is doing some laboratory research as well. Next the position of the Soviet Union seemed to be firmer, that any kind of prototypes and certain kinds of systems shouldn't be tested, and that was a harder line than existed back in June. Now the Soviet Union is talking about something a little closer to the June position.[4] I think, given the progress that was made by the two superpowers in a number of dimensions of arms control and disarmament in Iceland, that we may have some movement not too far away that would better define what ABM research is and what SDI research is and combine that research with these cuts that you mentioned. I think we're closer to an agreement than to the doom and gloom that followed two days after the summit.

Axworthy

First, I don't think Tom's right historically; the meetings of Soviet Foreign Minister Eduard Shevardnadze and U.S. Secretary of State George Schultz were held just two or three days ago and totally broke apart. Second, it's quite clear that the United States is substantially expanding the definition of the ABM Treaty to include testing and deployment, and that is against the original intentions of that treaty. The Canadian government should be saying so in unequivocal terms so that the United States and the Soviet Union can get back to the table and negotiate something; we should not give in to the American interpretation, which is what I think is happening now.

Hockin

No, that's not true. I'm sorry, Lloyd, I know of no statement by the United States saying that it wants the right to deploy SDI.

Axworthy

After the Reykjavik summit, President Reagan said, "We have a right to test and develop the SDI concept." That's against the ABM Treaty.

Jewett

That's correct.

Hockin

It's not true. In fact, the United States said before the NATO assembly last September that it will adhere to a strict interpretation of the ABM Treaty. That's its position, and it does not include deployment, and it certainly doesn't include testing in the environment or in space; that's been its position all along. I have not seen any changes in that.

Jewett

But the United States is already doing testing and development of components in space as well. President Reagan, unfortunately, has never distinguished between research, testing and development; he calls it all research. Everything short of deployment, he calls research.

Axworthy

This may be an example of how governments sometimes make policy by not getting confused by the facts.

Noel Keough (Calgary, Alberta)

Some speakers at this conference speak of the necessity to align ourselves with like-minded allies. They assume our main ally is the United States because we share democratic principles. Can we really assume this premise, given that the so-called democratic principles of the United States have always included the right of military intervention in democratic countries, such as we see in the present arming, training and directing of terrorists who are seeking to destroy the democratically elected government of Nicaragua?

Hockin

I do not want to get into an argument about the moral equivalence of the Soviet Union and the United States, but let me tell you this. In terms of history, defence policy, foreign aid and foreign policy, the United States is not to be compared with the Soviet Union. The Soviet Union attacked and occupied Eastern Europe. What the Soviet Union is doing in Afghanistan today is absolutely unconscionable, and this was said by Ambassador Stephen Lewis in great detail last week in the United Nations. I will not—I repeat, I will not—involve myself in a debate about the equivalence of these two superpowers. The United States makes mistakes, and when it makes mistakes we speak up, but let us not forget what the Soviet Union does.

Jewett

There should be no doubt that all three parties share, and indeed the whole of the United Nations with the exception of a few countries shares, our abhorrence of the Soviet occupation of Afghanistan. There is no question about that, nor has there ever been. Indeed, I would like to see the Conservative government pay a little more attention to the Afghan refugees; the government does nothing, absolutely nothing. We could debate forever the actions of the Soviet Union and the United States. I remind Tom that the Soviet Union has been left with two allies in the Middle East—Syria and South Yemen (and the former can be doubtful)—three or four in Africa, one and a half at most in the Caribbean and Latin America. You could argue, looking at it from the Soviet Union's perspective, that we are the danger and the threat—when I say we, I mean primarily the United States. I think it's only fair when we're noting our sharing of many of the democratic values of the United States, that we equally understand that its values also embrace interfering in the affairs of its neighbours if they're in its so-called sphere of influence.

Darren Kelly (Students' Union President, Ross Sheppard High School, Edmonton, Alberta)

If Canada expects to help make our world a peaceful world, we must act to bridge the gap that divides the Americans and the Soviets. As it stands right now, neither side would trust the other enough even to talk with each other regularly. Both sides have repeatedly proven that covertness and lying are integral parts of their method of government. How would each of your parties, if in power, direct Canada as a negotiating peacemaker to ease the tensions between the United States and the Soviet Union and develop that essential element of international peace—trust between nations?

Jewett

You could cover a million things that we haven't already covered in response to an enormous question like that. One of the first things we must try to do as Canadians is to recognize what the two superpowers are or are not doing. I find that, for example, if I say in the House of Commons that the United States has been the driving force in the nuclear arms race in the last few years, I get called a Commie. If I state what is a fact, that it's the Soviet Union and not the United States that has placed a moratorium on nuclear testing—a unilateral act—I get told I'm pro-Soviet. I think what Canadians must do, if we are going to act as a country that can help develop trust and confidence between the two superpowers, is to be honest.

Axworthy
The first priority would be to have our country take a major lead in developing coalitions of other states of similar size and interests to restore the effectiveness and the utility of our international institutions and international law. For too long we've allowed both superpowers to use a Rambo mentality to dominate international affairs. We've moved away from the wonderful vision we had after the Second World War—that we could actually establish some rules by which we could play, and that all people would play by them. It wasn't simply a question of who had economic or military might or power. We've lost that commitment. We don't fight for that basic purpose of re-establishing some rules and guidelines by which the world governs itself. I think that Canada must restore that sense of commitment to the internationalizing of this world in bringing together the kind of collective security that we need. If we don't do that, then we're simply going to have the law of the jungle apply, and eventually the law of the jungle consumes all.

Hockin
Darren, I want to congratulate you for your question because it poses the theme of this whole meeting this morning. The greatest book I've ever read on promoting international security is a book by Kenneth Waltz called *Man, the State, and War* (New York: Columbia University Press, 1959), and he answered your question very succinctly with three sentences. He said there are three ways to promote trust among rival powers. First of all, work on the level of psychology and build trust at the psychological level, not only between the governments but between people. Second, at the state level, make sure that the state relationships are more open and cooperative and build a sort of mutual interdependence between states. And third, make sure the international system doesn't, through accident or through overdevelopment of weaponry, trip the two major powers into starting a war. We must work on all three dimensions: the psychological level, the state level and the international level.

Don McKinnon (Project Ploughshares and Lawyers for Social Responsibility, Saskatoon, Saskatchewan)

My question is for Tom Hockin. Canadian arms control policy is supposedly in favour of major, radical weapons reductions. Given that priority, do you agree with Paul Warnke[5] when he says that SDI and major weapons reductions are fundamentally irreconcilable, and if you agree with him, then why hasn't Canada said to the United States in the aftermath of Reykjavik, "Rethink SDI and abandon it, please"?

Hockin

The government's statement on SDI is that since the Soviet Union is doing this research, it's prudent for the United States to do it too. In terms of the actual development and deployment and workability of SDI, my private view is that I don't think SDI will work. (This isn't the government's view and I haven't asked everybody in the Cabinet their view on this.) Therefore, I don't think that it's going to be a major force in our lives ten years from now, because it's not going to work. I think that there could be a lot of military expenditures by the United States and the Soviet Union on ABM defences that are going to be a waste of money. The fiscal crunch will probably point this out down the way, but that's just my private view. The third comment I'd like to make about SDI is that the original impetus for SDI was not to give a new step to the arms race but to try to find a replacement for mutually assured destruction. The world desperately wants to get out of mutually assured destruction as a system of deterrence. Perhaps you and many others feel that the ABM approach or the SDI approach is not the way to get out of it, but we must do something about diminishing the great dangers that face us through mutually assured destruction. This was President Reagan's approach. It's not very workable and we should find other approaches.

Joanne Oldring Sydiaha (Women in Peace and Interhelp, Saskatoon, Saskatchewan)
Nuclear arms technology, the nuclear energy industry, and uranium mining and exportation are inseparable. Mines in Saskatchewan and Ontario, and other potential Canadian reserves, are primary world sources for uranium, thus contributing to the total cycle. I would like your comments about uranium mining and its contribution to the arms race, first from your knowledge and experience as individuals and second, from your parties' policies.

Axworthy
Last spring in the House of Commons the matter came forward that the uranium exported to the United States (clearly limited by law to peaceful purposes) was, in fact, in a diffusion reactor plant in Tennessee, and parts of the uranium were being reallocated for weapons production. We had

several very extensive questioning sessions in the House of Commons and in the External Affairs Committee about the matter. We were given assurances by the Canadian government that the uranium was not being used for weapons purposes, and that goes into the technicality of how you mix uranium. Canada has taken the lead over the years in establishing the rules and laws against the use of uranium for weapons purposes, but part of the problem is that those rules and laws are not as effective as they should be. It has to be brought forward as one of the items that both the government and Parliament have to address in order to see whether it's really valid to continue in that export market.

Jewett

The New Democratic Party's policy is that we would end uranium mining. There were some differences within the party on this matter, coming from our friends in Saskatchewan. But it has now been accepted, in Saskatchewan as well, that we would cease all uranium mining, because we do agree with the questioner. Matters relating to nuclear arms and uranium mining and, indeed, to CANDU reactors, are inseparable. The federal NDP now has a task force studying the whole nuclear fuel cycle. We have asked the government repeatedly to live up to a commitment to do this. It hasn't, and so we have set up our own task force, which will be travelling across the country.

Hockin

The government's position on the use of uranium is very similar to what it was before we were elected. To prohibit the use of uranium in weapons is a profound objective of government policy. I believe it was before we were elected; therefore, my answer is very similar to Mr. Axworthy's.

Notes

1. "Independence and Internationalism," a report of the Special Joint Committee (Ottawa, 1986).
2. "Challenge and Commitment: A Defence Policy for Canada" (Ottawa, 1987).
3. Wilson was referring to her comment after William Arkin's speech, p. 93.
4. In November 1986, Soviet Foreign Minister Edward Shevardnadze said that laboratory research, including the building of samples and prototypes, could be permitted for ten years, but not cosmic tests. After ten years, he suggested, the sides would negotiate to ensure that further developments conformed to existing treaties.
5. Paul Warnke is the former director of the U.S. Arms Control and Disarmament Agency. He was the chief U.S. negotiator during the Strategic Arms Limitation Talks in 1977 and 1978, which led to the SALT II agreement.

CHAPTER 18
Science for a Peaceful Future

DAVID SUZUKI

Science is the most powerful factor shaping our lives in society today—science as applied by industry, medicine and the military. Yet, strangely, if you measure the amount of space in our newspapers and the amount of time on television and radio devoted to various stories, you would never know that science is so important. Looking at media coverage, we would have to conclude that Canadians are obsessed with political issues (whether Mr. Chrétien will displace Mr. Turner), economic issues (falling oil prices, the value of the dollar), sports issues (whether Mr. Gretzky will be able to hold off Mr. Lemieux), "glamour" issues (whether Sean Penn and Madonna will stay together), and so on. Judging by the amount of time and space devoted to these items, it would appear that we are obsessed with political and economic issues, athletic competitions and glamorous personalities.

As a society, we are blind to the central place of science. And the reflection of that blindness is in the kind of people we elect to political office. Of course, in a democratic country, the officials we elect reflect our perceived priorities. And as you all know, eighty to ninety per cent of all elected representatives, whether at the federal, provincial or municipal levels, come from two fields: business and law—eighty to ninety per cent of our politicians are business people or lawyers.

I've said over and over again, I'm not a bigot. I have nothing against business people and lawyers, although none of my four daughters had better marry one. What worries me about having such a disproportionate representation from business and law is that this skews the sense of what Canadians feel are important issues. It is not an accident that Canadian

183

David Suzuki

politicians are obsessed with economic and jurisdictional issues when so many of them are lawyers and business people. Yet, when you assess individual comprehension of very simple terms and issues in science, you find lawyers and business people come out absolutely rock bottom. They are simply scientifically illiterate. They are making major decisions about the future of fission versus fusion reactors, about SDI, about acid rain, about microelectronics, about biotechnology, and so on. As a society, we are out of control of our own destiny because the people making the decisions on our behalf cannot begin to assess the scientific and technological issues involved.

A classic example, and I say this in all seriousness, of the problem we face with the scientifically illiterate politician is President Reagan. Here is a man who grew up in a time long before computers, televisions, jets, rockets, satellites, nuclear bombs or birth control pills. He is making major commitments to SDI because he was nurtured on Buck Rogers comics. He understands science and technology so little that he believes in biblical creation. Now, I think that indicates the real problem we face. If we are to come to grips with nuclear and environmental issues, we first have to understand the relationship between science and society in a profound way. And I find that most of these discussions are so superficial as to be useless in any kind of long-term planning. So let me now discuss the relationship between science and society in a way that will perhaps be useful.

Scientists now begin to specialize very early in their training. When students take a bachelor of science degree, they have to accumulate an enormous amount of information. Yet they may go through four years in a Canadian university with little more than a freshman English course in addition to their science courses. Very few scientists today have ever studied history, philosophy, religion or literature. They know nothing of

David Suzuki is a native of Vancouver, British Columbia. He received his B.A. from Amherst College, Massachusetts, and his Ph.D. from the University of Chicago. A prominent geneticist, he has taught in the Department of Zoology at the University of British Columbia since 1963. He has worked extensively on the popularization of science, through articles, radio, television and film. Best known for the television series "The Nature of Things" and "A Planet for the Taking," he has always advocated a responsible relationship between people and the earth. Dr. Suzuki has also been active in numerous civil rights organizations. His numerous honorary degrees and awards include the Order of Canada, the United Nations Environment Program Medal (1985) and the Royal Bank Award (1986).

the limitations of the scientific method or of the sense of responsibility that should accrue to scientists. They know nothing of the history of their own activity or of the social context within which science is carried out and applied.

If you talk to scientists today and ask them questions, the vast majority of them will tell you: (1) that science is value free—it is a search for objective truth; (2) that science is an international activity that transcends national boundaries; and (3) that the application of scientific knowledge is the responsibility of all members of society and not the special responsibility of scientists themselves. And I think that such classic responses illustrate the enormous lack of knowledge on the part of scientists.

Science is *not* a value-free search for objective truth. Science is an activity carried out by human beings with all the foibles, idiosyncracies and limitations of any other group of human beings. The questions they ask and the way they interpret data are reflections of the values and beliefs of the practitioners themselves. So if, as now, most scientists are upper middle-class white males, the nature of science itself will reflect their particular values, assumptions and beliefs.

If you believe that science transcends national boundaries, you only have to look at the response in Canada to John Polanyi's Nobel Prize[1] to realize that this simply is not true. Science is very much a national activity; it is paid for by the taxpayers and representatives of individual nations. Indeed, if you look at the history of science, the reason we use English in science today is because the German community, which dominated science before World War I, came to be regarded as the enemy. The French and English then broke away from their German colleagues and decided to use English as the common scientific language. You only have to look at the scientific contributions of the Nazis in World War II to realize that science is far from being devoid of patriotic and nationalistic fervour. It is clearly a national and not an international activity.

And, finally, to say that scientists do not have special responsibilities is a total denial of reality. Today, over half of all scientists around the world carry out research directly for the military. The majority of the remainder of the scientific community carry out work for private industry. This means that the priorities driving the application of science are destructive power and profit.

Much newly acquired scientific information is not made generally available because it is classified for military or industrial reasons. And those papers that *are* published in the open literature are usually incomprehensible to the vast majority of the public. Surely, at the very least, scientists have a special responsibility to demystify the activity they're involved in, to allow people other than the military and private industry to take advantage of their information.

186

It is not politicians or military leaders who come up with ideas for their arsenal of weapons. It is not President Reagan or the Pentagon or the Kremlin that developed the idea of binary chemical weapons or conceived of the current biological weapons, neutron bombs, SDI or ethnic weapons. It is scientists like Edward Teller and Bob Jastrow who are the driving forces behind SDI.[2] The people developing the weapons are scientists and engineers. They are the colleagues and students of scientists. Surely, then, scientists bear a special responsibility. Yet unlike virtually any other group in society—including physicians, who traditionally have been the most conservative members of society—scientists have no formal codes or guidelines to direct their ethical and moral conduct.

Today, human beings are the most ubiquitous and numerous large mammal on the planet. Armed with science and technology, humans are exerting a profound impact on the planet—an impact that is out of all proportion to the rest of nature. The rate of extinction of species of plants and animals today is now approaching the rate that occurred when the dinosaurs disappeared. We are like a feral species, an exotic animal or plant introduced to a new habitat. And now, with our science and technology, we lack all the biological controls that keep our species in balance.

For ninety-nine per cent of human history we have invented new technologies slowly. They came about through observation, invention and painstaking trial and error. In the past, new technologies developed long before people had any idea of their scientific basis. But Hiroshima signalled a profound change in the relationship between science and technology. The atomic bomb was conceived by the greatest scientists of the day, sold to politicians by scientists and then built by scientists. And ever since, science, technology and the military have been inextricably linked. Modern warfare is unimaginable without science and technology, and science would be radically different without defence support.

Science is the source of most of the ideas and inventions that are being developed and applied. It is said that over ninety per cent of all scientists who have ever lived are alive and publishing today. So we get a huge outpouring of knowledge and invention that allows us to bludgeon nature into submission and perpetuate an illusion of control. We have become intoxicated with the revolutionary new insights gained into DNA, the atom and the brain. We are developing revolutionary technologies to exploit these insights: recombinant DNA, artificial intelligence, space labs and lasers. Today, we worship the power of technology. As its inventors, we believe that we remain its masters. Yet history informs us that every technology has a cost. However beneficent, there is no such thing as a cost-free technology. The more complex the technology, the greater the probability of accidents and a detrimental effect on the environment and on people.

Today, the most reliable cause of technological breakdown is human error. Bhopal, the *Challenger* explosion, Three Mile Island and Chernobyl attest to that. No technology today is foolproof, because every human being is a fool at some time in his or her life.

Nothing illustrates the ludicrous faith in technology better than nuclear weapons. You all know the technology much better than I—the warheads, the delivery systems, the surveillance satellites, the supercomputers. None of these systems has ever been tested under real conditions and let's pray they never will. But you can bet from the history of technology that they would never work as planned anyway. Anyone who believes that the components of weaponry will work as planned simply does not know history. A simple crude technology like a cruise missile plunges straight down onto Alberta soil because someone forgot to pull the plug. SDI will not, cannot, work as expected, any more than airplanes can be made crash-proof. I don't believe for a minute that all the technological problems will ever be overcome, but even if they were, even if you could redesign SDI, you could not design perfect human beings to run it.

Canada has traditionally underfunded science. There has been much more pressure on scientists in the last few years to do work with an immediate social pay-off, and I believe that part of the free-trade initiative is aimed at making the U.S. research money more readily accessible to Canadian scientists. The pull of enormous defence dollars is going to prove irresistible to our chronically underfunded scientific community.

Ever since human beings began thinking and creating, their inventions have had both beneficial and destructive potential. This is seen from the taming of fire to the development of knives, bows and arrows and dynamite. I don't think you can distinguish between research for peace and research for military purposes; any scientific invention can be used for peace or for destruction. The challenge is to change the nature of scientific funding, to establish an ethical framework governing scientists' activities, and to better inform the public and political communities.

QUESTIONS

Leonard Johnson
Dr. Suzuki, a conference was held on accidental nuclear war at the University of British Columbia in May 1986. It concluded that the risk of accidental war is probably very much higher than we've ever believed it was. This has also been affirmed in *American Scholar* and I believe that there's some general scientific concern about it. Could you comment on this problem and tell us how serious it is.

David Suzuki
You only have to look at the history of the NORAD supercomputer. In one eighteen-month period, I think there were one hundred and fifty mistakes, things like a flock of geese being mistaken for a Russian missile. There is no such thing as a foolproof technology unless you remove the fool, which is any human being. I've said over and over again, human beings fall in love and lose fifty IQ points; they get drunk and get hungover; they get the flu. We do all kinds of things that prevent us from acting one hundred per cent efficiently. Invariably, when a plane crashes out of the sky, for example, it's a result of human error. There are over a hundred thousand people in the American military who have direct access to at least one missile. They're screened very, very carefully because you don't want some insane person running around in there playing with a live missile, and yet every year over four thousand people are drummed out of the U.S. military for drinking on the job, for being stoned on marijuana, for taking heroin or for some psychological breakdown.

Cynthia Cannizzo
My question may be a little longer than usual. When we talk about the relationship between the military, science and society and about an individual scientist's responsibility for his or her own research, there are four potential obstacles to breaking the relationship between the military and science that I would like you to comment on.

First, an individual has a free choice in a democracy as to what kind of research he or she does. In other societies that choice is not free. Sometimes that free choice may be to work for the military. Sometimes the "unfree" choice may be to work for the military. How do we deal with that problem?

The second type of problem is that it's often hard to tell where some research is leading. Research at Ohio State University on repairing damaged retinas with lasers led to the creation of a very fast and efficient "fire-and-forget" firing control system for jet pilots.

A third problem is that money may sometimes not be available elsewhere for basic scientific research. Bishop De Roo told me a wonderful story about a young man who had a mathematical formula for fixing a point in space. No one would fund his research except the military. His research has a very wide application in all of our space activities, both peaceful and military.

And the fourth problem concerns the need for self-defence. While I think we would all like to see a completely disarmed world, as long as some people have weapons and as long as those people might attempt to impose their will on others (including Canadians), it seems to me that we must make reasonable efforts at self-defence and have a certain amount of weaponry that can respond to the threat with which we are faced.

Suzuki

Do I have an hour to respond to these four questions? First question, Does the individual have free choice? You contrasted different societies where the individual does and doesn't. Quite frankly, I can't say anything about the Soviet system. I am a Canadian citizen, and I can only speak for Canada; here we do have free choice. In the education of our students, we don't even face the fact that they may have to make such a choice and that they will ultimately have to respond as individuals. We give them no sense of the philosophical and moral questions that their choice raises. I think, at the very least, we ought to have a community that thinks about these issues in terms of making such a choice.

As to the second question, that you can't tell where research is going, you're absolutely right. That's why I didn't want to make a distinction between peace research and war research. I think one of the great examples is John Polanyi, a leading member of the peace movement in Canada, who nevertheless has seen one of his great inventions, the chemical laser, being touted as a potential weapon in SDI. So there is no such thing as a new idea that can be used only for peace or only for war. We must have scientists who say, "I will do research wherever my curiosity leads, but I must make the results accessible to the public." I believe that public knowledge will minimize the potential for research to be used in a deleterious way.

Your third point is that dollars for basic research are often available only from the military. In Canada that is especially true. As long as I've been back in Canada, and that's twenty-four years, the government has drastically underfunded research in this country, and scientists who remain in Canada have often secured American military money. I, for example, existed for five years on an Atomic Energy Commission grant, but there were no strings attached to that grant in the sense that I could publish and talk about anything I discovered in open literature. And I think that's the crucial point.

As long as there are weapons, we must make efforts to ensure normal self-defence. Obviously, we're never going to get back to being able to fight with our bare fists. We're going to have to have conventional weapons. But it all sounds insane when we talk about being able to have on-site inspection and have some kind of anti-ballistic missile treaty, and so on. The technology is totally out of control; it's beyond human control. To speak as if we can control this by further technological devices simply perpetuates a myth that we are in command of this technology. I think that we should decide right now, as a country, that nuclear weapons are insane and we don't want to have anything to do with them. I feel the same about chemical and biological weapons. I'm very nervous about the current trends in the United States, and I can tell you now that the American military is funding recombinant DNA work in universities in the United States. I think that's something you have to pay attention to. It's very, very worrisome.

Lois Wilson
We've talked about the rather complicated reasons for conflicts between nations; one that has not been mentioned very often is that people don't have enough to eat. There are lots of people out there who really won't work at the business of sharing resources. Do you see any possible role for science and scientists in feeding a hungry world?

Suzuki
I don't think that the problem is a scientific problem. It's a political and economic one because scientists are opportunistic and want to get money wherever it's available. You find a lot of genetic engineers, for example, who are arguing that we have to support biotechnology in order to improve our efficiency of food production to feed the Third World masses. That's absolutely ludicrous. We reached the first billion on this planet in the last century. In only a hundred and fifty years we doubled twice to reach four billion and we're going to double again to eight billion in another fifty years. Science, no matter how much you pour into it, will never keep up with that. That is a major problem we have to face. It's not a scientific issue.

Rick Gunther (Dawson Creek, British Columbia)
This question is coming from a science teacher, so if you detect any bias that's where it is. It's directed to both Dr. Suzuki and the panel. Because of the conservatism imposed on the public school systems by elements of the public and by many parents who are ill-prepared to have their science, non-science and nonsense beliefs questioned over the supper table, and by politicians like British Columbia's Premier Vander Zalm, who stated that facts rather than opinions should be taught, how can educators and the public education system in this country address the issues of sovereignty, security and the idiocy of nuclear weapons?

Cannizzo
We have to become aware of and work to overcome a tendency to think that young people can't understand some of these issues. Given proper information, given a chance to explore their views, and given a chance to hear two, three, or four sides of a single issue, even young students can

begin to grasp some of the issues. Obviously the older you are and the more experience you have, the more subtly you can see various positions, but I think there has been a tendency to believe that we have to dole out information in very tiny doses. That is beginning to change within the school systems. In Calgary, our Strategic Studies Program has requests from high schools for speakers, and we've even had requests from junior high schools. There is a lot of work going on to develop sound educational materials for the elementary schools, the junior highs and the high schools.

Suzuki

As parents and teachers and people concerned about young people, we have to understand that our youngsters today are going to spend the vast majority of their lives in the twenty-first century. My two youngest children will become adults long after the year 2000. They're going to grow up in a world radically different from ours, so the idea that we are educating youngsters who are kept out of science or ignorant of science is really a terrifying thing to me, because I think that's the way the educational system is set up.

Premier Vander Zalm's emphasis on facts indicates a total lack of understanding of the nature of scientific fact. When I tell my students the kinds of ideas we believed in 1961 when I graduated as a fully licensed geneticist, they fall on the floor laughing. They say, "How could you have believed such stupid ideas?" And I say: "You know, you're absolutely right. What we geneticists believed in 1961 seems really stupid and naive today. But then, in ten years people are going to say about today's hot ideas, 'My God, what stupid ideas those are!'"

If you look at the history of science, the great bulk of science is involved in proving that current ideas are wrong. So then, what does it mean to give the facts? If we are giving youngsters the facts that science says are true today, then we are giving them only stuff, the bulk of which is going to be wrong tomorrow. We should be trying to understand the nature of knowledge, of reality. Is there such a thing as subjective reality? What is the sex bias in the accumulation of information? What are the social contexts within which science is carried out and applied? Those are the important things.

There's a second part to Mr. Gunther's question: in my experience, the vast majority of Canadians feel completely estranged from science. I've gone out in the streets and done what we call "streeters," where you go with a camera behind you and you do person-on-the-street interviews in downtown Winnipeg at forty below in February. People are coming out of grocery stores with fresh bananas and tomatoes and you say, "Do you think science and technology affect your daily life?" And the vast majority of people say, "No, not really." Now where do you get bananas and tomatoes at forty below? But the interesting thing is that many will say: "Gee, you know, science doesn't affect me. I was never any good at math." So I think that it's really weird, and wonder why they think that. And of course the reason is they've been taught that. In the education system, Johnny and Mary, and disproportionately Mary, are told they're having trouble with math. We're told that if you can't do well in math you're not going to do well in science. If we want to have a scientifically literate public, the challenge is in the first creative five years of elementary school; that's when we lose the bulk of the youngsters, and after that they're cut off from science.

Peter Sherrington (Nuclear Disarmament Group, Cochrane, Alberta)
As you have rightly stated, Dr. Suzuki, the ultimate responsibility for the good or bad application of science and technology rests with individual scientists. That being the case, however, what do you see as the responsibility of the universities as institutions in addressing the moral and ethical issues inherent not only in specific research programs but also in the fundamental general education of our scientists and technologists?

Suzuki
I'm very worried about what the universities are doing today because I think the universities are getting themselves into a terrible hole. Universities in the past fifteen years have sold themselves to the public by acting as if the correlation between going to university and getting a better job is a direct one. The universities have taken the credit for any correlation and said, "You've got to go to university to get a better job." Now we're locked into the expectation that we have to "service" students coming to university, not expose them to the vast range of human thought and the excitement of exploring ideas. Universities, which are now committed to giving students an education that will let them get jobs, find themselves more tightly bound to interfacing with industry and the military and any source of outside funding where they can expect to find a payoff. For example, universities in the United States are allowing a lot of military money into funding biotechnology research. I'm concerned because these are going to be secure areas where scientists cannot publish except in classified literature, so their research is going to be out of bounds to other scientists and the public.

An academic community offers tenure so that scientists and academics will be able to explore new ideas fully and openly without fear of political interference. When there is a tight tie between scientists or academics and industries, then that possibility of openness is closed. Let me give you a classic example of this. A few years ago, when OPEC had imposed its oil embargo, there was a great deal of interest in exploiting the tar sands of Alberta, so we decided to do a one-hour program on the tar sands. At that time, Syncrude was a model and we were projecting ten Syncrude-sized, or bigger, plants in another ten years. Syncrude pours out fifty tons of sulphur dioxide a day. That would make a lot of acid rain, and ten more plants of this size would make a lot more acid rain. We thought we had better ask ecologists at the university what the consequences would be. We went to the University of Alberta in Edmonton, and nobody would talk to us. We went to the University of Calgary, and nobody would talk to us. Why? Because they were all getting grants from the oil companies. Now I say that that is a denial of what an academic community is all about, and I am terrified at the encouragement universities are given for the development of such things as biotechnology companies. What discourages me even more is that historians and philosophers in the university ought to know better. They ought to be up there screaming and yelling, and they're not.

Monty Bauer (County of Thorhild Central High School, Thorhild, Alberta)
With all the research that has been done to produce ways of killing people, there's no doubt that science has led us to the brink of nuclear destruction. Do you think that the scientific community can reverse this process and correct the wrong that has been done, and if so, what should be done?

Suzuki
I don't feel that you're going to see the major change coming from within the scientific community, although there are organizations, such as Scientists for Social Responsibility and Science for Peace. They are small groups, but they can have an enormous impact, comparable to the impact of Canadian Physicians for the Prevention of Nuclear War. The way you change the scientific community is for the public, which controls the purse strings, to demand that scientists develop a moral and ethical framework within which to act. It has to be audiences like this that are going to put the heat on the scientific community.

Notes

1. John Polanyi was awarded the Nobel Prize in Chemistry in November 1986, along with two Americans. Polanyi, a professor at the University of Toronto, is a prominent peace activist.

2. Edward Teller is a prominent theoretical physicist, centrally involved in the development of the hydrogen bomb. He had a major influence on President Reagan in his pursuit of an impenetrable defensive shield (SDI). Bob Jastrow is another U.S. scientist who believes in the technical possibility of SDI.

CHAPTER 19
A New Role for the Military

C. G. GIFFORD, D.F.C.

I bring you greetings from American Veterans for Peace. They believe they did not risk their lives and that their comrades did not die in battle so that their government could violate international law and disregard the judgement of the International Court of Justice. They know about us here and they want you to know that they are marching side by side with us to make a world without war.

Dr. Ignatieff mentioned this morning the need for a Canadian parallel to the Center for Defense Information in Washington and I'm glad to be able to report that we have set up the Canadian Defence Research and Education Centre.

I've been asked to comment on the defence of the North, on Canada's military alliances and on whether the Canadian military should be doing things differently, and if so, how. I was not a career officer and I speak here as an individual citizen.

First, I'll give you the context of Canadian military policy:

1. War has become obsolete, and the institutions to replace it are already in operation.

2. The arms race between the superpowers has accelerated, daily increasing the risk that the war nobody wants will be triggered by accident or misjudgement.

3. The military situation in Europe has been a stalemate for the last thirty years. There are no foreseeable circumstances in which the Soviets will deliberately invade Western Europe. Neither side has any possibility of breaking the stalemate in its own favour. The stalemate is a fine source of profits, promotions and power for the military, industrial and scientific complexes of both sides, but the military complex is an expensive, waste-

C.G. Gifford, D.F.C.

ful, highly dangerous and useless institution from the perspective of most citizens.

4. The real power struggle is taking place in the Middle East, Asia, Latin America and Africa. It is here that the Soviets twice considered initiating the use of nuclear weapons before establishing their no-first-use policy. It is here that American presidents have considered the use of nuclear weapons, risking World War III, at least fifteen times since World War II. It is here that intervention by the superpowers takes place daily, some by the Soviet Union and more by the United States. The spark of World War III is many times more likely to occur in the developing world than in Europe, where there is a stalemate.

5. The United Nations is an absolutely essential institution for our world. Its greatest weakness has been that the United States, the Soviet Union, France and Britain have not wanted it to diminish their unilateral power.

6. Whatever has been the case in the past, the Soviet Union appears to recognize present realities. I have a long quotation from the *New York Times*. I'll just quote part of it. At the twenty-seventh Communist Party Congress in February 1986, General Secretary Gorbachev said: "There is no alternative to cooperation and interaction between all countries. Thus the objective conditions have taken place in which confrontations between capitalism and socialism can proceed only and exclusively in forums of peaceful competition and peaceful contest."

Words are one thing and deeds are another. The Soviet moratorium on testing (and the promise to continue it indefinitely if we match it) is an action, and it's an action that we can verify. It does not depend on trust. The evidence is strong that the Soviet Union is ready to begin dismantling the arms race.

In the case of the U.S. government, the evidence points in the opposite direction. For nine years, U.S. administrations and the Congress have been expanding the surplus of nuclear weapons; they have been spreading that surplus around the world on the oceans; they have shown a renewed readiness to intervene in the Third World; and with SDI and Strategic Defense Architecture 2000 they have been preparing to militarize space. All these bespeak an expansion of reliance on military force, a rejection

"Giff" Gifford, D.F.C., received his B.A. in 1939. After serving as an RCAF air navigator in the Pathfinder Force of the RAF during World War II, he returned to university. He received his M.S.W. in Pittsburgh in 1947 and began working in the field of social work. After being director of the schools of social work at the University of Manitoba and Dalhousie University, he retired in 1984. He has devoted himself to disarmament work and is the chairman and founder of Veterans Against Nuclear Arms.

of negotiation and the arms control process of the 1960s and 1970s, and a rejection of the United Nations and the International Court of Justice.

7. From the perspective of history, a warless world is quite near. It will come in one of two ways: either we will stumble into World War III, after which the planet will be a very peaceful place; or the citizens will make it unthinkable for their governments to resolve disputes with other countries by any means other than negotiation and resort to the International Court of Justice. It is an outrage that any government deliberately chooses violence rather than accepts the jurisdiction of the International Court of Justice.

Are Canada's military forces to be primarily devoted to maintaining the useless stalemate in Europe? Is our territory to be used for the destruction of the arms control process? Is our military policy to be a silent collaborator in U.S. violation of commitments to the United Nations and to NATO and the Third World? In other words, is our military policy going to continue to be one of collaboration in the preparation for World War III? Or is our military policy going to help dismantle the European stalemate, to make our territory a factor in strengthening international law and the arms control process, and to take realistic steps to eliminate the many flashpoints that might result in a nuclear conflict in the Third World? If we are to work for survival, we have to choose the latter path.

We must recognize that a choice for world law and international collective security means standing against the whole thrust of the present U.S. policy.

What are the implications for Canadian policy? First, NORAD and the North. With regard to NORAD, the choice has become absolutely clear. NORAD cannot avoid being a vehicle for the Unites States' war-preparation plans. Therefore, our government should announce at the earliest possible date that it is going to cease military integration with NORAD, that it will replace it with a Canadian air defence command, and that the territory north of the Arctic Circle will be demilitarized under surveillance by Canadian means with international observers, giving the United States and the Soviet Union assurance that our territory will not be used to threaten either.

The overall function of NATO now is to find ways of dismantling the stalemate and replacing it with a system of international policing and the use of the International Court of Justice. This can be broken down into at least six components:

1. accepting that NATO's current forces are more than adequate to prevent Soviet delusions of grandeur;
2. stopping the introduction of new, threatening weapons and strategies like Follow-On-Forces Attack;[1]
3. researching, developing and implementing non-provocative, truly

defensive technologies and strategies as self-defence measures;
4. matching such unilateral Soviet steps as a no-first-use policy and a nuclear test moratorium;
5. negotiating mutual steps such as creating a demilitarized zone between the two blocs in the centre of Europe and establishing an international arms reduction inspection regime;
6. abolishing the two military blocs.

The citizens of many NATO countries are going through the same struggle that we are to redefine their countries' policies. The political situation in several NATO countries, including Britain and West Germany, makes changes of policy like those advocated here realistically possible within two or three years. In particular, our Nordic NATO allies see things in much the same way as we do. It is in Canada's interest to join these NATO allies in changing NATO's direction.

At the same time, acting for our own and the planet's survival requires us to separate ourselves from the present U.S. policy. It will be harder to do this alone than in the company of these NATO allies because of the U.S. pressures that can be expected. Thus, it makes sense for Canada to stay in NATO. If nothing happens within a few years, we would still be free to withdraw unilaterally.

I believe that our defence priorities should be:
1. United Nations peacekeeping;
2. surveillance of our own territory, especially the North;
3. military contribution to NATO without upgrading.

It may be that we can only afford the first two of these goals, or the first two and part of the third. If we have to withdraw our military forces from NATO, then, like France and Spain, we should keep our seat at the table and work with like-minded countries for change in NATO. We should also be part of the current discussions of Northern and Pacific nuclear-weapons-free zones.

As far as these difficult choices of allocation of resources are concerned, I have a rule of thumb. Will the strategy or the weapons system under consideration only be used in World War III? If so, there is no point in pursuing it. World War III will be the end, and we are overprepared for it already. There is absolutely no sense in allocating new resources to preparing for World War III, especially when resources are so desperately needed and means are so clearly feasible to work on preventing it.

Some people say that we should not deny our territory to the U.S. Department of Defense because the United States will violate it anyway. Those who say this do not grasp that what is at stake is our physical survival and possibly the survival of the planet. It is too late to try to appease the U.S. Department of Defense for fear that we might otherwise have to pay a price. In any case, we will have to pay a price. What is our survival worth to us?

There are some who still dream of influencing the U.S. government. The power and momentum of the U.S. military, industrial and scientific complex make such a hope unrealistic. There is no evidence that any country has moved the U.S. government towards disarmament and world law in recent years.

The only path open to friends of the United States is to limit the damage the U.S. government can do. We can't stop the United States from destroying us all if it so decides, but we can limit its scope for doing so and we can send a firm, clear message by our actions. This is a necessary effort for our safety, but a secondary result could be to give heart to the majority of U.S. citizens who want non-intervention in Latin America, who want a freeze of nuclear weapons, who want an end to SDI, and who want multilateral disarmament.

I said earlier that the real military action is in the Third World. The most important area of policy, and the one in which there seems to be the greatest gap, is that of finding ways to quarantine the indigenous conflicts there and disengage the Soviets, the Americans and other industrial states. International developments, such as the International Law of the Sea Agreement,[2] and the role of the International Atomic Energy Agency vis-à-vis the Chernobyl disaster,[3] show how an international framework of institutions to replace the operations of raw national power is emerging. The trade in drugs, the trade in arms, the activities of terrorists—all must become as reprehensible as the trade in slaves and the trade in women have become. There is surely no vehicle for such developments but the United Nations.

What are the implications of these policies for Canada's military? These priorities and goals do not suggest a new role for Canada's military so much as a shift in emphasis—from emphasizing NATO to emphasizing peacekeeping, international surveillance, verification and policing. They involve giving up the tired clichés and misleading statistics of NATO and giving up preparation for World War III. They involve a shift of emphasis from participating in expensive and unrealistic NATO North Atlantic convoy exercises, for example, to using our skills in resolving "neighbourhood" conflicts, which is the day-to-day experience of peacekeeping forces. They involve a shift from thinking in terms of the Pentagon to thinking in terms of Canada and the United Nations.

These policies also involve a shift in the political exploitation of the military. It will be a great day for Canada when our military forces refuse to be used to deceive the public through misleading NATO estimates of the NATO–Warsaw Pact military balance or dishonest statements about the warheads of cruise missiles. The killing of women, children and old people through weapons of mass destruction has become the chief characteristic of modern war. This violates the Geneva and Hague Conventions on the protection of civilians. The morality of industrialized war has sunk below that of Genghis Khan. What the public needs from our military is a return to the concept of military honour, which rejects acceptance of atrocities as the daily task of the soldier and which, above all, refuses to let soldiers be merely tiny cogs in the race to oblivion.

Our military forces have a fine record of bravery in action. What we need from them now, above all, is career and political bravery—the kind of bravery shown by General Gert Bastian of Germany when he resigned from NATO Command in opposition to the spread of nuclear weapons in Europe; the bravery of Major Helmut Priess and his uniformed colleagues in the Bundeswehr, who sacrificed the opportunity for promotion by organizing the Darmstadt Appeal against the placing of cruise and Pershing II missiles on West German soil. This, too, is not a change of role but is an emphasis on the kind of Canadian patriotism shown by such leaders as Sir Arthur Currie, Lieutenant-General A. G. L. MacNaughton, Major-General Worthington, Lieutenant-General E. L. M. Burns and Major-General Leonard Johnson. These Canadian generals— all patriots and independent thinkers—recognized that the institution of war must, in the long run, be replaced by world law.

QUESTIONS

Cynthia Cannizzo
On the one hand, you argued that NATO levels are currently adequate to prevent Soviet delusions of grandeur and that we should continue our contribution to NATO. On the other hand, you argued that the stalemate based on military alliances in Europe was useless and that there was no need for deterrence as the Soviet Union does not want to invade. I have difficulty reconciling those two positions, both of which you gave. I sense a certain contradiction there. Would you please explain that?

Giff Gifford
I believe that unilateral disarmament would be dangerous, and therefore our problem is to start from where we are with mutual dismantling. I don't see a contradiction.

Lois Wilson
You mentioned the necessity for quarantining Third World conflicts from

both the Soviet Union and the United States. I presume you would think that might be done through the United Nations, and if so, what is your prescription for the UN, which is suffering a lot of brickbats from citizens and countries these days? There isn't much expectation that the UN is able to act.

Gifford
There isn't such an expectation at present, but I think it comes back to the citizen and especially to the middle powers, if I may use that term in spite of Lloyd Axworthy's comment about it earlier. The UN is in financial trouble, and yet Canada's contribution to the basic funding of the UN is roughly the cost of one CF-18 and its upkeep. The budget of the United Nations is less than that of any Canadian province except Prince Edward Island, and it's perfectly within the capability of the middle powers to correct that situation. We also have to persuade the members of the Security Council that it is in their interest to move towards international border control, border protection and inspection regimes. That seems to be the next stage. Nobody says these things are easy. It's just that they are a lot easier than nuclear war and the nuclear arms race.

Cannizzo
While the UN does have a mandate to isolate conflicts and to put in peacekeeping forces and so forth, the use of that mandate in any particular situation depends on the countries in the conflict themselves allowing the peacekeeping forces to come in. How are we going to get around that problem? Canada cannot simply say, "We're going to establish a quarantine."

Gifford
No, that's right, but if we were to offer Nicaragua and Honduras, and possibly also El Salvador now, a UN border control force to protect these countries from intervention, they would be quite likely to accept it voluntarily. I think the front-line states in Africa that are dealing with South Africa on their border would be quite likely to accept an offer of a UN-sponsored border control force to protect them from intervention.

Julien Kinsale (Citizens Against Racism and Apartheid, Edmonton, Alberta)
I love where your heart is and your revelation that both the superpowers at some point considered using nuclear weapons in Africa. I like your clear vision of the evil deeds of the United States and its NATO allies in Africa and your realization that in the 1940s, after the defeat of Germany, care-

ful thinking went into the reasons for Canada joining NATO. Did the Allies also use their brilliant minds to visualize that Africa would be in such a sad state today because of the total chopping up of Africa by the Europeans and the eventual dogfight between East and West over political ideologies? Does the affluent, benevolent West also know that the very bombs we have been discussing for these past two days have been falling on the poor, mainly people of colour, even before the birth of communist Russia.

Gifford
I'm glad you used the phrase *the benevolent West*. It's witness like your own that makes people like me feel that our claims to Christian values, to democratic values, and so forth, ring a little bit hollow. We say we're defending these values in NATO when we are party to so much violation of those values in countries like your native South Africa. I just hope we've learned from history and that we're beginning to take some of those values more seriously than we did in the past. I am glad to see that our own government has taken steps in relation to the economic boycott of South Africa, but we have a long way to go, I'll agree with you there.

Wilson
Christian values and democratic values have been automatically joined, and I don't think that's necessarily so.

Gifford
Okay.

Lance McFadzen (M.E. Lazerte High School, Edmonton, Alberta)
You claim that war is obsolete, and your speech suggests that if there is a war it will be instigated by the United States. I'll point out that war is far from obsolete and it's very effective. Just ask Yasir Arafat, Ho Chi Minh, Daniel Ortega, Moammar Gadhafi and, from his marvelously successful actions in Afghanistan, Mikhail Gorbachev. The examples of Laos, Cambodia, Mongolia, Vietnam, Angola, Zimbabwe, Mozambique, Poland, Czechoslovakia, Hungary and East Germany are far too numerous to ignore. Why do you see the Americans as the only threat to Canada? Can't you see that the Soviet Union is not to be trusted either?

Gifford
Did I say the Soviet Union was to be trusted? We seemed to agree in the first half of this conference that the threat to Canada is a nuclear conflict between the superpowers. That's the enemy. When I use the phrase *pre-*

paring for World War III, I am referring to the belief that it is possible to fight World War III. In *Defense Guidance—84 to 88,* U.S. Defense Secretary Caspar Weinberger says we have to be prepared to fight and win an extended nuclear war. Now the fact that a person in such an important position can believe such a concept and put it in writing scares me. We see that policy being implemented in the U.S. forward defence strategy, and we need to witness far more firmly and in our actions the idea that has been widely expressed that World War III must not start, that nuclear war cannot be won and that it must not be fought. But Canada's actions are not based on Mr. Weinberger's concept of fighting and winning a nuclear war. The actions of our allies and of the Soviet Union do not reflect it. So our target needs to be the war system in which both sides are involved. The countries that you've mentioned are a small part of the problem. It's true that war is taking place in many places in the world now, but getting the industrialized countries, which provide the arms for these wars for both sides, to engage in a warless system is what we have to do if we're going to tackle this problem the world over.

Carmen Macklin (Edmonton, Alberta)
In this inquiry we seem to be focusing on a direct reduction of arms, but we also seem to be still unprepared to live without our military forces, hence living with power vacuums. Considering that the best way of combatting evil is to make energetic progress in the good, I want to suggest that it is on the level of building international trust, confidence and brotherhood that we need to work to take away the threat of war. An initial thrust towards disarmament that the peace movement should make is to get the nations of the world today, large and small, to commit themselves to non-aggressive, non-expansionist foreign policies. By the time the world knows that such treaties have been made and will be honoured, arms and armies will be obsolete. Why not?

Gifford
The problem is to get the treaties honoured. NATO countries have all committed themselves, first under the Atlantic Charter, then under the UN charter, the NATO agreements and the Hague Convention. They have undertaken, first of all, not to make civilians the target of military activity and yet that's what we're doing. They have undertaken also not to interfere by force in any country which has not first interfered by force with them; unfortunately, it's a matter of record that NATO countries have intervened in more than seventy per cent of the violent conflicts that have taken place since World War II. So our problem is to mobilize ourselves as citizens to get our governments to adhere to what they've already promised.

Macklin
The United States is a NATO country. What's it doing in Nicaragua?

Gifford
I agree with you.

Brian Roadhouse (United Church of Canada and Farmers for Peace, Lashburn, Saskatchewan)
I am a dedicated member of the peace movement and also the child of a Second World War veteran and a nephew of two uncles who died in the war. What might I say to veterans of the world wars when I do not, I cannot, believe in war? Second, is pacifism a possibility both for individual Canadians and for us as a nation, for it has not been spoken of much at this conference?

Gifford
I'll tell you how we feel in our organization about what you can say to veterans. We believe we have some unfinished business. We enlisted in World War II because our country was in danger, because our children's future was in danger and because it was necessary to stop Hitler. Our country is in greater danger today than it was in World War II, and our children's future is in greater danger because nuclear war encompasses all children, and so we have re-enlisted. We perceive ourselves as having re-enlisted for exactly the same reasons that we enlisted so many years ago. I mentioned American Veterans for Peace at the beginning. I had the privilege of being one of the speakers at their convention in Portland, Maine, in August 1986. I met there a U.S. Marine Corps colonel with thirty years of service who served in combat in Korea and twice in Vietnam and commanded nuclear weapons for ten years. What he said would, I hope, make sense to any veteran: "After commanding nuclear weapons for ten years, I've come to the conclusion that war is obsolete and we have to find another way of doing business. Period." I have yet to meet a senior Canadian military officer, serving or retired, who does not think there are too many nuclear weapons around the world, and I think you'll find that with most veterans too. Their concern is about the methods for dismantling these weapons.

As far as pacifism is concerned, if by that you mean non-violent resistance, I think we can see from the Philippines, we can see from the civil rights movement in the United States, we can see from Haiti, we can see from Iran (where unarmed civilians stopped the tanks), that unarmed civilian resistance can be an effective force and we don't need to put all our eggs in the nuclear basket. In fact, we are stupid to put any of them in the nuclear basket. There are other forms of deterrence such as civilian resistance, which has been demonstrably effective in the face of overwhelming military superiority.

Peter Langille (Ottawa Disarmament Coalition, Ottawa, Ontario)
We've been asked to think anew, to move beyond the alliance context in our thinking and to consider defence alternatives. There are a few powerful impediments, vested interests, that stand in the way of this transition, and I'd like to ask how you propose we begin. It's my impression that the study of Canadian strategy and defence requirements reflects the pervasive extension of an American influence over both our governments and our academic communities, certainly in strategic studies. Do you think it's presently possible to get a fair assessment of new alternative defence requirements from a Canadian government or bureaucracy, such as the Department of National Defence or the Department of External Affairs, or even from within a Canadian strategic studies program? If not, will the new Canadian Defence Research and Education Centre attempt to fill the void?

Gifford
I haven't had much contact with strategic studies centres outside the Centre for Foreign Policy Studies at Dalhousie, which is essentially a strategic studies centre; people there have not yet started studying non-provocative defence, but they do welcome members of our organization to their seminars, and we do have the opportunity there to exchange views with both retired and serving senior military people. I would not consider it beyond the realm of possibility that some of the centres of strategic studies might begin studying non-provocative defence, of which Project Ploughshares is providing interpretation at the moment. I think these alternatives will be studied when we, as citizens, say, "Look, you're losing credibility." Our Department of National Defence is losing credibility because it has been on a one-track course and some of the citizens are becoming better informed than our so-called military experts on the real alternatives to the course we're on.

Carolyn Pounder (Strathcona Composite High School, Edmonton, Alberta)
Why don't you consider that the real problem Canada faces is that we should be trusting the Soviet Union and the United States. And without that essential trust we can never hope to attain peace or nuclear disarmament. And that is what scares me.

Gifford
I don't think we have to rely on trust. When I buy a car, I don't rely on

trust to make a deal; I get the car checked out by an independent source to tell me it's okay. The car salesman has an interest in selling it to me, and I have an interest in buying it, but we don't have to go on trust. Arms control agreements don't rely on trust; they rely on mutual agreement and inspection, and I apply this to our own government as well as to the U.S. and U.S.S.R. governments. In the last six to eight years, and possibly going back further, we've had too many attempts by our government to obscure the realities. I'll take the question of testing of the cruise missile. I heard Harriet Critchly of the University of Calgary and Mr. R. P. Cameron (formerly in External Affairs) on public national radio arguing that the warhead of the cruise missile would be conventional. Now, why did they do that? And why did our military collaborate in this misinformation? Some of us in the peace movement dug out the information that the nuclear warhead of the cruise missile is two hundred kilotons, fifteen times the power of the Hiroshima bomb. We've had too much of that kind of misleading information seriously advocated, and if the people in government advocating this kind of thing don't know the facts, they should keep quiet. If they do know the facts, they should tell us. I'll get in one more plug on that one, if I may. We say we're to defend democratic values. What about truth?

Notes

1. Follow-On-Forces Attack (FOFA) is a current NATO military doctrine of preparing to attack enemy concentrations and command posts far behind the front line of any presumed conflict.

2. The third UN Conference on the Law of the Sea concluded successfully in 1982. The convention was offered for signatures from December 1982.

3. Following the nuclear reactor disaster at Chernobyl in 1986, fifty nations affiliated with the International Atomic Energy Agency signed two accords. One requires notification of all other signatories of leaks at civilian nuclear reactors, and the other requires other signatories to be available with assistance.

Laurie MacBride

CHAPTER 20
The Economics of Conversion

LAURIE MACBRIDE AND DOUGLAS URNER

Several years ago the *New Internationalist* reported that the money required to provide adequate food, water, education, health and housing for everyone in the world had been estimated at $17 billion a year, or about as much as the world spends on arms every two weeks. A couple of years ago the estimate was revised to the amount spent on arms every ten days.[1]

Although we have the necessary resources to provide well for everyone on the planet, we are choosing not to do so. Instead, we are allowing our leaders to build and institutionalize a permanent war economy—an economy in which we allocate resources, plan production and set social priorities as if we were constantly in a state of war.

Throughout both the developed and developing worlds, military spending is causing huge government deficits, high interest rates, inflation and

Laurie MacBride is a Vancouver Island peace activist and former teacher. In 1984, she helped found the Nanoose Conversion Campaign (NCC), with the goal of ending all weapons testing in Georgia Strait and seeing the Nanoose Bay naval weapons testing range converted to peaceful, economically productive uses. She now lives on nearby Gabriola Island and works as a volunteer for the NCC. She has been involved in extensive public outreach work, travelling in British Columbia, eastern Canada and the United States to present the NCC slide show, to speak on economic conversion, and to gather support for the campaign. She has made a number of media appearances, spoken at peace walks, and written articles on Nanoose for a variety of publications. At the public inquiry, Laurie MacBride gave this speech, which was co-authored by Douglas Urner.

unemployment and is channeling money away from desperate human needs.

Canadian military spending is accelerating rapidly. Since 1980, defence expenditures have shown the highest rate of growth of all government spending other than servicing the public debt. Defence spending currently consumes about two per cent of our Gross National Product, about ten per cent of federal government spending, and about forty per cent of federal discretionary spending.[2] With the Department of National Defence receiving almost half of discretionary funds, it is inevitable that other government programs—those designed to meet social needs—will suffer.

Military production undermines our economic security. Military goods and services are economically useless in terms of ordinary consumption and they have no economic value for further production. You cannot produce anything else with a CF-18. Defence spending is highly inflationary as it pumps money into the economy and competes for scarce human and material resources but produces nothing socially useful. With more money in the economy but fewer consumer goods available, demand exceeds supply and prices rise. Inflation is further fuelled by the massive borrowing needed to pay for the present arms buildup. Tied as we are to the U.S. economy, Canadians are deeply affected by U.S. military policies.

Perhaps we could excuse some of this inflation if it produced jobs, but in real terms military spending does not create employment. Many studies have confirmed that more jobs can be created by investing in virtually any other sector of the economy.[3] One study shows that a net increase of 111,000 jobs would have resulted during the fiscal year 1984/85 if Canadian military spending had been diverted to consumer spending.[4]

In fact, despite higher levels of military spending, employment in defence production is actually dropping throughout the world. For ex-

Douglas Urner is co-author of the speech given by Laurie MacBride at the public enquiry. A recent immigrant to British Columbia, he has lived in a number of places in the United States, including Ohio, where he attended Antioch College, and Oregon, where for eight years he was active in the labour, peace, and justice movements. He has worked as an electrician in the construction industry of New York City and in the shipyards of Portland, Oregon. He was a shop steward for the International Brotherhood of Electrical Workers and worked on occupational health and safety issues. With the decline of heavy industry in the Pacific Northwest he went to work as a computer programmer. Douglas Urner now lives on Gabriola Island and is a member of the Nanoose Conversion Campaign.

ample, since 1935 half a million jobs have been lost in Britain's defence industries, despite rising levels of defence spending. Compared to civilian industry, military production is capital-intensive and requires a high proportion of skilled, well-paid engineers and technicians. Few jobs are created for those who need them most.

This war economy is not a secure source of employment. Defence priorities change, and if a community is caught unprepared, the economic effects of a cutback can be devastating. Such surprise cutbacks are unfortunately common. Recent Canadian examples include the planned closure of seventeen Pinetree radar stations over the next three years and the loss of a major weapons contract by Spar Aerospace of Toronto in August 1986. These cutbacks were the result of decisions made in Washington, and they underscore how vulnerable Canadians are to sudden changes in U.S. policy.

Military spending does not promote economic growth. Countries with a high proportion of capital investment and research and development moneys committed to the military have slow economic growth and low productivity increases. A prime example is the United States, where from 1965 to 1984 the average increase in the annual rate of productivity in the manufacturing sector was the lowest of any industrialized country. At the high end of the productivity scale is Japan, which commits only a small portion of its resources to military purposes.[5]

Military spending removes useful resources from civilian use, slows the rate of productivity growth and diverts new knowledge and technologies away from productive social uses. Yet we are told by proponents of military spending that this is good for the economy—that we must continue and even increase our spending if we are to create employment and have the benefits of sophisticated technology for use in civilian industry. This myth serves to bind us to a permanent war mentality and keeps us from seeing beyond our short-term economic survival. If we are to break the cycle of inflation, unemployment, declining productivity and economic decay, we must expose this myth and begin to look seriously at alternatives.

Economic conversion is a central strategy for reversing this economic decay and for decreasing the threat of nuclear war. If we are to survive into the twenty-first century, we must begin the process of disarmament in earnest. But unless we create practical alternatives for those presently dependent upon the military economy, we will understandably face resistance to change. Through developing and carrying out these alternatives, the conversion process can become a framework for the creation of a permanent peace economy.

For this process to work, we need a thorough and well-planned conversion strategy which includes the following: advance planning; local decision making; alternatives that are in harmony with local values and meet social needs; diversification and strengthening of the local economy and skill base; employment of all who choose to stay in the area; retraining and reorientation of managers, technicians and production workers; and funding to provide for retraining, relocation and other benefits for affected people.

While these criteria can be met fairly easily, there are a number of significant problems to overcome. Basic structural changes will have to be made in the way that military contractors operate. Many previous conversion efforts failed because management did not recognize the differences between military and civilian production practices and attempted to enter the civilian market without making the necessary adjustments.[6]

Military contractors have grown accustomed to secure profits through having a guaranteed buyer and cost-plus contracts. Major military contractors have almost never been barred from further contracts as a result of poor product performance. These factors mean that management has not been required to learn the skills necessary for survival in a civilian market. Other military industry practices such as concurrency—the simultaneous design, testing, and production of a product—have also been blocks to serious, successful conversion.[7]

Many past conversion efforts were initiated in response to the announcement that a defence facility was to be closed. What prevented success was often the failure to deal with the fears of a community faced with the loss of a major employer.

Studying the effects of the closure of Canadian Forces Base Gimli, a researcher for the Department of National Defence concluded that local fears, especially the community's failure to accept the irreversibility of the base's closure, hindered conversion. Had more effort gone into convincing the local population that the closure was an opportunity for economic growth, less time would have been wasted before planning was started, and the self-fulfilling prophecy of defeatism could have been overcome.[8] Studies of conversion efforts from the U.S. Department of Defense reinforce the importance of developing a positive community attitude.

Conversion efforts initiated by workers or the community face a further problem, that of overcoming the resistance of those in positions of authority. An example was the attempt by workers at Lucas Aerospace in Britain to prepare for anticipated defence cutbacks after the election of the Labour government in 1975. The workers drew up a detailed plan that included an inventory of the company's human and material resources; an analysis of the problems facing the aerospace industry; social needs that alternative production could meet; and detailed proposals for new products, financing, marketing, production processes and employment development programs. However, management refused to discuss the proposals and fired the engineers who led the effort. As expected, defence cutbacks resulted in significant layoffs.

In spite of all these challenges, conversion can and has worked. The most extensive efforts have been in the United States, where military facilities in over three hundred communities have been closed since World War II. A Pentagon study of base closures since 1961 found that after an average transition period of two to three years, there had been an increase of over fifty per cent in the civilian employment.[9]

Unions at one of Italy's largest arms manufacturers, Oto Melare, have convinced the company to divide production at its new plant equally between military and agricultural vehicles. At several Italian factories a similar agreement has been reached, and they are now producing radio equipment for civilian airports.[10] Economic conversion literature cites many more examples.

Currently, neither Canada nor the United States has any conversion legislation. Such laws could provide considerable support to communities wanting to convert local military bases and industries. In the United States, despite the opposition of every president from Kennedy to Reagan, numerous conversion bills have been introduced. An example is a 1985 resolution introduced by representative Ted Weiss, a Democrat from New York, and co-endorsed by fifty-four other representatives.[11] The bill has all of the essential components for sensible economic conversion, including early notice of cutbacks to allow for advance planning on a local level, decentralization, a workers' trust fund and a national coordinating council. If passed, every U.S. defence facility employing over one hundred people would have to establish a local alternate-use committee and develop detailed plans for conversion and re-employment. All defence contractors would pay into a national fund to provide retraining, relocation and other benefits to displaced workers.

We need similar initiatives in Canada. Along with an overall reduction in defence spending, we need a national framework for conversion to support communities attempting to plan for the future. Federal legislation could require defence contractors to investigate alternate products and markets, fund the establishment of alternate-use committees in military-dependent communities, or set up a national conversion council to sponsor research projects on conversion.

Those of us in the peace movement are trying to bring about a profound change in our society, and conversion offers us a practical tool to help initiate that change. Conversion speaks of options, and this is important, for in order to make change, people need a new vision; they cannot be asked to step into a void.

While we need to lobby for national conversion legislation, action at the community level is essential. This is where the work of grass-roots groups such as the Nanoose Conversion Campaign fits in. Through patient and steady work in our community, we are trying to build a climate in which change is possible, in which community dialogue will lead to empowerment and, ultimately, to community action. We believe that our efforts are laying the groundwork for this possibility, and we hope that they can be of use to other groups working on similar campaigns. There is a great deal that all of us can do at the community level.

First, we must listen to working people's concerns about military cutbacks. Particularly in a time of high unemployment, it is hard to convince someone to make a change that he or she believes may threaten jobs. Under these circumstances, skepticism or even defensiveness is perfectly reasonable. Acknowledging this is a step towards building alliances with labour that will help create a will for conversion.

Our research and information-sharing networks must be extended. We need to be well prepared to demonstrate how conversion can and has worked. Equally important, we need to analyse the failures in conversion history and learn from them.

An important part of our job is to create practical and positive visions of conversion. This does not mean that we should impose "solutions" on a community. Rather, we must be catalysts for dialogue, giving imaginative, life-affirming suggestions that will get others thinking creatively and envisioning further possibilities.

Even if community leaders want no part of a change towards peaceful production, it's up to us to show them that it's in their economic interest to begin conversion planning. We know from experience that the military is an insecure source of employment, particularly when we are so dependent upon decisions made in the United States. So it's important to bring historical examples to people's attention in order to show them the benefits of being prepared for conversion ahead of time.

We need to take advantage of every opportunity to address this issue among all the varied constituencies within our communities—labour, management, defence employees, business, churches, universities and public interest groups—and to promote a real exchange of ideas. We must be prepared to listen to the ideas and concerns that come forth and to work with others towards a broad consensus. We should encourage the establishment of local conversion committees to explore alternatives and design detailed plans for conversion. This will be a long-term process, so patience and persistence will be vital.

The biggest challenge facing all of us is to change people's attitudes so that they are able to see decreased military spending as an opportunity for positive change rather than as a threat. Only when enough people understand the benefits that can come through conversion will there be a political and social will to bring it about.

In the meantime, those of us working on the issue must find effective ways to support each other so that we are not merely isolated voices within our separate communities. It's essential that we have a vision of what we want for the future and that we keep this vision clearly before us. We are at a time of crisis in terms of both our physical and economic survival, but the word *crisis* comes from a Greek word meaning *to decide on a course of action,* and this is what we now must do.

Notes

1. From posters published by the *New Internationalist* (Toronto). See also Ruth Leger Sivard, *World Military and Social Expenditures* (Washington, D.C.: World Priorities, 1985), p. 5.

2. Peter Chapman, "Canadian Defence Spending: The 1985–86 Estimates," *Ploughshares Monitor* (June 1985): 6–7.

3. For example, the U.S. Department of Labor found that a billion dollars spent on military production created an average of 22,000 fewer jobs than the same amount spent on social programs or consumer production. See statistics quoted by John Calvert, "Military Conversion: Turning Arms Spending to Social Uses," *CUPE Facts* (May 1984): 14.

4. Study commissioned by the Canadian Union of Public Employees and written by Toby Sanger. Published in *CUPE Facts* (January/February 1986).

5. See David Langille, "The Arms Race: It's as Wasteful as It Is Dangerous," *CUPE Facts* (February 1984): 14; Seymour Melman, "The Economics of Permanent War," *Ploughshares Monitor* (June 1984): C1; and Sivard, op. cit., p. 23.

6. For example, Rohr Corporation's attempt to produce cars for San Francisco's rapid transit system (BART). Rohr, which had built its reputation in the aerospace industry, entered production without re-orienting its managers, engineers or production workers. The system opened four years late, and there were enormous problems with costs and repairs. See Lloyd Jeff Dumas, "Economic Conversion, Productive Efficiency and Social Welfare," *Peace Research Reviews,* Vol. VII, No. 3.

7. For example, Boeing-Vertol's attempt to produce trolley cars and subway trains for the Massachusetts Bay Transportation Authority in the 1970s. See Seymour Melman, "Swords into Ploughshares," *Technology Review,* Massachusetts Institute of Technology (January 1986): 67.

8. Peter Edward Buker, "The Closure of CFB Gimli and the Post-Closure Development of the Gimli Region," Operational Research and Analysis Establishment Project Report No. PR 317 (Ottawa: Department of National Defence, July 1985).

9. President's Economic Adjustment Committee, "1961–1981: 20 Years of Civilian Reuse; Summary of Completed Military Base Economic Adjustment Projects," (Washington, D.C.: Department of Defense, November 1981).

10. "Transforming the Economy for Jobs, Peace and Justice," *Proceedings of the International Economic Conversion Conference* (Boston: Boston College, June 22–24, 1984).

11. The Defence Economic Adjustment Act (DEAA), HR 229, a bill introduced to the 99th Congress, 1st Session, January 3, 1985.

Wendy Wright

CHAPTER 21
What Individuals Can Do

WENDY WRIGHT

What can individuals do—what I can do? This is probably the most important question concerning the issue of nuclear disarmament.

The nuclear arms race is the most urgent issue humanity has ever faced. The fact that we live under the threat of annihilation from one year to the next makes it no less urgent, no less terrifying. But the continuous increase in the nuclear stockpile, the development and deployment of ever more lethal weapons systems, talk of war-fighting strategies from the mouths of powerful public figures, and the failure of every international forum to generate any momentum towards arms control—all of these seem uncontrollable and irreversible.

We have lived under the nuclear threat for a long time and the nuclear threat continues to increase. The doomsday clock moves closer to midnight. Perhaps it is inevitable that, in this environment, the sense of fear and urgency gradually gives way to feelings of hopelessness and fatalism.

The five thousand people gathered at this inquiry are not the only ones

Wendy Wright was born in New York and educated in Welland and London, Ontario. Presently the coordinator of the Toronto Disarmament Network, she has been active in the peace movement and the women's movement since 1972. Wendy Wright coordinated the Toronto Peace Petition Caravan Campaign in 1984 and has been responsible for outreach activities, campaigns and events. She is currently writing a chapter for an anthology, "Feminism and Peace—Canadian Women 1910–1986" (working title) to be published by Women's Press.

sharing this concern. Most other Canadians and people around the world are desperately hoping for an end to the arms race and the removal of the threat of nuclear war.

People in this society are not raised to believe they can cause change. Rather, they are raised to feel isolated, cut off and fragmented, with no hope of being able to make change. They are not raised to feel an integral part of the decision-making apparatus of this society. The arms race is proof of this isolation. Who wants the arms race? Whose interest does it serve? The arms race continues because people believe they cannot cause change. Against the huge power structures of the government and the military, people feel isolated, alone and overwhelmed.

As a democracy, our system is at best imperfect. Most people have little or no access to the political process. The political process is organized to exclude the majority of people. Elections are the exception to the rule.

For most of us, everyday life is more important and more time-consuming than the political process. Politics takes a back seat to school, home and family. And even if we manage to watch the news or read the papers regularly, we still don't have an opportunity to express an opinion. Our relationship to the media, and via the media to the actual events, is a passive one. We may not like it, but we are observers of not participants in the political process. Lives are lived in isolation, each of us pursuing private goals, making and changing our personal plans.

The individual pursuit of happiness would be just fine if the world was just fine. But the world is not just fine. In the face of monstrous and criminal policies, personal isolation is a form of oppression. We all want to see what is going on, but we have no voice.

Perhaps some of you may not experience this sense of isolation. But my experience as a peace activist tells me that most people feel this way. Most people feel indifferent to governments and their policies because they believe they can't do anything anyway. Most people want peace. Most people are disgusted by a society that can plan a trillion dollar space weapons program but can't stop hunger, even in the richest of countries. But the bottom line is that most people don't have any say in these things. They are cynical and fatalistic because they are politically isolated.

This brings me to answer the first question. What can individuals do? The answer is that they can begin to overcome their isolation. They can turn a sympathetic opinion into deliberate action, because even if the political process is restricted, it is not closed. Politicians are elected and defeated by voters. As a result, there are many forms of pressure that can be effectively exerted.

Individuals, organized as a collective force, can do almost anything. There has never been political change without a political movement.

When enough people joined together to oppose slavery and child labour or to demand the forty-hour work week or the vote for women, they achieved their aims.

If we are looking at how to achieve change today, we must look at how major social change has occurred in the past. All major change has been preceded by a period of consistent activity by many people throughout the society. Through this process of mass organizing, their collective will has been brought to bear and has brought about, over time, the change they desired.

What can individuals who are collectively organized do? They have already stopped nuclear war. It is clear from Richard Nixon's own memoirs that in 1969, during the Vietnam War, he seriously considered using nuclear weapons. This action would probably have caused a nuclear response from the Soviet Union. In Nixon's memoirs it is also clear that it was the size of the anti-nuclear movement in 1969 that prevented him from taking such action. And it was this same anti-war movement that eventually caused the Americans to withdraw from Vietnam.

The Canadian peace movement has celebrated its first direct political victory in recent years. In 1985 Prime Minister Mulroney's government was forced to take a position it was fundamentally against, a position opposing government-to-government participation in the American Star Wars program. The Canadian government's position did not go far enough, but it will make participation in the program more difficult. Mulroney didn't say that Star Wars was a bad thing, that it represents one of the most serious threats to world peace since the arms race began, that it opens the door to a first-strike policy, and that it is based on a belief that we can survive a limited nuclear war. But the peace movement said these things, mobilized unprecedented numbers of people and presented a well-documented case to the government.

Twenty million Canadian people, eighty per cent of the Canadian population, favour a nuclear freeze; twelve and a half million, fifty per cent of the Canadian population, support an end to cruise testing. The polls, which have consistently shown these results, make it easy to forget that these figures represent individuals—real people.

We've heard a lot about the issues surrounding the arms race this weekend. Knowing and understanding the issues is important; it provides a knowledgeable base for our work, but concentrating on issues alone will bring us no closer to nuclear disarmament. The peace movement doesn't just need to *tell* people about the concern. The situation itself creates concern. The role of the peace movement is to organize that concern into a force that can help prevent nuclear war. When enough people see what needs to be done, believe it can be done and organize together, then we will achieve our goal. If each of the twelve and a half million who support an end to cruise missile testing (or better yet, the twenty million who favour a nuclear freeze) did something to prevent nuclear war, Canadian support for the arms race would be over tomorrow.

All of us who are here this weekend are concerned. If each of the five thousand of us left here with a greater understanding of the issues, this meeting would only be a partial success. What we have to leave here with is not just a concern about the issues but a commitment to be actively involved in the process of bringing about change.

That involvement should focus on asking ourselves, What can I do to encourage more people to become involved? Change won't happen just because we want it to. It will be a slow process, at times painfully so, of building and organizing, a process of helping people break down everything they have been taught. If a building is built with a poor foundation and with structural problems, it comes down easily. In the same way, breaking down the isolation of our society—something unsound—can be done.

Two areas of work have been critical to the regrowth of the peace movement: grass-roots and Canada-wide organizing. There are few communities in Canada that do not have a peace movement. Just to look at the Alberta groups endorsing this convention is impressive, and Alberta has more peace groups than are listed.

The peace movement began to grow again in the early 1980s when concerned individuals began talking to their friends, neighbours, co-workers and church members. They found others sharing their concern and organized groups in these sectors. Individuals donate money, write letters, make phone calls and do an incredible number of other tasks. Many of the ninety peace groups comprising my organization, the Toronto Disarmament Network, were formed this way. Every one of these groups includes individuals who have raised the issue of peace and disarmament in every conceivable way and in every imaginable place—at school, at work, at church, with friends, through community or professional organizations and in the street.

I want to emphasize that the net effect, the aggregate of these individuals' activities, has been to transform public awareness of this issue. Millions of people have become sensitized to and educated about nuclear disarmament as a result of the work of thousands of individuals.

These, though, are really only technical points. The fundamental question is how are we going to take this powerful force and intervene in Canadian political life? My organization will be participating in a campaign for the next federal election organized by the Canadian Peace Alliance. The goal will be to get voters to vote only for candidates who take a positive position on specific issues concerning peace and disarmament and to get candidates to state publicly where they stand on these issues. The timing is good for a number of reasons. There is a good possibility of a minority government being elected, and a minority government would be a lot more responsive to the demands of the peace movement. Also, all of the political parties are looking to new areas for support. This issue is not new. For the first time in years, peace was part of the political agenda during the last federal election. Peace movements have successfully intervened in other countries. New Zealand, as a nuclear-weapons-free zone, is a very good example of this. Each and every candidate must feel the peace movement breathing down his or her neck; I encourage everyone to support this campaign.

What can individuals do? What can individuals not do? It is not a question of what individuals *can* do but what we all *must* do. We must recognize our inherent strength as rightful owners of this world. We want it for ourselves and for our children.

In conclusion, I would say that we are faced with two choices. Either we can do nothing and allow a society bent on breaking down and destroying life to continue a military system that not only is capable of terminating life on this planet but is already doing so by abusing and assaulting the earth and its inhabitants. Or we can all choose to do everything we are able to do to work together for something different—nuclear disarmament. The process of organizing and working together is an alternative process to the way in which society is currently structured. We would not be just ridding the world of nuclear weapons but would be accepting a new way. We are changing the priorities of our society. It's a lot of work. We stand to lose everything if we fail. The role of the individual is to do everything possible to ensure that nuclear disarmament is achieved. The activity and growth of the peace movement over the last few years shows that success is possible. It's up to all of us to make it happen.

CHAPTER 22
Question Session

LAURIE MACBRIDE AND WENDY WRIGHT

Lois Wilson

Laurie MacBride, you said that federal legislation could provide some national framework for economic conversion and you mentioned some of the sectors of our society that need to know about this. What encouragement have you received from the three political parties? What other sectors of society have shown some interest and support?

Laurie MacBride

I can't say we've received a lot of encouragement from political parties, but we have received some. We haven't received any encouragement from the Conservative government. We have received some on an individual level from some Liberal politicians in Ottawa, but only from a very small number of them. We're working on getting support from more of them. We have received very strong support from both the federal New Democratic Party and the provincial NDP caucus in British Columbia. The federal NDP passed a resolution at its 1985 convention that essentially supported what we are after, and in the spring of the same year the NDP in British Columbia passed a resolution that adopted the same goals that the Nanoose Conversion Campaign has advocated for Nanoose Bay, that is, an end to the Canada–United States agreement that allows Nanoose to be used for weapons testing, an end to all weapons testing there and the conversion of the facility to peaceful purposes.

As for the second question, the other sector of society that obviously has a great interest in this is labour. There have been some encouraging developments in the labour movement around conversion. The Canadian Labour Congress is very interested in conversion and has put out some good publications on it. I was really glad to hear Shirley Carr say that the CLC now has a full-time peace worker. The Quebec-based labour federation also has a full-time peace worker. That group has undertaken research work on conversion along with Project Ploughshares. So there is some good response by various organizations in the labour movement, and we're hoping to bring some of the grass-roots labour people into the movement on a community level as well.

Cynthia Cannizzo

Laurie MacBride, you gave an example of the United States and Japan and the relative amounts of their military spending; Canada has low military spending (about two per cent of its GNP) yet has serious economic problems, while Norway, with higher defence expenditures (over three per cent of its GNP), has fewer economic problems than Canada. Can you explain this?

MacBride

I'm sure there are a lot of factors involved in that. No, I can't explain it. I've never made a study of Norway. I'm not convinced that Canada has low defence spending, though. I would question that assumption. Yes, it's two per cent of our Gross National Product but I still think that's too much. It's also ten per cent of the federal government spending and forty per cent of federal discretionary spending. Discretionary spending is made up of those funds over which Parliament exercises direct annual decision making, funds that can be spent in various ways each year. I think that Canadian defence spending is too high, so I disagree with your assumption on that question.

Leonard Johnson

Laurie MacBride, you mentioned the Nanoose Conversion Campaign. I wonder if you could tell us a little about what has been happening on the conversion side of that. What have you proposed and what success have you had in getting public support for it in Nanoose?

MacBride

We've been doing a lot of work on the research end of it and putting out information to the community in the form of pamphlets and in our report to the People's Enquiry into the Canadian Forces Maritime Experimental and Test Ranges (CFMETR) at Nanoose, held in Nanaimo in January 1986. Since then we've spoken on conversion in various forums in British Columbia and a few times in the local community to a couple of Chambers of Commerce. This month we're approaching other Chambers of Commerce in the area, and over the next few months, we're going to be approaching the base workers at Nanoose, the labour councils in the area, the B.C. Federation of Labour and other groups for support for conversion.

We haven't put out specific proposals for Nanoose; we have put out ideas. We don't think that it's our role to propose specific projects because we see our role more as catalysts to get dialogue going in the community. It's very important that the community together make the decision about what best should take place in Nanoose, and we're one constituent of that community, but not the whole community, so we're trying to get a dialogue going. We will be working over the next couple of years to get an alternate-use committee set up in the community that would include a wide constituency of community people.

We have put out some ideas, though, to get thinking started. Some of these include a marine research station and a station for alternate energy research and development. We also suggested a plant for things such as recycling pulp-mill waste; producing fertilizer from the fish and shellfish wastes that are common in that area; producing advanced industrial materials, which might include wood-fibre composites and particle products; making ceramics; and recycling. Recently, somebody in our group suggested that it might be a lovely spot for a retirement village. There are all kinds of ideas. They are just ideas to get the community thinking, but not specific proposals.

Johnson
Wendy Wright, is your organization encouraging peace workers to join riding associations and to run as candidates in the next federal election?

Wendy Wright
The Toronto Disarmament Network is a non-partisan organization, so it's up to individuals to decide which party they want to join. We want to bring a peace presence forward during the election and to bring strong community pressure to bear on all of the candidates at the grass-roots level. At the same time, we will be working with other peace groups to bring pressure to bear on the parties and will try to affect party policy directly.

Cannizzo
Wendy Wright, could you please estimate the proportion of your funding that comes from the government or from quasi-government organizations such as the Canadian Institute for International Peace and Security (CIIPS)?

Wright
I know exactly where our funding comes from; a lot of our time is spent fund raising. This year our budget is $200,000 and we expect to raise all of that through the donations of individuals. We had a grant of $5,000 from CIIPS last year to use towards an educational program, and we have had a number of different grants from the Employment Development Branch of the federal government for summer students, for instance, but that money comes specifically tied to hire people who fit the criteria.

Wilson
Wendy Wright, does your organization do anything to assist people to demolish the image of the enemy, or do you just urge them to do that?

Wright
One of the things that's changing within the peace movement is the attempt to develop a much more positive image of peace and disarmament. You see that in the artwork that the peace movement produces. It's now showing more of what we stand for as opposed to just what we're opposed to.

Peter Horsfield (Nanaimo, British Columbia)
Laurie MacBride, to a very large extent, it's due to you that we have this meeting. I want to know what you've been doing in Nanoose, where Nanoose is and what you want to convert.

MacBride
Thanks, Peter. Obviously I can't give a full answer to that, because there's not enough time. Starting with the middle part of your question first: Nanoose is on the east coast of Vancouver Island, north of Nanaimo and across the Georgia Strait from Vancouver. We want to convert the facility known as the Canadian Forces Maritime Experimental and Test Ranges, or CFMETR. It's a Canadian-owned facility with an underwater weapons testing range; it is used primarily by the United States Navy and was built at the request of the U.S. back in the 1960s.

In this short time I can't give an adequate answer to the first part of the question concerning what we've been doing. Our work covers a whole range of education and outreach, environmental research, conversion research, speaking to people, and taking action when U.S. nuclear-capable vessels come in, actions that range all the way to civil disobedience.

Rafael Yutes (Exchange student from Heidelberg, West Germany)
As an exchange student from West Germany, I have enjoyed for the last three months Canadian hospitality and friendliness. Through the German

225

Guild for World War II, Germany feels a certain and very special responsibility to do everything to avoid another war. I want to underline that. Many people have mentioned the need for trust between the nations, but how are you going to achieve this when governments all over the world are cutting back money on exchange programs that promote understanding of different cultures and languages?

Wright

I agree that it's going to be extremely difficult for us to do that, because one of the most important ways that we build trust is person-to-person contact. When a person gets to know someone of another nationality or another race, then that person is not a foreigner anymore but is a contact. That's how we break down prejudice and build up trust. It is going to be very difficult to promote contacts and exchanges when governments are cutting back money in these areas. I think our role, though, is to exert every type of pressure to insist that these programs not be cut, that an environment of friendship be fostered, and that funds not be cut back.

Dieter Simonkowski (Calgary, Alberta)

I have a question for Lois Wilson and for General Johnson. In view of the stated goals of world communism by the Soviet Union and in view of the total enslavement of their societies, and in view of the aggression on this entire planet, especially in Afghanistan where there has been a loss of one million lives and where fifty thousand children have been kidnapped to the Soviet Union for indoctrination, would you say that this conference is concentrating too much on the United States? Do you really believe that the Soviet Union will change its goals and disarm voluntarily? Would you trust the Soviet Union if it tells us that it is doing so?

Wilson

The answer is no; I wouldn't trust it if it says it is doing so nor would I trust the United States if it said it was doing so. The proof of the pudding is in the eating, and I think that's been demonstrated throughout this conference. It would be very useful in a future conference to have people from both those countries present if we're going to talk about them and to try and build the bridges in that way. I feel very uncomfortable talking about absentee people and absentee governments.

Johnson

Part of the problem here is that we have stereotypical perceptions of the Soviet Union and we must get a better picture of it. Certainly, everyone in this room will agree that the Soviet Union's behaviour in Afghanistan is absolutely reprehensible, and nobody is endorsing it. However, the question of world domination is an assumption that you and some others hold. The Soviet Union does not have the capabilities to achieve that; history is not on its side. Soviet influence has been receding, if anything, in the last twenty-five to thirty years and the Soviet Union repudiated those goals a long time ago. There will always be difficulty in our relationship with the Soviet Union and we should not make it worse by perpetuating the stereotypes and acting on less than good information. What we need are these cultural exchanges; we need better coverage on the CBC and the media of the Soviet Union. We need to get the Soviet people down to human proportions and deal with them as human beings in order to prevent the differences between us from becoming a source of war. There's nothing in that relationship that justifies the dangers that we live under.

Wilson
Part of my motive for asking the question about the activity of the peace movement in reducing the enemy image, or exploding it, or diminishing it, was that I think the perception of the enemy is one of the main things that contributes to conflict.

Ron Aspinall (Green Party and Canadian Physicians for the Prevention of Nuclear War, Tofino, British Columbia)
John Kenneth Galbraith, the famous American economist, suggested that the military industry needs a possible enemy in order to justify not only its existence and growth, but also to maintain the confidence of the taxpayers and voters who support it. Do you think the arms race is driven primarily for security or primarily as a financial business venture riding on this capitalization of fear?

MacBride
I'll just have to give my opinion rather than empirical evidence as an answer. Certainly there are all kinds of arguments either way on that. My instinct is that it's driven by profit.

Darlene Konduc (Edmonton, Alberta)
From December 31, 1986 to January 3, 1987 in Long Beach, California, an International Human Unity Conference will have a simultaneously timed, worldwide, mass meditation and candle lighting for peace. Many efforts of individual snowflakes, as Dr. Goresky alluded to, are often met with apathy and accusations of "busy work," making individuals feel powerless. What role do you see the churches, governments and universities playing in raising human consciousness beyond our own Canadian context to encompass the oneness and similarities of our humanity as men, women and children worldwide?

Wilson
I'd like to speak on behalf of faith communities, not just the churches, because we live in a very pluralistic world. I think it's incumbent on faith
communities to address this issue in terms of their perceptions of what the
human community is about and in terms of their understanding of the nature of persons—what makes a person a person—which, in some traditions, is a person who must be in just and reciprocal relationships with
others and with the created order and the Creator. Thirty years ago, when
we didn't have the communications media that we have now, it was much
easier to believe that the human community was the one I belonged to; all
people had to do was join it, and if only everybody would join it, everything would be fine. We know now that this is a very naive assumption,
and we have to develop our concepts of how there can be a sustainable
human community that can affirm our deep diversities and yet keep us in
reciprocal relationships. So I think the contributions of the faith communities in this effort ought to be in terms of their ideas of what a person is
and what a human community is.

Wright
The advantage of people organizing within a church, a school or a university is that these are places where people are already congregating.
Churches are already part of an organized institution, as are schools. So it
means that part of our work as organizers is already done. It's a matter,
then, of just getting people to discuss the issues. Also, peace groups that
start from existing groups have a stronger sense of support when they begin, and they often have a better chance of longevity.

Carl Rosenbaum (Strathcona Composite High School, Edmonton,
Alberta)
Laurie MacBride, at the beginning of your presentation you drew the
common comparison between defence spending and the far lesser cost of
feeding the hungry. However, how much of this diverted spending will be
able to control the arms race and go towards feeding the hungry?

MacBride
That's entirely dependent upon the political will to do so, and I think
that's a decision that we people must make. We must start creating the
political will to meet people's social needs—feeding people, housing
people, giving them clean safe water to drink, giving them a future and
teaching them how to feel empowered enough to demand their future.
That's what I'm talking about. Economic conversion is very dependent
on the empowerment of people, which then creates the political will to do
exactly things like that.

228

Monty Bauer (County of Thorhild Central High School, Thorhild, Alberta)
Wendy Wright, in your speech you were very negative about our political system in Canada. Would you support the idea of proportional representation in this country?

Wright
My negativity about the political system isn't so much due to how it's organized but to how we participate or don't participate in it. That's not just because of the structure of government itself but because of the structure of our society, which breaks us down, makes us feel alone, and doesn't encourage a person to feel part of a political process. That's what I'm most critical of, and our work involves trying to change our attitudes, recognizing that we have the right to participate politically and to organize to achieve certain goals.

Ruth Loomis (Ladysmith, British Columbia)
Since we have talked about the Strategic Defense Initiative and various protection umbrellas, what about Canada declaring itself neutral and putting up its own umbrella, thereby putting defence money to economic conversions?

MacBride
Certainly I think there would be a lot of money freed up for other spending if we were neutral, and I believe Gwynne Dyer addressed that yesterday. The money that would be available from getting out of NATO wouldn't need to be spent defending our European allies, and that money could be spent any way we wanted it to be spent if we create the political will to do so. I think an excellent way to spend Department of National Defence money would be in planning and preparing for conversion. That's a long-term solution, and I think we need long-term solutions not just short-term ones.

Johnson
Before we squander the defence budget, we'd better find out what we're going to do and the needs we have for it.

Selected books from
Gordon Soules Book Publishers Ltd.

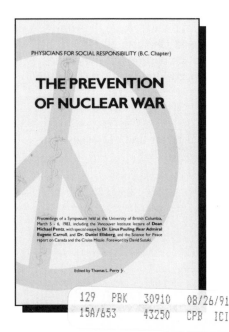